PALGRAVE Studies in Oral History

Series Editors: David P. Cline and Natalie Fousekis
Founding Series Editors: Linda Shopes and Bruce M. Stave

Editorial Board

Rina Benmayor
Division of Humanities and Communication &
Oral History and Community Memory Archive
California State University Monterey Bay
United States

Indira Chowdhury
Archival Resources for Contemporary History
India

Pilar Domínguez
Department of Historical Sciences
Division of Political Thought and
Social Movements
Universidad de Las Palmas de Gran Canaria
España

Sean Field
Centre for Popular Memory
Department of Historical Studies
University of Cape Town
South Africa

Alexander Freund
Department of History &
Oral History Centre
University of Winnipeg
Canada

Anna Green
College of Humanities
University of Exeter
United Kingdom

Paula Hamilton
Faculty of Humanities & Social Sciences &
Australian Centre for Public History
University of Technology Sydney
Australia

Paul Ortiz
Department of History &
Samuel Proctor Oral History Program
University of Florida
United States

The Order Has Been Carried Out: History, Memory, and Meaning of a Nazi Massacre in Rome, by Alessandro Portelli (2003)

Sticking to the Union: An Oral History of the Life and Times of Julia Ruuttila, by Sandy Polishuk (2003)

To Wear the Dust of War: From Bialystok to Shanghai to the Promised Land, an Oral History, by Samuel Iwry, edited by L. J. H. Kelley (2004)

Education as My Agenda: Gertrude Williams, Race, and the Baltimore Public Schools, by Jo Ann Robinson (2005)

Remembering: Oral History Performance, edited by Della Pollock (2005)

Postmemories of Terror: A New Generation Copes with the Legacy of the "Dirty War," by Susana Kaiser (2005)

Growing Up in The People's Republic: Conversations between Two Daughters of China's Revolution, by Ye Weili and Ma Xiaodong (2005)

Life and Death in the Delta: African American Narratives of Violence, Resilience, and Social Change, by Kim Lacy Rogers (2006)

Creating Choice: A Community Responds to the Need for Abortion and Birth Control, 1961–1973, by David P. Cline (2006)

Voices from This Long Brown Land: Oral Recollections of Owens Valley Lives and Manzanar Pasts, by Jane Wehrey (2006)

Radicals, Rhetoric, and the War: The University of Nevada in the Wake of Kent State, by Brad E. Lucas (2006)

The Unquiet Nisei: An Oral History of the Life of Sue Kunitomi Embrey, by Diana Meyers Bahr (2007)

Sisters in the Brotherhoods: Working Women Organizing for Equality in New York City, by Jane LaTour (2008)

Iraq's Last Jews: Stories of Daily Life, Upheaval, and Escape from Modern Babylon, edited by Tamar Morad, Dennis Shasha, and Robert Shasha (2008)

Soldiers and Citizens: An Oral History of Operation Iraqi Freedom from the Battlefield to the Pentagon, by Carl Mirra (2008)

Overcoming Katrina: African American Voices from the Crescent City and Beyond, by D'Ann R. Penner and Keith C. Ferdinand (2009)

Bringing Desegregation Home: Memories of the Struggle toward School Integration in Rural North Carolina, by Kate Willink (2009)

I Saw It Coming: Worker Narratives of Plant Closings and Job Loss, by Tracy E. K'Meyer and Joy L. Hart (2010)

Speaking History: Oral Histories of the American Past, 1865-Present, by Sue Armitage and Laurie Mercier (2010)

Surviving Bhopal: Dancing Bodies, Written Texts, and Oral Testimonials of Women in the Wake of an Industrial Disaster, by Suroopa Mukherjee (2010)

Living with Jim Crow: African American Women and Memories of the Segregated South, by Anne Valk and Leslie Brown (2010)

Gulag Voices: Oral Histories of Soviet Incarceration and Exile, by Jehanne M. Gheith and Katherine R. Jolluck (2011)

Detained without Cause: Muslims' Stories of Detention and Deportation in America after 9/11, by Irum Shiekh (2011)

Soviet Communal Living: An Oral History of the Kommunalka, by Paola Messana (2011)

No Room of Her Own: Women's Stories of Homelessness, Life, Death, and Resistance, by Desiree Hellegers (2011)

Oral History and Photography, edited by Alexander Freund and Alistair Thomson (2011)

Place, Writing, and Voice in Oral History, edited by Shelley Trower (2011)

Oral History, Community, and Displacement: Imagining Memories in Post-Apartheid South Africa, by Sean Field (2012)

Second Wind: Oral Histories of Lung Transplant Survivors, by Mary Jo Festle (2012)

Displaced: The Human Cost of Development and Resettlement, by Olivia Bennett and Christopher McDowell (2012)

Exodus to Shanghai: Stories of Escape from the Third Reich, by Steve Hochstadt (2012)

Oral History in Southeast Asia: Memories and Fragments, edited by Kah Seng Loh, Stephen Dobbs, and Ernest Koh (2013)

Oral History Off the Record: Toward an Ethnography of Practice, edited by Anna Sheftel and Stacey Zembrzycki (2013)

Sharecropper's Troubadour: John L. Handcox, the Southern Tenant Farmers' Union, and the African American Song Tradition, by Michael K. Honey (2013)

Tiananmen Exiles, by Rowena He (2014)

Black Leaders on Leadership: Conversations with Julian Bond, by Phyllis Leffler (2014)

Oral History and Digital Humanities: Voice, Access, and Engagement, edited by Douglas A. Boyd and Mary A. Larson (2014)

The End of the Cold War? Bush, Kohl, Gorbachev, and the Reunification of Germany, by Alexander von Plato (2015)

Memory, Subjectivities, and Representation: Approaches to Oral History in Latin America, Portugal, and Spain, edited by Rina Benmayor, María Eugenia Cardenal de la Nuez, and Pilar Domínguez Prats (2016)

Memory, Subjectivities, and Representation

Approaches to Oral History in Latin America, Portugal, and Spain

Edited by

Rina Benmayor, María Eugenia Cardenal de la Nuez,
and Pilar Domínguez Prats

palgrave
macmillan

MEMORY, SUBJECTIVITIES, AND REPRESENTATION
Selection and editorial content © Rina Benmayor, María Eugenia Cardenal de la Nuez, and Pilar Domínguez Prats 2016
Individual chapters © their respective contributors 2016
Softcover reprint of the hardcover 1st edition 2016 978-1-137-43869-0

All rights reserved. No reproduction, copy or transmission of this publication may be made without written permission. No portion of this publication may be reproduced, copied or transmitted save with written permission. In accordance with the provisions of the Copyright, Designs and Patents Act 1988, or under the terms of any licence permitting limited copying issued by the Copyright Licensing Agency, Saffron House, 6–10 Kirby Street, London EC1N 8TS.

Any person who does any unauthorized act in relation to this publication may be liable to criminal prosecution and civil claims for damages.

First published 2016 by
PALGRAVE MACMILLAN

The authors have asserted their rights to be identified as the authors of this work in accordance with the Copyright, Designs and Patents Act 1988.

Palgrave Macmillan in the UK is an imprint of Macmillan Publishers Limited, registered in England, company number 785998, of Houndmills, Basingstoke, Hampshire, RG21 6XS.

Palgrave Macmillan in the US is a division of Nature America, Inc., One New York Plaza, Suite 4500, New York, NY 10004-1562.

Palgrave Macmillan is the global academic imprint of the above companies and has companies and representatives throughout the world.

ISBN: 978–1–349–56646–4
E-PDF ISBN: 978–1–137–43871–3
DOI: 10.1057/9781137438713

Distribution in the UK, Europe and the rest of the world is by Palgrave Macmillan®, a division of Macmillan Publishers Limited, registered in England, company number 785998, of Houndmills, Basingstoke, Hampshire RG21 6XS.

Library of Congress Cataloging-in-Publication Data
Names: Benmayor, Rina. | Domínguez Prats, Pilar. | Cardenal de la Nuez, María Eugenia.
Title: Memory, subjectivities, and representation : approaches to oral history in Latin America, Portugal, and Spain / co-edited by Rina Benmayor, María Eugenia Cardenal de la Nuez, Pilar Domínguez Prats.
Description: New York, NY : Palgrave Macmillan, 2015. | Series: Palgrave studies in oral history | Includes bibliographical references and index.
Identifiers: LCCN 2015020265
Subjects: LCSH: Oral history—Latin America. | Oral history—Portugal. | Oral history—Spain. | Memory—Social aspects—Latin America. | Memory—Social aspects—Portugal. | Memory—Social aspects—Spain. | Latin America—Historiography—Social aspects. | Portugal—Historiography—Social aspects. | Spain—Historiography—Social aspects. | BISAC: HISTORY / Latin America / Central America. | HISTORY / Latin America / General. | HISTORY / Europe / Spain & Portugal.
Classification: LCC F1409.7 .M467 2015 | DDC 980—dc23 LC record available at http://lccn.loc.gov/2015020265

A catalogue record for the book is available from the British Library.

Contents

List of Figures   ix

Acknowledgments   xi

Introduction: Bridging Boundaries   1
*Rina Benmayor, María Eugenia Cardenal de la Nuez, and
Pilar Domínguez Prats*

Part I   Collective Memory and Identities

CHAPTER 1
"I Was Just One More among Many": A Mosaic of
Ex-combatant Voices from the Portuguese Colonial War   19
Ângela Campos

CHAPTER 2
Voices of Spanish Socialist Trade Unionism during the End of
the Franco Regime and the Transition to Democracy   37
Pilar Domínguez Prats

CHAPTER 3
"Gendered" Memories: Women's Narratives from
the Southern Cone   57
*Cristina Scheibe Wolff, Joana Maria Pedro, and
Janine Gomes da Silva*

Part II   Subjectivity and Identity Construction

CHAPTER 4
The Healing Effect of Discourses: Body, Emotions, and
Gender Subjectivity in Basque Nationalism   77
Miren Llona

CHAPTER 5
Lola's Story: The Struggle to Build a Professional
Identity with No Good Jobs in Sight 93
María Eugenia Cardenal de la Nuez

CHAPTER 6
"Getting Ahead": The American Dream in the California
Agricultural Fields 111
Magdalena Villarreal

CHAPTER 7
Migration, Sex Work, and Stigma: An Analysis in
Biographical Code 129
*Ángeles Arjona Garrido, Juan Carlos Checa Olmos, Estefanía
Acién González, and Francisco Majuelos Martínez*

Part III   Memory and Public Representations

CHAPTER 8
Oral Accounts and Visual Inscriptions: Narratives under
Heavily Tattooed Skin 149
Vitor Sérgio Ferreira

CHAPTER 9
The Black Movement and Race Relations in Brazil: Building
New Knowledge through Online Oral History Materials 167
Verena Alberti and Amilcar Araujo Pereira

CHAPTER 10
Images and Words: Photography and the 1968 Student
Movement in Mexico 187
Alberto del Castillo Troncoso

CHAPTER 11
"A Living Museum of Small, Forgotten and Unwanted
Memories": Performing Oral Histories of the Portuguese
Dictatorship and Revolution 207
Joana Craveiro

List of Contributors 231

Index 237

Figures

9.1	Screen shot of video interview, with accompanying transcript, interview details, narrator biographical data, and contextual background	173
9.2	Naming and describing source files	174
9.3	Affirmative Action activity worksheet	181
9.4	Fishbowl activity structure	181
10.1	"Blood Was Spilled." *La Prensa*, September 25, 1968	193
10.2	Military occupation of the Central University City Campus. Front page of the daily *El Universal*	195
10.3	Protest march of President Barros Sierra, August 1, 1968, annotated by Marcelo Brodsky	198
10.4	Burning of the gorilla, August 13, 1968	200
11.1	Part 1, "Small Acts of Resistance"	209
11.2	Part 2, "Invisible Archives of the Portuguese Dictatorship"	212
11.3	Part 6, "When Did the Revolution End?"	224

Acknowledgments

This book began with a conversation at the Oral History Association Annual Meeting in Denver, Colorado, in October 2011. Linda Shopes and Bruce Stave, the founding coeditors of the Palgrave Studies in Oral History series, met with Rina Benmayor and Pilar Domínguez to explore the idea of publishing an anthology in English of oral history essays from Latin America. We were enthusiastic and proposed including work from Spain and Portugal, given the intellectual, linguistic, and historical transatlantic connections. We also suggested that including work from related fields would provide a wider view of the use of oral sources in these regions. Soon thereafter, sociologist María Eugenia Cardenal joined us as our third coeditor.

This is the first volume in the Palgrave Studies in Oral History series to anthologize a collection of translated essays from Spanish and Portuguese. Compiling such a volume was quite a challenge, given the enormous amount of oral history scholarship produced over the last 20 years, especially in Latin America and Spain. We felt that such a volume, although a drop in the bucket, would make a useful contribution to the field, especially since, for years, members of the International Oral History Association have been calling for publications of scholarship in translation.

The many months of reviewing proposals, identifying contributors, losing some, adding others, revising, editing, and polishing these 11 essays have been demanding, but also enriching and satisfying. Our intense and often lengthy editorial discussions, conducted in two languages over Skype and email, enabled us to engage our different critical perspectives, as well as our editorial and organizational strengths, in a highly collaborative way. The essays themselves gave us new insights into a variety of interpretive approaches—historical, sociological, cultural, and ethnographic—as well as the development of these approaches within each country or region. And, quite simply, we found the constellation of topics and themes created by these essays to be captivating. Each of us came away from this process with an expanded scope of reference and deeper appreciation of the scholarship on oral narratives in these regions. We hope our readers will find the experience of reading these 11 essays to be equally stimulating and enriching.

We have many people to acknowledge and thank in this endeavor. First and foremost, on behalf of the authors, we wish to appreciate all the narrators who shared their stories and gave of their time to be interviewed. It is thanks to them that this book is even possible. Of course, there would be no book without the intellectual labor and perseverance of its 17 authors. We celebrate their strong and insightful work, and thank them for their patience and willingness to entertain multiple rounds of rewrites and editorial revisions in another language. We have "lived" with these authors for many months and enjoyed working with each and every one. We also thank our colleagues, Gerardo Necoechea, of Mexico's Institute for Anthropology and History (INAH), Jack Tchen (New York University), and Barbara Stauber (University of Tübingen), for recommending the work of Alberto del Castillo, Joana Craveiro, and Vitor Ferreira, respectively.

In terms of the editorial process, we owe special thanks to Linda Shopes for her invaluable guidance and support throughout this project, even after her term as coeditor of the Palgrave series came to an end. From the earliest proposal to the final stages of the manuscript, her astute questions and insightful suggestions significantly enhanced this volume. Our Palgrave editors were lovely to work with as well. We are especially grateful to our Palgrave editorial team: Kristin Purdy, who carefully shepherded the production of this volume; Brigitte Shull; Michelle Smith; Bhavana Nair; Tanuja Kumar, our benevolent copy editor; and indexer Suzanne Sherman Aboulfadl.

If identifying 11 strong essays from a voluminous corpus of oral history and related research was difficult, even more challenging was the added issue of translation, particularly in the absence of a budget. Finding professional native-English translators who could produce idiomatic academic translations from Spanish and Portuguese, and at the same time render oral narrative speech into colloquial English, is nothing short of daunting, especially without a budget. Translation is never literal and sometimes necessitates complete rewrites, as we indeed discovered. *Tradunet* Canarias, facilitated part of the Spanish–English labor. Genoveva Armas gave us prompt and professional assistance in finding a wonderful translator, although for contractual reasons we are not permitted to know her name. Nonetheless, we wish to thank and tip our hats to our anonymous translator, for her smooth and highly nuanced renditions of four essays (Cardenal, Arjona et al., del Castillo, and Domínguez). Chris Paetzhold translated an early conference version of Domínguez's essay. Rina Benmayor translated Llona, Wolff et al., and Alberti and Pereira's essays, as well as portions of our introduction, and produced idiomatic renditions of four essays written originally in English (Campos, Villarreal, Ferreira, and Craveiro).

In the midst of draconian budget cuts in Spain, several institutions and individuals facilitated the resources to translate three essays (Domínguez, Arjona et al., and Cardenal). Their authors acknowledge and thank the Largo Caballero Foundation of Madrid, the Laboratorio de Antropología Social y Cultural of the Universidad de Almería, and the following individuals from the Universidad de Las Palmas de Gran Canaria: José Manuel Izquierdo, chair of the Department of Psychology and Sociology; Alberto Bachiller, chair of the Department of Historical Sciences; and Josefina Domínguez, director of the "Atlantic Society Studies" research group.

Finally, we want to thank Serafín and Diego Torres for their steadfast support during this long process, and especially salute María Eugenia's son Juan, for his patience and good humor in sacrificing his bedtime stories when his mother periodically disappeared to talk instead to a computer screen. At the same time, across an ocean and a continent, we also thank Panchito, who waited dutifully for his pack leader to put aside that silver object that perpetually sat on her lap and occupied so much of her attention, and finally take him out for his daily walk!

Introduction: Bridging Boundaries

Rina Benmayor, María Eugenia Cardenal de la Nuez, and Pilar Domínguez Prats

Oral history and related scholarship is thriving in Latin America, Portugal, and Spain. This book is an effort to disseminate some of this work in English. The 11 chapters in this collection represent oral narrative research in Brazil, Mexico, the Southern Cone of South America, Portugal, and Spain. The authors come from the fields of oral history, biographical approaches in sociology, and anthropology, and are both young and established scholars who have not published before, or at least not extensively, in English. While this volume does not pretend to offer a comprehensive overview or a representative sample of the voluminous research on oral narratives in these geographical regions,[1] the chapters give access to and insight into how Latin American, Portuguese, and Spanish scholars approach theoretical, methodological, interpretive, and representational issues in their work. These chapters come together around three major themes that have long concerned oral historians: memory, subjectivity, and representation. They reflect current and ongoing research on the relationship of political identities and collective memory, the turn toward subjectivities and the construction of personal and social identities, and the public representation of memory through oral narratives.

This volume bridges several divides—geographical, linguistic, and disciplinary. Oral history scholarship is global, but access to it is not universal. Language continues to complicate the field, frustrating and excluding scholars who are not polyglots from knowing and referencing work from other cultural regions and contexts. Rather than "lost in translation," we might say that oral historians are often lost for lack of translation. One need only think about the linguistic difficulties at International Oral History Association (IOHA) conferences, where despite a bilingual mission and the publication of abstracts in the two official languages, English and Spanish, communication across languages is still experienced as a chasm. Several bilingual efforts are demonstrating sensitivity to the importance of linguistic diversity: IOHA's biannual *Newsletter/Boletín* and its online journal *Words and Silences* have been publishing in both languages since 1998. More recently, the Canadian Oral History Association's online journal, *Oral History Forum d'Histoire Orale*, published a special issue on Latin America (2012), guest edited by three noted scholars from the region.[2] By making this set of 11 chapters available to English readers, this volume adds to, and hopes to stimulate further cross-linguistic communication and dialogue in the international oral history arena.

Along with bridging linguistic divides, this collection crosses geographical boundaries, traveling transatlantic routes forged by histories of empire and colonialism. Networks of oral history collaboration between Latin America and the Iberian Peninsula have been ongoing since the early 1980s, with the expansion of the oral history movement across the globe. The incorporation of the International Oral History Association in 1995 strengthened these ties, especially with the biennial conferences held in Spain, Brazil, and Argentina. Groundbreaking journals like *Historia, Antropología y Fuentes Orales* (founded in 1989 as *Historia y Fuente Oral*), and the Brazilian Oral History Association's *História Oral*, have provided spaces of critical exchange for Spanish- and Portuguese-speaking scholars. Building on a longstanding oral history movement in the region, Latin American oral historians have formed the new and vibrant Red Latinoamericana de Historia Oral (RELAHO) [Latin American Oral History Network], which holds biennial conferences and disseminates news and articles through its website. Additionally, attention to oral history and oral narratives has been on the rise in Portugal since the 1990s (Oliveira). The Portuguese Red Ibero-Americana Resistencia y Memoria (RIARM) [Iberoamerican Resistance and Memory Network] is a more recent effort to bring together Spanish, Portuguese, and Latin American oral historians. In framing this volume, therefore, we purposefully include three chapters that reflect a range of approaches to oral narratives in Portugal.

The chapters in this collection also construct bridges across disciplines. The volume's subtitle, *Approaches to Oral History*..., signals what oral historians have always recognized: that the boundaries between historical, ethnographic, sociological, literary, linguistic, psychological, pedagogical, and artistic analyses of oral narratives are porous. As Alistair Thomson has pointed out (2007), interdisciplinarity is one of the paradigm shifts that mark contemporary oral history. Early oral history collections, dominated by historians, introduced sociologist Daniel Bertaux's work on biography (1981) and Alessandro Portelli's highly insightful applications of literary and folklore studies (1997, 1998, 2005) to the understanding of memory and oral narratives. Bertaux, Isabelle Bertaux-Wiame (1982), and Joanna Bornat's studies (2001, 2012; Chamberlayne et al. 2000) are well known in both oral history and sociology circles, and, as such, stand as exemplary bridges.[3] In Latin America and the Iberian Peninsula, the field of oral history is largely comprised of historians. However, interdisciplinary collaboration has been strongly supported by institutional structures such as Mexico's Instituto Nacional de Antropología e Historia (INAH) [National Institute of Anthropology and History], the Instituto Mora, and the Mexican Center for Advanced Research and Postgraduate Studies in Social Anthropology (CIESAS), the Instituto de Ciencias Sociais [Institute of Social Sciences] at the University of Lisbon, and national and international meetings like the European Social Science History Conference, that attracts many oral historians.[4] And yet, on the whole, few published oral history collections in Spanish or Portuguese explore different disciplinary perspectives in an intentional way.[5] This volume offers readers examples of the diverse ways in which oral historians, ethnographers, qualitative sociologists who use biographical methods, and scholars in cultural and performance studies analyze and interpret oral narratives. Not all consider themselves oral historians, however, all use the in-depth, one-on-one life narrative interview as materia prima to reconstruct the past, analyze memory, interpret subjectivity, and challenge official interpretations of the past—all key concerns in the field of oral history.

The chapters in this volume could be clustered in different ways to highlight these linguistic, geographical, and cross-disciplinary interconnections. However, we chose to organize the volume around three central issues in oral history research. In Part I—Memory and Collective Identities—oral accounts speak to the formation of collective identities in contexts of political dictatorships and their aftermaths. Part II—Subjectivities and Identity Construction—focuses on individual narratives and the construction of personal identities, in this instance, of women in nationalist movements, economic migrations, and contracting labor markets. We devote Part III—Memory and Public Representations—to the uses and "performances" of oral history and memory in particular public contexts in order to transform collective consciousness and historical discourses.

Collective Memory and Identities

The development of oral history in Portugal, Spain, and the Southern Cone of South America has been profoundly marked by the political struggles of the recent past: decades of authoritarian regimes, resistance to those regimes, and transitions to democracy. Consequently, the testimonies of social actors, long kept "underground," have been critical to understanding and interpreting the histories that official written documents have silenced. Since the turn to democracy in these countries, studies of collective memory and identities have flourished, recognizing oral history's unique capacity to connect the past and the present, and contribute to the creation of a public memory. Argentine sociologist Elizabeth Jelin (2002) argues that the representation of the past involves a struggle among diverse social actors to officialize and institutionalize *their* narrative of the past. As Paul Ricoeur (1999) points out,

> The past cannot be changed. One cannot erase events or undo what has transpired... [but] the meaning of the past is not fixed forever, and the events of the past are open to varying interpretations. (48–49)

Ângela Campos; Pilar Domínguez; and Cristina Wolff, Joana Pedro, and Janine da Silva; all historians by training, take up the question of competing memories and contested interpretations in the personal narratives of Portuguese ex-combatants of the colonial war in Africa, Spanish trade union leaders, and women in armed resistance movements in the Southern Cone respectively. All three chapters interrogate the relationship between history, memory, and identities, attending to individual standpoints in reconstructing collective histories. The unifying thread in these chapters is the formation of collective political and gendered identities based on shared experiences and reinforced by collective reminiscence in the present. They also illustrate the impact of public discourse on individual rememoration constructed from the vantage point of the present.

With the end of the dictatorships in Portugal (in 1974) and Spain (in 1975), social and political changes enabled the consolidation of democracies and generational shifts. These events impacted the social perception of the past and encouraged public commemoration of that past. In both countries, there exists today a complex and fraught public memory of these dictatorships, a memory that is shaped in part by the life histories of those who lived through those decades. The 36 war veterans that make up Campos's

"Mosaic of Ex-combatant Voices from the Portuguese Colonial War" have very diverse experiences and recollections of that conflict, memories and perspectives that clash and contrast with dominant "public cultural discourses" about that war. Analysis of their oral narratives reveals how decades after their return, the ex-combatants maintain a group identity as soldiers of Ultramar who want official public recognition as historical actors and protagonists in the colonial war. Campos suggests that the life story is a complex meshing of memories and reflections about the past elaborated in the present. She takes into account the subjective dimensions of their narratives, pointing out how the individual narrators voice the "positive" aspects of their war experiences and downplay or omit memories of trauma and violence. "The oral historian," she argues, "creates an interpretative bridge between biography and history and enables further understandings of the conflict." Her work is an important addition to oral history's longstanding concern with memories of war, genocide, and dictatorship. However, more importantly perhaps, is the contribution these narratives make in understanding the complex relationships between individual and collective identity, collective memory, and forms of public commemoration.

Pilar Domínguez's "Spanish Socialist Trade Unionists during the End of the Franco Regime and the Transition to Democracy" examines the political trajectories of five labor militants in the socialist UGT, the General Union of Workers. In analyzing their life history interviews, she finds that the narrators follow certain patterns of self-representation. Their narratives offer a genealogy of their union militancy, charting a collective story of political protest and organizational activism and strategies both during the regime and the transitional period. She finds that official discourses and media representations of these political changes shaped the way union leaders retell the past. The choral character of their accounts shows that over the years, trade unionists have forged a collective memory that has cemented their identity as a group. Those interviewed describe how they wholeheartedly embraced common political ideas at the time, although today some of them take a more critical view of the ideas and values that characterized socialist unionism. The depictions of that period suggest that that memory has undergone reinterpretation, weakening the cohesion of the group and its collective identity. This reminds us that the telling of the past always bears the stamp of experiences and events that transpired since the time of the events recounted.

Wolff, Pedro, and da Silva's collection of 170 personal narratives of militant women in the armed struggles against dictatorship in Argentina,

Bolivia, Brazil, Chile, Paraguay, and Uruguay, offers an excellent example of what Passerini (2010) calls the "gendering" of history, acknowledging the importance of gender subjectivity in both the private (traditionally assigned to women) and public spheres. Passerini asserts, "To discover subjectivity in memory is to restore to the narrator her full condition as a subject capable of making her own life decisions and forging her own strategies" (120). Like much feminist research in Latin America, the authors also draw on the theoretical contributions of Judith Butler and Joan Scott, proposing that just as women's bodies are gendered, so also are their narratives. The chapter explores a range of gendered themes in militant women's narratives: maternity, personal male-female relationships, and discrimination against women in political organizations. Most interesting is the discussion of "memories of the female body." Narrators recollect how in order to be fully accepted in their respective political organizations, they had to discard their femininity and adopt masculine corporeal attitudes—to look and act like men. The authors highlight the importance of recognizing the use and abuse of power over the female body, as their narrators' engaged in the difficult and traumatic process of remembering experiences of torture and other brutalities at the hands of dictatorial regimes. In reflecting on the relationship between past and present, the authors note that the expansion of feminism in later years, coupled with the rise of three former militant women as democratically elected presidents in Argentina, Brazil, and Chile, has reshaped the ways in which these militant women have come to understand and explain the past.

Subjectivity and Identity Construction

Complementing collective aspects of memory, we turn to considerations of individual memory and subjectivity, the stock-in-trade of oral history. The four chapters that comprise this section concern the most personal aspect of identity, the creation of a self—one that must be reinvented. They also all concern women. Although not all the chapters specifically address the question of gender or engage it as the theoretical frame, each examines women's struggles to redefine their identities under conditions of subordination, humiliation, physical displacement, and economic marginalization. In each case, the narrator's quest for identity is marked by current social realities—migration, precarious labor markets, discrimination, and the impact of social origins and political activism on identity. These conditions and social circumstances challenge women's subjectivity—disrupting their senses of self and their place in the societies they inhabit. Each narrator grapples with what Villarreal calls a "reframing" that involves reflecting on the past self, adopting a new persona—a new "I," and adjusting frames of reference to shifting realities. These chapters also demonstrate the particular attention the authors give to open and attentive dialogue and establishing a trusting connection with their "storytellers" (Portelli 2005: 6).

Miren Llona's chapter, "The Healing Effect of Discourses: Body, Emotions, and Gender Subjectivity in Basque Nationalism," connects the political and the personal, collective memory and personal subjectivity. To inform her inquiry, Llona approaches Basque nationalism, a major topic in contemporary Spanish political history, through feminism, cultural studies, US Chicana studies (Moraga), and pathbreaking work in the field of emotion studies (Passerini; Matt; Reddy). Particularly significant life experiences, Llona argues, leave an emotional imprint within us, searing these experiences into what she calls "enclaves of memory," moments of deep significance in the shaping of our identities. As memory is embodied, she contends, we experience our identities as a natural, intrinsic, part of our beings, rather than as something constructed or learned. In analyzing the life narrative of Basque nationalist Polixene Trabudúa, Llona finds clues to the enclaves of memory in the affective qualities of her narrator's performance: her tone, recurrent use of the verb "feel," modulations of voice, and laughter. Llona's narrator relives her process of identity transformation from a rural Basque woman, ashamed of her traditional origins, to an ardent nationalist, proud of her roots. Attending to the gendered dimensions of Trabudúa's experience, Llona underscores the emotional power of political ideology in restoring a sense of personal integrity and dignity, transforming a subordinated subjectivity into an integrated identity in which the personal and the political are inextricably intertwined.

In "Lola's Story: The Struggle to Build a Professional Identity with No Good Jobs in Sight," María Eugenia Cardenal, like Llona, adopts a strategy of close textual reading and attention to emotive expression. She examines the story of a young social educator, whose attempts to find employment in her field and forge a professional identity are frustrated by the 2008 labor market collapse in Spain. To analyze Lola's construction of identity, Cardenal provides a very interesting step-by-step textual analysis using Chamberlayne and Wengraf's (Wengraf 2001) Biographic Narrative Interpretive Method (BNIM). This method is based on the open-ended interview, in which the interviewer closely follows the narrator's thread. According to the method, Cardenal identifies and juxtaposes two tracks of information: the biographical facts of Lola's "lived life" and actual professional trajectory, and the narrative itself, the way in which Lola "tells her story." Identifying the internal structure of each track and the relationship between them, Cardenal finds that Lola's educational and employment history reveals an intermittent downward trajectory. In her telling she adopts a matter-of-fact tone, showing little or no emotion when talking about her "downs." However, she expresses passion and engagement when describing her "ups." This change of tone provides an interpretive clue. Despite Lola's downward trajectory and the precariousness of her present employment, the stable core of her self is constructed around a story that highlights her worth, effort, and competence.

Mexican anthropologist Magdalena Villarreal also examines a single life story in order to understand how and why Mexican migrant farmworkers construct their claim to the "American Dream." Crossing the border into the California fields, she establishes a relationship with María, a Mexican migrant woman who works as a picker and a field forewoman. She visits María in her home, follows her into the fields, attends community festivities with her, records interviews, and annotates informal conversations. In "Getting Ahead: The American Dream in the California Agricultural Fields," Villarreal contextualizes María's life history accounts (formal and informal) in relation to the realities of hard physical labor, poverty, economic instability, limited rights, and lack of legal status in the United States. Within all these constraints, the expectation of a better future is the engine that drives María and allows her to "reframe" her identity as a responsible "cultural citizen," community leader, capable worker, consumer, and generous hostess who recreates a sense of family community in "el norte." Villarreal illustrates how this constructed dream rationalizes María's economic subordination and precarious legal status, filling day-to-day hardships with optimism and hope. As was true of Lola, María is aware of her place in the economic and social ladder, but she overlooks the obstacles and reframes her persona—a new I, for what matters to her are the steps she is taking to achieve her American Dream.

Similar to Villarreal, Arjona, Checa, Acién, and Majuelos take up the theme of women's economic migration, and use mixed field methods of informal and formal interviews, participant observation, and even advocacy to establish relationships of trust with their narrators. In "Migration, Sex Work, and Stigma: An Analysis in Biographical Code," they analyze the responses of immigrant sex workers from Latin America, Africa, and Eastern Europe, to the social stigma they experience in Almería, Spain. Their narratives provide a vivid portrait of women who enter sex work out of economic and legal need, only to find themselves in debt, undocumented, and trapped in a sex trade network that brought them to Spain. Displaced from home and culture and highly conscious of the stigma attached to sex work, they must find an "acceptable" identity under circumstances of great economic and gender subordination. The authors describe the multiple protective strategies that the women devise to negotiate the boundaries between their daily lives and their work, and between their work and their desire for legal status. Some defend their work, affirming that it fulfills a social need. However, an emotional distance from sex work predominates in these accounts. The women find themselves obliged to invent a provisional persona, one that can withstand personal shame and social opprobrium in the hopes that their situation will improve and they can leave behind their present way of life.

Memory and Public Representations

Oral history's democratic impulse suggests that, along with collecting, archiving, and interpreting oral narratives, we also consider their public uses and potential for social transformation. Beyond the mere display of oral texts in public settings like museums, exhibits, documentaries, or archives, representation concerns the production of meanings, the public contexts and venues for their production, and the audience's interpretations of these productions. Just as memory and subjectivity are contingent and changeable, so also are the meanings derived from the re/presentational strategies we use to bring oral narratives into public view.

All four chapters in this section—from Brazil, Mexico, and Portugal—deal with the relationship between narrative and image, in what Freund and Thomson refer to as the "visual turn" in oral history (1). They highlight the relationship between the oral and the visual, memory and document, and propose unusual and creative spaces of representation: the body, the Internet, memorial exhibitions, and dramatic performances. Each suggest ways in which oral narratives and their public representations resignify the past from the perspective of the present, reshaping and undermining official narratives and social attitudes, and opening spaces for new meanings.

In "Oral Accounts on Visual Inscriptions: Narratives under Heavily Tattooed Skin," sociologist Vitor Ferreira explores how the body is at once a private site of personal memory (a *lieu de mémoire*) and a living museum of visual public representation. Through a combination of informal conversations, observation, and recorded interviews with young adults in the Lisbon tattoo scene, Ferreira demonstrates how biographical narratives are critical to decoding the tattoos and to understanding their role in the construction of identity. He argues that tattoos "express the embodied struggle to conquer and maintain a desired identity." Each tattoo permanently inscribed on the skin is auto-bio-graphical, representing an affirmation of selfhood that talks back to social exclusion and to cultural attitudes that stigmatize the heavily tattooed as deviants.

In "The Black Movement and Race Relations in Brazil: Building New Knowledge through Online Oral History Materials," historians Verena Alberti and Amilcar Pereira engage a rich trove of oral histories to address a different social concern—racism in Brazil. Their work combines the visual and disseminative capacity of the Internet with the representational and emotional power of videotaped oral narratives to produce curricular materials for use in public education. Their materials challenge, for example, the discourse of *mestizaje* (racial mixing) that continues to mask the existence and persistence of racism and prejudice in the country. Through pedagogical exercises juxtaposing oral narratives and other historical sources, students become their own historians, deriving new historically informed interpretations and understandings of colonial and postcolonial race relations. In this way, oral histories play a vital role in reshaping the national consciousness on race, and the Internet provides all teachers and students access to this material. Alberti and Pereira's work is part of a conscious effort in Latin America and Spain to integrate oral history in school curricula, providing younger generations with new sources for understanding the national political past (Benadiba in Argentina and Spain; Castro Bueno and the Oral History Collective in Colombia, among others).

In "Images and Words: Photography and the 1968 Student Movement in Mexico," Mexican historian Alberto del Castillo challenges official narratives and popular discourses about Mexico's recent national past. In oral history interviews with newspaper photographers who captured for posterity the story of the student massacre at Tlatelolco in 1968, Castillo explores how their images were/are both used and understood in the past and present. Rather than legitimizing the past, these interviews, conducted in 2008 for a photographic exhibition at the site's memorial museum, illustrate the power of images and words to reshape collective, public, and political "imaginaries." The photographers' compelling images circulated widely in newspapers at the time, and were manipulated to bolster the official government narrative that condemned the students as the perpetrators of lawlessness. Today, those same images have become part of a new official national discourse that honors the murdered students as martyrs. Castillo's work exemplifies how "photographs and oral narratives play on each other during the interview [to] construct rather than simply reveal, recover, or retell the past" (Freund and Thomson 10). In analyzing what the images said then, how they were used then, and what they say now, del Castillo illustrates how the visual and the narrative open up the past to new critical interpretations.

Finally, theatrical artistic director and performance artist Joana Craveiro explores the production and contestation of memory by taking oral history to the stage. In "A Living Museum of Small, Forgotten and Unwanted Memories," a one-woman "performance/lecture" in seven acts that premiered in Lisbon in 2014, Craveiro reenacts official and private memories of the 1974 revolution in Portugal. Her objective, in this highly imaginative stage creation, is to provoke her audiences into self-reflection and to critique official commemorations (or lack thereof) of this critical period in the country's recent past. She takes the stage as an "Archivist," sitting at her desk, sorting through, arranging, and commenting on the rich array of materials before her—oral histories, historical documents, images, and music. As the performance proceeds, the Archivist morphs into her oral history narrators, embodying and voicing their testimonies "word for word, utterance by utterance," presenting various aspects of this national story. The performance concludes with an open forum in which the audience is invited to comment on the performance itself, a kind of reenactment of the popular assemblies of the revolutionary period. This becomes an active *lieu de mémoire* (Nora), a space of memory, meaning-making, and healing. By witnessing the juxtaposition of positions and emotions on stage, audiences with varying perspectives on the revolution see themselves represented and are moved to comment on what they have seen and felt. The discussion becomes a testimonial space to enact the complex and contested nature of memory and, as Craveiro suggests, to move beyond binary Left/Right positions into the "im/possibility" of reconciling the past.

Overall Highlights

As we wrote at the beginning of this introduction, we designed this collection to extend bridges across linguistic, geographical, and disciplinary divides in the study of oral narratives. We intentionally chose a set of chapters that demonstrate the variety of themes, approaches, and uses of oral narratives in

Latin American, Portuguese, and Spanish scholarship. As the volume took shape, however, we took notice of several distinctive, cross-cutting features regarding oral narratives and memory that invite comment.

In the introduction to *Oral History and Public Memories* (2008), Paula Hamilton and Linda Shopes note, "As areas of research and writing, oral history and memory studies have had very different historiographic trajectories" (viii). Although their statement is primarily in reference to Holocaust studies, it caught our attention since in Latin America and the Iberian Peninsula the trajectories of oral history and memory studies have not been distinct. Oral historians in these regions have been profoundly influenced by theoretical studies of social, collective, and individual memory. Halbwach's writings on memorialization and collective memory, Nora's concept of "sites of memory" (*les lieux de mémoire*), and Ricoeur's work on the relationship between narrative, memory, and identities, have been fundamental to the development of oral history scholarship in Spanish and Portuguese. Josefina Cuesta's (1998) interpretations of Halbwachs, Ricoeur, and Nora, and Enzo Traverso's popular volume on the uses of the past (2011), translated into Spanish and Portuguese, made these and other theoretical work on history and memory widely accessible to oral historians, and many authors in this collection cite these sources. Many also look to more recent writings on memory coming from cultural studies, as noted by several references in this volume of Marianne Hirsch's theorizations of visual culture and postmemory (1997, 2012).

A second overarching highlight of this volume is the attention given to the relationship between memory and the body. The body harbors the most intimate aspects of the self and memory, but at the same time it is part of the surrounding social world, bridging the personal and the social, the intimate sphere and the public, individual subjectivity and collective identities. Several chapters express particular sensitivity to the embodied emotional dimensions of memory, as influenced by feminist theory and the more recent area of emotion studies. Llona and Arjona et al. explore narrators' feelings of shame; Wolff et al. analyze women's memories of "masculinization" in political underground movements. Alberti and Pereira foreground responses of black Brazilians to the racialized body. Ferreira presents the tattooed body as a canvas for individual expression, and, in Craveiro's work, the body becomes a performative incarnation of political and cultural meanings. This attention to the body, emotions, and subjectivities in oral narratives now shares intellectual space with the more traditional concerns of political history in Latin American and Iberian oral history research.[6]

A third thread that we observed across many of the chapters is the conscious awareness of the multilayered dialogic relationships that researchers build with their subjects and their narratives. Some of the chapters pay attention to the moment of encounter in the interview itself, articulating the methodological strategies of the interviewers for building rapport with their narrators (Cardenal, Campos, Villarreal, Ferreira, Arjona et al.). Others reflect on a second dialogic moment of meta-conversation as researchers enter into dialogue with their narrators' voices and detail their steps in analyzing and interpreting the interviews (Campos, Llona, Cardenal, Ferreira, Alberti, and Pereira). Another group of chapters foregrounds the influence of public memory on the accounts the narrators construct in the present moment of the interview (Domínguez, del Castillo, Campos). Finally, some researchers reflect on power dynamics and their roles in shaping the narratives (Cardenal, Campos, Craveiro). Craveiro's work is especially multilayered as she reflects on her role as researcher, performer, and catalyst for audience dialogues about remembrance. While these considerations are not new to oral history research, they reflect a post positivist, constructivist consciousness that is now common among humanists and qualitative social scientists.

And yet, despite the shared approaches and practices among those who work with oral narratives, the strong pull into disciplinary silos remains striking. While compiling this volume, we discovered that there is comparatively little cross-disciplinary referencing across the chapters. Many of the authors do not know each other or each other's work. Scholars outside the field of oral history are often not conversant with its literature or the insights it offers into the analysis of life narratives. Conversely, oral historians stand to gain from exploring new developments in ethnographic life history and biographical treatments in sociology. It is our hope that this volume will encourage greater mutual curiosity, access, and cross-disciplinary dialogues in oral narrative research, not only across linguistic and disciplinary divides but also among this volume's authors themselves, who can learn much from each other's work.

Notes

1. Two important topics that, for various reasons, we were unable to incorporate in this volume include virtual archives and museums and the struggles and political debates surrounding them in Argentina, Chile, Brazil, Mexico, and across the autonomous regions of Spain; and oral traditions and narratives in indigenous communities.

2. Gerardo Necoechea (Mexico), Pablo Pozzi (Argentina), and Robson Laverdi (Brazil), coedited this special issue along with the journal's editor, Alexander Freund (Canada).
3. Since 1984, the International Sociological Association has sponsored a Research Committee on Biography and Society, to "help develop a better understanding of the relations between individual lives, the social structures and historical processes within which they take shape and which they contribute to shape, and the individual accounts of biographical experience (such as life stories or autobiographies)" (http://www.isa-sociology.org/rc.htm). The European Sociological Association also sponsors a Research Network on Biographical Perspectives on European Societies.
4. Mexico's interdisciplinary National Institute for Anthropology and History [Instituto Nacional de Antropología e Historia, or INAH], established the first oral history spoken word archive in Latin America, the Archivo de la Palabra. The Instituto Mora, renowned for its work in history and social sciences, is a major center for oral history research in Mexico City. The Mexican Center for Advanced Research and Postgraduate Studies in Social Anthropology (CIESAS) is home to anthropologists who also publish in oral history. In Portugal the Centro de Estudios Sociais (Center for Social Studies) and the Instituto de Ciências Sociais da Universidade de Lisboa (Institute of Social Sciences of the University of Lisbon) have been meeting grounds for scholars who work in qualitative methods across such disciplines. In recent years, the European Social Science History Conference has become another cross-disciplinary meeting ground for oral historians and social scientists.
5. More recently, Miren Llona's anthology *Entreverse* (2012) brings Spanish-speaking cultural historians, sociologists, and anthropologists together around theory, method, and use of oral sources.
6. Antonio Montenegro y Gerardo Necoechea's 2011 volume, *Caminos de Historia y Memoria en América Latina,* illustrates the persistent centrality of politics in Latin American oral history. The essays address issues related to the public sphere, conflicts over urban spaces, class and gender, the organized Left, and social movements during the dictatorships and in the present day.

Works Cited

Benadiba, Laura. "Proyecto ArCa: 'La Persistencia del Silencio después de la Dictadura.' La Escuela como Lugar de Memoria." *CONHISREMI, Revista Universitaria de Investigación y Diálogo Académico* 5.1 (2009): 1–12. Web.

Bertaux, Daniel. *Biography And Society: The Life-History Approach in the Social Sciences.* London: Sage, 1981. Print.

Bertaux, Daniel and Isabelle Bertaux-Wiame. "Stories as Clues to Sociological Understanding." *Our Common History: The Transformation of Europe.* Ed. Paul Thompson. London: Pluto Press, 1982. 93–108. Print.

Bornat, Joanna. "Reminiscence and Oral History: Parallel Universes or Shared Endeavor?" *Ageing and Society* 21.02 (March 2001): 219–241. Print.

———. "Remembering as the Politics of Later Life." *The Oxford Handbook of Oral History*. Ed. D. Ritchie. New York: Oxford University Press, 2012. 202–218. Print.

Butler, Judith. *Gender Trouble: Feminism and the Subversion of Identity.* New York: Routledge, 1990. Print.

Castro Bueno, Fabio, et al. "La Investigación Histórica Escolar con Fuentes Orales como Estrategia para la Formación y Desarrollo del Pensamiento Histórico en la Educación Básica y Media." Web.

Chamberlayne, Prue, Joanna Bornat, and Tom Wengraf. *The Turn to Biographical Methods in Social Science: Comparative Issues and Examples.* London: Routledge, 2000. Print

Cuesta Bustillo, Josefina. "Memoria e Historia. Un Estado de la Cuestión." *Memoria e Historia*. Ed. Josefina Cuesta. Madrid: Pons, 1998. 203–224. Print.

Freund, Alexander and Alistair Thomson. *Oral History and Photography.* New York: Palgrave, 2012. Print.

Halbwachs, Maurice. *Los Marcos Sociales de la Memoria* [English: *On Collective Memory*]. Barcelona: Anthropos, 2004. Print.

Hamilton, Paula and Linda Shopes. *Oral History and Public Memories.* Philadelphia, PA: Temple University Press, 2008. Print.

Hirsch, Marianne. *Family Frames: Photography, Narrative, and Postmemory.* Cambridge, MA: Harvard University Press, 1997. Print.

———. *The Generation of Postmemory, Writing and Visual Culture after the Holocaust.* New York: Columbia University Press, 2012. Print.

Historia, Antropología y Fuentes Orales [formerly *Historia y Fuente Oral*]. Barcelona: Asociación Historia y Fuente Oral, Universitat de Barcelona.

História Oral. Journal of the Brazilian Oral History Association (ABHO). http://revista.historiaoral.org.br/index.php?journal=rho

Jelin, Elizabeth. *Los Trabajos de la Memoria* [*State Repression and the Labors of Memory*]. Madrid: Siglo XXI, 2002. Print.

Llona, Miren. *Entreverse. Teoría y Metodología Práctica de las Fuentes Orales.* Bilbao: Universidad del País Vasco/Euskal Herriko Unibertsitatea, 2012. 15–61. Print.

Matt, Susan J. "Current Emotion Research in History: Or Doing History from the Inside Out." *Emotion Review* 3.1 (2011): 117–124. Print.

Montenegro, Antonio and Gerardo Necoechea, eds. *Caminos de Historia y Memoria en América Latina.* Buenos Aires: Imago Mundi, 2011. Web.

Moraga, Cherríe and Gloria Anzaldúa. *This Bridge Called My Back: Writings of Radical Women of Color.* New York: Kitchen Table, Women of Color Press, 1983. Print.

Newsletter/Boletín. International Oral History Association. http://www.iohanet.org/ioha-newsletter

Nora, Pierre. "La Aventura de *Les Lieux de Mémoire*." Memoria e Historia. Josefina Cuesta, ed. Madrid: Marcial Pons, 1998. 17–34.

Oliveira, Luisa. "A História Oral em Portugal." *Sociologia, Problemas e Práticas* 63 (2010): 139–156. Print.

Oral History Forum d'Histoire Orale. Special Issue/Edición Especial: Oral History in Latin America/Historia Oral en América Latina. Pablo Pozzi, Alexander Freund, Gerardo Necoechea and Robson Laverdi, eds.

Passerini, Luisa. "La Memoria como Subjetividad e Intersubjetividad en las Narraciones de Memoria de las Mujeres." *Subjetividad, Cultura Material y Género: Diálogos con la Historiografía Italiana*. Ed. Pilar Pérez Fuentes. Barcelona: Icaria, 2010. 115–131. Print.

Portelli, Alessandro. *The Battle of Valle Giulia: Oral History and the Art of Dialogue*. Madison: University of Wisconsin Press, 1997.

———. "What Makes Oral History Different." *The Oral History Reader*. Ed. Robert Perks and Alistair Thompson. London: Routledge. 1998. 63–74. Print.

———. "A Dialogical Relationship: An Approach to Oral History." *Expressions Annual 2005*. http://www.swaraj.org/shikshantar/expressions_portelli.pdf.

Reddy, William M. "Historical Research on the Self and Emotions." *Emotion Review* 1.4 (2009): 302–315. Print.

Ricoeur, Paul. *La Lectura del Tiempo Pasado: Memoria y Olvido*. Madrid: Universidad Autónoma, 1999.

Scott, Joan W. *Gender and the Politics of History*. New York: Columbia University Press, 1988. 28–50.

Thomson, Alistair. "Four Paradigm Transformations in Oral History." *The Oral History Review* 34.1 (2007): 49–70.

Traverso, Enzo. *El Pasado: Instrucciones de Uso* [The Past: Instructions for Use]. Buenos Aires: Prometeo, 2011. Print.

Wengraf, Tom. *Qualitative Research Interviewing: Biographic Narrative and Semi-Structured Methods*. London: SAGE. 2001. Print.

Words and Silences: The Journal of the International Oral History Association. http://www.iohanet.org/call-for-articles-word-and-silences-2/.

PART I

Collective Memory and Identities

CHAPTER 1

"I Was Just One More among Many":
A Mosaic of Ex-combatant Voices from
the Portuguese Colonial War

Ângela Campos

The Portuguese Colonial War (1961–1974) and
Its Memorial Legacy

I was just one more [soldier] among many, one more to add to those thousands who have been there, one more—who went there—among so many, from so many villages, mountains, cities—I was just one more who went to the *Ultramar* [overseas provinces]...[Now] I am part of this group [veterans]. I too got drafted.[1]

Joaquim Azinheira, whose words these are, was, indeed, one of the nearly one million Portuguese conscripted men who fulfilled their military service from 1961 to 1974 in Angola, Mozambique, and Portuguese Guinea (now Guinea-Bissau), then colonial territories of Portugal. Not recognizing the independence aspirations of those African "overseas provinces," the Portuguese regime responded with counterinsurgency. By 1964, the Forças

Armadas Portuguesas (Portuguese Armed Forces) were fighting on three fronts in Africa, commonly known as the "Portuguese colonial war."[2] The conflict ended in 1974 with the April 25 Portuguese Revolution. Initiated by a coup led by the Portuguese military, the "Carnation Revolution," as it came to be known, marked the end of the Salazar dictatorship, the Estado Novo (New State), and the Portuguese rule in Africa.[3] Overnight, Portugal embraced democracy after 48 years of dictatorship (1926–1974), and was the last European nation to relinquish protracted conflict and centuries-old claims to an overseas empire.

Given the mobilization of over 90 percent of male youth during that period—1 percent of the Portuguese population—Azinheira and his family were, indeed, one of many, since practically every Portuguese family was affected by the conflict, at the time and afterward.[4]

The move from a decades-long dictatorial regime to a newborn democracy in 1974 confers complexity to the public memory of the conflict. There are memorial difficulties associated with the dictatorial, colonial legacy and the lack of real national unity around the cultural memory of the war. Consequently, official, public, and private silences, indifference, and ruptures in the memorial transmission of the past have long engulfed this conflict and its combatants, generating a "collective amnesia" (Medeiros 202). Displaying features of a "traumatized community" or "transitional society" (Dawson 207), Portugal's remembrance dilemmas became significant aspects in defining the memorial aftermath of the colonial war and its combatants.

Despite prolonged dismissal of the war in public memory, from the 2000s onward, the Portuguese colonial conflict has generated new and wider forms of commemoration and higher veteran visibility, particularly informal, veteran-promoted ones. Changing sociocultural circumstances—such as a sense of chronological and generational distance, the maturing of Portuguese democracy, expansion of various cultural sectors, and the impact of international remembrance frameworks—have played a part. "Now," as narrator Daniel Cunha remarked, "these issues are talked about a bit—although not enough."

Notwithstanding this revival, in Portugal, remembrance of the colonial war and its ex-combatants remains uncomfortable and laden with divisiveness, shame, and political polarizations. In 2011, the fiftieth anniversary of the beginning of the conflict, the Portuguese Ministry of Defense declared, "We are still ashamed of the war."[5]

This sensitive relationship with the colonial conflict paradoxically allows Portuguese society to simultaneously engage in increasing war remembrances while producing continued instances of forgetting. The history of this war, in particular, remains largely unwritten, suggesting historiographical dismissal and postponement (Barata 5: 197). In our interview, and echoed by others, Manuel Loureiro described this as "one of the great failings of our country," a history that is "already long overdue."

My oral history research illuminated the fact that in their role as soldiers of the Portuguese army in Africa, the ex-combatants are, to a great extent, positioned as "untidy reminders" of the colonial past (Evans 1997). In attempting to find the identities of these veterans, I encountered a group of embarrassing historical actors portrayed disparately as dutiful citizens fulfilling military service; committed patriots; last defendants of the Portuguese empire; obedient thugs serving fascism; or young, inexperienced, conscripted victims of the dictatorship. Their position is a dubious one, permeated by political contradictions and guilt surrounding participation in the colonial war.

Whatever the viewpoint, most of the hundreds of thousands of veterans living in Portugal, like Azinheira, were born in the 1940s and 1950s and were conscripts doing their military service—which, after 1968, included a training period in Portugal and at least two years in the African theater. Fighting was a "national mission assigned to them by the political power" (Antunes 7) and, adhering or not to the ideals of the regime, most fulfilled their duty. Those who chose insubordination (by leaving the country before conscription) or desertion would face the regime's harsh penalties. Those who served—veterans like Azinheira and thousands of others—nowadays represent a generation whose shared identity is brought into existence by the war experience.

Demographically still a very significant section of Portuguese society, many of these ex-combatants, now mainly in their sixties and seventies and embarking on a life-review phase, acquire a new, reflective awareness of their involvement in this conflict. Aware of the passage of time and the specter of their physical disappearance, these war veterans stand between shifting memorial developments and their own negotiated concessions to forgetting and remembering. They are often plagued by the double trauma of having been compulsorily conscripted to fight and then having their society deny acknowledgment of that experience.

More noticeably in the last decade and a half, the aging and mostly retired veterans group has emerged with a stronger and clearly distinguishable generational identity, higher visibility, and greater social mobilization power, particularly toward claims for support and recognition.[6] Struggles for wider public recognition made the country comparatively more sensitive and informed about many aspects of the veterans' war, more aware of the importance of their first-hand experiences and of the need to question a persistent indifference surrounding the topic.

Interviewing Ex-combatants of the Portuguese Colonial War

The typical underinclusion of war veteran's lived perspectives in the historical record and wide historiographical disagreement over the positioning of the colonial war have limited interpretative angles and blocked more inclusive, fuller accounts of the conflict. Albeit challenging, such circumstances created an ideal platform for an oral history assessment of the ex-combatant experience. These veterans provide a unique opportunity to explore the war's subjective and experiential side and in so doing, to understand the new group identity forged through a common war experience.

Seventy veterans agreed to participate in my doctoral oral history research, focused on gathering accounts of their lived experiences of this war (Campos 2014). I interviewed 36—of wide geographical, chronological, class, and educational backgrounds—who served in different branches of the armed forces on the three African fronts. Conducted in Portuguese across continental Portugal between 2005 and 2008, these interviews followed a simple but encompassing guideline that focused not only on the war experience, but also on the period before and after the conflict, providing ample contextualization of each individual's life story.

Rather than advancing claims for absolute representativeness, my sample constitutes an experiential range—a rich composite portrait of diverse war memories. Their narratives give insight into the servicemen's typical military path, from conscription, training, mobilization, departure to and service in Africa, to return to Portugal.

Inspired by Portelli's (2010) image of each interviewee's story as an individual "tile" in a composite "mosaic" of human experience, I investigated this war generation through the meanings and historical patterns contained in the veterans' oral histories. I argue that we can reach a wider, more meaningful and inclusive understanding of this war by crafting a multifaceted picture of how these men perceive themselves as war veterans and manifest their group identity in contemporary Portuguese society.

Adopting Thomson's approach, I embraced a historiographical inquiry that acknowledges the subjectivity of memory—as object, subject and source (2011:80, 86). A revealing asset rather than a debilitating flaw, the subjectivity of the interviews encompasses the partial and retrospective nature of any traditional historical source, in this case, mediated and cocreated by the researcher.

My oral history practice suggested that in Portugal there exists a common perception (expressed by interviewees too) that the voice of the average war participant is undeserving of academic interest, and that hierarchy and traditional politico-military historiography should be privileged. Such historiographical conservatism, alongside a visible resistance to address the topic more widely in the here and now, has often pushed oral history contributions to the margins. Besides generating a platform to assess the memorial complexities of this conflict, the oral history approach was also a chance to uncover the frequently neglected standpoint of ordinary servicemen, and their personal everyday experiences during and after the war. Significantly underrepresented are the perspectives of working-class soldiers, the injured and disabled combatant, and the lower rank noncommissioned officers.

Having been given "a listening space" (Rogers and Leydesdorff 9–10), the veterans who participated in this project offered insight into how this conflict is remembered and interpreted by those who fought it. While simultaneously documenting their war trajectories, I sought to critically assess the meanings they attributed to their war experiences, focusing on "[individual] feelings, attitudes and motivations (Evans 231–232)." Interviewing these veterans was challenging on many levels. It meant addressing traumatic elements that frequently emerged as difficult remembering during the interview. For Portuguese ex-combatants, such aspects appear to be heightened by the divisive nature of the conflict, its associated shame and guilt, and the historical neglect its veterans have experienced for decades.[7] Talking to and about live historical actors who have felt long-term marginalization meant that many perceived the interview as an opportunity to not only articulate their stories but also voice claims for recognition and support. Throughout this project, I encountered many examples of the consequences of lack of veteran recognition. Sensitive personal scenarios are often associated with physical and psychological disability, violence, family breakdown, and social maladjustment. All these aspects shape the testimonies I collected.

Furthermore, their retrospectively "composed" individual narratives—to employ Thomson's concept (1994: 215–16)—are necessarily interwoven with available public cultural discourses at the time of telling, reflecting Portugal's democratic sociopolitical shifts and cultural developments. Such narratives also express the veterans' evolving life stages and choices. The chronological variation in their accounts reflects shifting personal and collective identity characteristics associated with different biographical phases.

My research suggested that, with the passage of time, most veterans acquired a notion of their historical significance as actors of the country's contemporary history, namely as participants in a divisive conflict of non-unified public memory. As the public remembrance of the war increased in the last decade and a half, many veterans developed an acute generational and group identity awareness, seeking to make sense of their war experience and comprehend the wider meaning of the conflict.

In composing a narrative mosaic from the many different tiles of individual voices, I underline the most prominent features of the ex-combatants' discourse on their collective identity as veterans in contemporary Portugal. Their words, structures, themes, and meanings repeated throughout many hours of interviews guide my analysis. I found that the most prevalent themes arise through notions of generational bonds, sacrifice and futility of war, fulfilled duty, official and social neglect and unrecognition, uneasiness about the past, disappointment about the public remembrance of the conflict, and the assertion that the ex-combatants themselves constitute a privileged memorial location aware of the duty of historical transmission.

Veterans in Their Own Words

Today, hundreds of thousands of Portuguese men who served the Portuguese Army in Africa between 1961 and 1974 are united by that transformative "collective" experience. Most veterans interviewed portrayed themselves as members of the "war generation," since "any [Portuguese] man [of a certain age] would have been in the *Ultramar*." Often aware of the sensitive social space they occupy, they frequently repeat that they "belong to a sacrificed and misunderstood generation...who lost two years of their lives...for nothing," feeling that their war experience confers a socially distinctive factor in relation to subsequent generations. As Manuel Figueiredo reasoned, "I was part of it....I was part of them [combatants], and all the rest is nonsense." Frequently, the ex-combatants used language that emphasized a certain individual powerlessness regarding the role they played in the national military process. This sense of powerlessness highlighted their group bonds. Some described themselves as "one more stone" comprising the military block, others as "a piece of a larger unit." Joaquim Piteira explained how he was

> a little matchstick, you know, a little matchstick, amongst thousands of matchsticks....This matchstick was a matchstick that...was lit...and

then slowly died out. There are thousands of matchsticks…and many of them have already died out, and many of them are about to…the soldier was like that…like a matchstick. We light it, it was…it was alive…it got extinguished, dumped to one side, it's done, and bit by bit, there they remained extinguished, forgotten.

Although not all think about the war experience on a daily basis, many perceived their military service in Africa as the most important event of their lives, the experience that "sticks out" from the rest, and one that shaped the course of their future and forged a common generational identity. That is true of Francisco Fitas, whose military service in Angola remains a pivotal life phase:

Want it or not, my subconscious is always thinking about it, because sometimes in life we have years and years and years that are routine-like. We almost don't even give them a second thought, but then there is a short phase…of our life, but it leaves such marks on one that, that it's always above the others, which is, which is this case…of going to Africa. It was a very turbulent period, unforgettable…it fills a lot of our life, that…that period. Perhaps…it is the most remarkable of my life…and that is the one which frequently is more in the subconscious, because here, this day-to-day life is everyday the same thing.…On the other hand this war period is different, it is a period which…arrived, is gone, but stayed in me…and, alright, I'm always remembering it…it was, of all phases of my life, the one which left more marks, because it was the most agitated period of my life.

Interestingly, when questioned about their feelings about having fought in the colonial conflict, a significant number of interviewees mention that they feel "rather proud" and "honored" to have "served" and fought for "our motherland," and for "having belonged to the Armed Forces," or "having served the Portuguese Army" during the 24 months spent in Africa. In these statements, most discard the political complexity of acknowledging their satisfaction in having taken part in a colonial army opposed to African liberation movements. Beyond political standpoints, these ex-servicemen also appear to associate traditional notions of masculinity to their military experience, ascribing to national military service a pride-inspiring rite of passage from youths into grown men. From that perspective, they see their participation in the conflict as "positive."

In their role as former soldiers, these men often emphasize that their bonds emerged from the hardships jointly endured in Africa. As Figueiredo noted, their identity bond was also forged in the deep-lasting solidarities created by the intensity of armed combat (Dawson 2007). Some stress that their comradeship and trust are so enduring that they are stronger than family ties. Many express their group solidarity by socializing in veteran associations, or formal or informal veteran gatherings—arenas that have increased in popularity over the last decade.[8] As the years advance, the ex-combatants become aware that they "are an endangered species," feeling the urgency to locate and interact with one another. Many find, in these spaces, the most comfortable location to "intensely" reconnect with their war past, a reconnection with "the youth of my time," and a sign "that we are alive." A significant number of my interviewees stressed the fact that only a comrade can understand another one. For instance, Daniel Cunha explained how upon meeting another war veteran, even a stranger, the conversation topic will frequently converge on the colonial war:

> We leave feeling relieved.... "What about you? Where have you been?"
>
> "In Angola"
>
> "Hey man, you've been there! You know"
>
> Yeah, I mean, that seems to take us back there again... seems to take us back to when we were twenty... I leave with a great feeling of friendship... and above all with... a burden is lifted from my shoulders.

Illustrating what Winter (1999) calls "fictive kinships" or "families of remembrance," such examples reveal how the veterans display a very clear sense of themselves as a distinct generation. As Cunha points out, it is significant to note that, even for veterans who did not fight together, a social group proximity can be forged in relation to the rest of society. However, that aspect certainly becomes more prominent regarding comrades-in-arms. Recollecting meeting the men of his combat group, Manuel Figueiredo emphasizes:

> We know what we have been through. Nobody else is able to interpret... no matter how much one talks, how much I say, that we trembled, what we did, we can't pass this message to anybody. Therefore that, on that occasion, this is our family... we will never separate in life... because I cover their back, and they cover mine. They always covered me.

Significantly, some veterans display awareness of the ambivalence contained in the fact that such extraordinary friendships, fundamental for thousands of ex-combatants, were formed in the context of a war most wish never happened. Fitas struggled to express the contradiction:

> This is hard to explain [laughs]—it is hard to explain because I didn't want the war, I wanted the war in another way. I wanted a war without war, but...I mean...regarding...comrades, servicemen and all that, I feel proud to be a part of this family, because it was a family that...has made us much closer.

Another strong, distinctive factor manifests in geographical knowledge. My interviewees perceive this in multiple ways, but most feel a strong connection with the African territories where they served and reveal a keen interest in the fate of these now independent countries. There they gave their "best" and "endured the worst." The intense experiences lived in Africa forged a deep, visceral bond with the land and its people that is still powerfully felt today. The veterans' facial expressions often change when talking about "that wonderful land"—which they speak about in highly emotional and sensory terms—"longing" to rediscover their youth spent there. They remain "fascinated with Africa" and want to "go back" to where they "had been." Provided that certain financial, health, and security requirements are met, many respondents declared they would be prepared to visit the former African province (or provinces) that left such a vivid impact on their younger selves. Some have already done so. This is a wish that others interpret as paradoxical, considering the hardships they endured in Africa. Such disparate perspectives illustrate well how subjective relationships are established through the geographical memory of the war veterans' past.

For some, fighting in this war remains an overpowering, disturbing, and confusing memory. José Marques remarked that "even nowadays, despite all these years gone by, it is still a bit difficult to understand what happened." At times paradoxically, these ex-combatants expressed the richness of subjective interpretations. The majority characterize their participation in the conflict as mainly negative and "worthless." It was "a waste of time," a "hurtful" experience, "the worst thing that could ever have happened" in their life, marking "the saddest years" of their youth. Since their "military number had flesh and bones," they were human "pawns" of war. Despite variations dictated by sociocultural backgrounds and political convictions, there is a widespread notion of having served the former regime as "cannon-fodder" in a political and military "effort in vain," for a "lost cause." Most emphasize that in serving in the war they were fulfilling a "duty" that was compulsorily demanded from them as Portuguese citizens. It was "an act of citizenship" they did not evade. As a result, they were now "even" with their mother country.

From this perspective, the veterans whose narratives are more embedded in contemporary democratic notions often undervalue their participation in the colonial conflict, frequently stating that they "don't feel proud" or "honored" for having taken part in a "war like that." They simply "fulfilled my duty." These ex-combatants often stress how they did not fight for the "motherland" or any patriotic values. They were "forced to participate" in an "unfair" war and simply tried "to survive." This reasoning is normally accompanied by a concept frequently invoked by these men, and one that appears to be rather common in Portuguese war veteran discourse: the refusal to be considered "heroes"—although they are "not coward[s] either." Some emphasize they have no reason to feel proud, although they are "not ashamed of having been there" either.

Furthermore, most interviewees highlight many negative lifelong consequences of this experience (physical, psychological, material, moral, among others), both for themselves and their families. Those who were affected physically and psychologically by their war experience, most of them disabled, often express anger "against the system, against the war that was waged, against what I've been through." Most in this situation keenly stress how their lives have become painfully interwoven with this war, which for them is ever present, as a constant indelible memory inscribed in their minds and bodies. For Artur Santos, this "unfair" war disabled him in Guinea in 1971, and left him feeling like "a victim of war." Another respondent questions why he "left a leg there [in Mozambique]" and nearly lost his life. Frequently expressing anger and disappointment, they condemn the lack of stronger official support and social involvement.

Overall, the veterans collectively assert that they were let down as citizens, believing that they were used by the previous regime and essentially left unrecognized and neglected by subsequent ones. They emphasize the sense of injustice regarding their compulsory conscription during the war and the social stigma and amnesia that followed in the postwar period. In the words of the veterans, they were "kicked away like dogs," "thrown into the rubbish bin," "discard[ed] after use, " making them feel "useless," or like "a used part."

Their narratives point to an underlying theme of ex-combatants as victims both of "the pointless war itself and of post-war neglect" (Ashplant 24).

In effect, an established public narrative of participation in the Portuguese colonial war that the veterans could embrace or reject did not emerge, pushing the emergence of a stronger ex-combatant identity into the social margins.

Most interviewees are very critical of public representations of the colonial war in Portugal. They regret the indifference as well as the superficial and polarized approaches to the topic. Above all, they emphasize that the typically available discourses and forms of public commemoration are incapable of satisfactorily representing their experiences. Such inadequacies leave their historical voices undervalued and unrepresented, and contribute to further difficulties in articulating and structuring the memory of their war experiences. Their accounts suggest that this lack of identification with circulating narratives and the absence of a cohesive discourse on the war produces identity fractures, which result in shame and avoidance. Contained in their accounts and in their private remembrances are alternative meanings to public narratives.

The ex-combatants expressed concerns about a historiographical deficit of the colonial war, particularly regarding its lived veteran perspectives. Conscious of the passage of time, and setting themselves apart from mainstream Portuguese society, the ex-servicemen stressed the notion of testimonial duty toward the historical transmission of the colonial conflict. The majority of interviewees asserted that the veteran group was a privileged experiential milieu for war remembrance since

> the authors of [more traditional] books about the colonial war—did not feel, did not step foot [there] like me and my colleagues and those who died, did not spend two years paddling in the mud, going through rivers, and with water up to our chests, didn't suffer... in the flesh, what we suffered... we soldiers.

From this standpoint, the veterans placed high expectations on historians to create a "future" history of the colonial war, focusing on its social meaning and consequences. They would value the reflective incorporation of personal war testimonies as rich historical sources underexplored in Portugal. Many interviewees believe that the shortcomings of memorialization could be overcome by fostering the pedagogical value of history and the promotion of intergenerational dialogue—aspects that might lead to a deeper and more beneficial social recognition of the colonial war and its participants.[9] In this context, many valued their oral history interview as a space to tell their story for history, counteracting the "historical black-holes" and "leaps of history," as Artur Santos put it. They felt that they were contributing to a complementary and innovative history of the colonial war by leaving oral testimonies for the "history of the future." I argue, however, that doing an oral history of the colonial war is writing this history now.

As contributions to this history, these interviews provide illuminating examples of subjective critical reflexivity about the past, evidencing not only an individual combatant's standpoint of a sociohistorical experience of war, but also a powerful shared group identity present in the interpretation of their past experiences (Thomson 2011: 80, 86). In effect, my interviewees often employ plural forms of speech when considering the value of their accounts, placing emphasis on themselves as a group rather than as individuals. In the process, the expectations placed on the oral historian as a channel to voice veteran experiences and concerns became clearer: "*We* thank you!" I have been told, for doing the interview. These narratives express the notion that, through oral history, their generation is able to convey a message to the future.

Most interviewees, preoccupied with their mortality, manifested an urgency to connect with the war past and transmit their experiences. Seeking a meaningful collective remembrance of the war exists in paradoxical tension with an often-acknowledged desire in individuals to forget their war past. Indeed, condemnation of official and social silence and indifference, longing for recognition, and an awareness of the value of providing testimonials for history coexist with an acknowledgment of the veterans' common reluctance or refusal to talk or even remember war experiences. These contradictory and uncomfortable negotiations between forgetting and remembrance uncover the complexities surrounding the expression of the lived memory of this war, revealing how veterans like my interviewees purposely or circumstantially hide their war experience in Africa in the 1960 and '70s from the mainstream.

Very often, ambiguous memorial conditions enveloping the ex-combatants are associated with varying degrees of guilt, shame, and uneasiness—normally complicating the veterans' wish to pass on their generation's testimony, pay homage to dead comrades, and generally make sense of their past. These remembrance difficulties are also related to the sudden disruption of sociopolitical contexts post-1974. The inadequacy of previous authoritarian sociocultural frameworks that the democratic regime discarded encumbers stable structures for autobiographical recollection.

Several of the veterans interviewed expressed greater attempts at reconciling the dictatorial, colonial past and their role in the war with their current selves. Most generally emphasize that they were forcibly conscripted at a specific moment in time. José Carvalho, for instance, explained how, having been raised in that cultural environment, the "values of the motherland" characteristic of the colonial war era did not really contradict the "ideology" he espoused at the time. He is keen to assert that today he holds different views yet does "not feel guilty" for that past allegiance. In this regard, Manuel Figueiredo provides a good example of this uneasiness: "Sometimes I like to say I was a combatant...but, on the other hand (sigh), I would like that to have never happened because it was wrong, because I am uneasy with my conscience." Those like Júlio Lobo, Victor Palma, and José Pinto were against the war from the onset. They express more articulately their discomfort at having taken part. Lobo considers himself "a huge victim" for having to "fulfill my role" in a conflict that was never "my war." Palma explains that it was "regrettable having been there!" and that he feels "ashamed" of having fought for the "wrong side." Since "one day history...will record there were colonial wars," Palma regrets having fought to maintain what he perceives as imperialistic exploitation, since, he says, by "being part of that [colonial] Army...I was on the side of the bad guys!" Some also feel "guilty" for the destruction of those territories, now independent countries. For a few interviewees, particularly officers, "there are no doubts that we collaborated with a dictatorial regime."

Besides being more generally linked with the colonial essence of the conflict, this uneasiness is also associated with the traumatic memory of war experiences, of having participated in or witnessed violent acts and enemy deaths. In his assessment of the Portuguese colonial war, Quintais (2000) highlights how many ex-combatants struggle to find a meaning capable of pacifying the memories of violence witnessed or perpetrated. From this standpoint, a moral puzzle of memory remains unresolved due to the impossibility of clearly identifying the veterans either as victims (of the dictatorial regime) or victimizers (of the enemy in combat). Obviously, not every ex-combatant was involved in extreme violence, nor became war-stressed or afflicted with guilt. However, if taking part in armed conflict is bound to be an impacting experience on many levels, for many of those who did engage in violence, memories remain challenging. José Gouveia, a former commando officer, explained, "I wake up with this massive anguish, do you know? I killed people! Do you understand? I killed!" This respondent admits that "say whatever they please, I don't feel good about myself" for having killed. Evaluating the "contrast in relation to what we were and what we are," Avelino Oliveira regrets the violence he committed in the name of "patriotism."

Despite these multiple layers of remembrance difficulties, the ex-combatants accounts normally relegate these troubles to the shadows, reinforcing instead group cohesion. Individually, and in veteran arenas, memories and identities tend to focus on more positive aspects of the war. Such narratives highlight comradeship, masculine pride in fulfilling military service, and national identity. A common element of nostalgic revisiting of a shared military past, reinforced by the need to pay homage to lost comrades and honor solidarities forged during combat, leads to a distinctive generational attachment to this historical period and also to Africa.

Conclusion: Oral History Contributions

Not often told in a history research context, the recorded personal memories of these veterans enable more innovative and comprehensive understandings of the Portuguese colonial war, which are unattainable otherwise. While Piteira employs the matchstick metaphor to convey individual powerlessness, Fitas conjures the war as his central life event. Figueiredo and Cunha emphasize lifelong ties of veteran solidarity. Santos and Moreira present themselves as disabled war victims. Santos champions a new history of the war featuring the veteran lived experience. While Carvalho negotiates Portugal's ideological past, Lobo and Palma repeatedly stress how uncomfortable they have been with the role they played in the war. Sousa and Gouveia struggle with the violence witnessed and perpetrated.

I argue that the nuances contained in these individual voices become all the more significant and revealing due to the characteristics of the Portuguese memorial context. The veterans emphasize a common fighting experience for the motherland, the family-centered nature of gatherings, the celebration of their military units, the erection of monuments and similar commemorative manifestations. In these respects, war commemoration for the Portuguese veterans' group resembles more closely conflicts of a noncolonial nature.

The ex-servicemen's testimonies give insight into how a significant commemorative focus on positive, and more comfortable, aspects of the war experience can develop into "fashionable" memorialization, to the detriment of deeper and more difficult explorations of remembering. The latter normally encompasses challenging, less-comfortable aspects of war: the conflict as a struggle for independence from the colonial system, the role of the authoritarian regime, and violence perpetrated and witnessed. Such superficial celebration of the ex-combatants' military past develops mainly in a noncritical, ahistorical manner. This often enables a condoning of the colonial conflict and the previous regime, frequently informing political usages of these memories—of which some interviewees were well aware. These tensions suggest the memorial complexities that the veteran group and Portuguese society in general have to tackle to expand their understanding of the colonial past.

Notwithstanding the veterans' contradictory positions, these commemorative developments have reinforced the creation of a distinctive and evolving group affirmation for the Portuguese ex-combatants. The fact that they still long for societal recognition and assert the need to overcome a sense of shame are further indicators that a meaningful engagement with the past—capable of producing more inclusive and wide-reaching forms of remembrance—is lacking in Portugal.

Therefore, my oral history of ex-combatants of the Portuguese colonial war in transitional, post-authoritarian Portugal also illuminates the importance of departing from traditional standpoints of Portuguese historiography by adopting the life history approach. Incorporating oral history into reflective historical research offers innovative contributions toward a richer social history of this event and period.

Together, the "historical narratives" contained in each interview provided a vivid composite portrait of both the diversity and uniformity of Portuguese war veteran memory and identity that I was seeking to attain. By assessing what it meant for individual participants to experience events that became collective history—attributing to their life experiences a historical significance and placement in the history of Portugal and beyond—the oral historian creates an interpretive bridge between biography and history and enables further understandings of the conflict.

An analysis of the colonial war based on personal narratives of its ex-combatants unraveled not only this historiographically unexplored lived experience but also produced significant insights into the individual and collective impact of the conflict. After decades of silence, unrecognition, media and political opportunism, and social stereotyping, this approach offers an increased historical understanding of an entire generation of combatants. It allows for a more accurate identitary repositioning within national Portuguese history, and promotes a democratic and responsible historiographical practice, aimed toward a more critical, reflective, and politically dispassionate assessment of the Portuguese colonial war.

Expansion of knowledge, methodological renewal, and the passing of time make further life history work on the colonial war and other contemporary topics all the more urgent. Thousands of voices who compose the wider mosaic of those who lived this war have not been heard and their mortality looms. Dialoguing with their voices widens our historical awareness and contributes to a more meaningful remembrance of the Portuguese colonial war. Being "one among many," Azinheira's narrative is one tile in the bigger mosaic constituted by the veteran group to which he, alongside others, is so acutely aware of belonging.

Notes

1. Throughout this chapter, citations of interview extracts are English translations of interviews originally conducted in Portuguese. These extracts were selected from the narratives of 36 interviewees (born between 1932 and 1954) whose period of service in Guinea, Angola, and Mozambique spans 20 years between 1955 and 1975. For full citations, please refer to Campos (2014). The Portuguese *Ultramar* refers to the Portuguese overseas provinces. These territories ceased to be called colonies in 1951.
2. Fighting in Angola began in 1961; in Guinea in 1963; and in Mozambique in 1964.
3. The Estado Novo (New State) was installed in Portugal in 1933, having evolved from the Ditadura Nacional (National Dictatorship) initiated in 1926. The Portuguese overseas provinces became formally independent between 1974 and 1975.
4. Comparatively, the Vietnam conflict involved 0.25 percent of the American population. In Portugal, the mobilized forces represented over 7 percent of the active population (Teixeira 77).
5. Stated by Aguiar-Branco, Portugal's minister of national defense, in a speech evoking the fiftieth anniversary of the beginning of the colonial war, December 19, 2011 ("Portugal Ainda...").
6. These claims have been voiced mainly through veteran associations, generating some improvements in veterans' retirement pensions, the national support network for PTSD sufferers, the rehabilitation of Portuguese military cemeteries in the former colonies, transference of fallen servicemen's remains to Portugal, and provision of care homes and other social support and health care services for ex-combatants.
7. Similar circumstances were faced by war veterans of the Algerian conflict (Evans 83).
8. There are many veteran associations in Portugal (and ten are particularly visible). Generally, these associations reunite servicemen of the same company, battalion, or other military unit, or those from a same geographic region.
9. On the complexities of overcoming trauma, see Dawson (2004: 180–204).

Works Cited

Antunes, José Freire. *A Guerra de África, 1961–1974*. Vol. 1. Lisbon: Círculo de Leitores, 1995. Print.
Ashplant, Timothy, Graham Dawson, and Michael Roper, eds. *Commemorating War: The Politics of Memory*. New Brunswick, NJ: Transaction, 2004. Print.
Barata, Manuel T. and Nuno Severiano Teixeira, eds. *Nova História Militar de Portugal*. Vols. 4 and 5. Lisbon: Círculo de Leitores, 2004.
Campos, Ângela. *Shifting Silence, Enduring Shame, Ambivalent Memories: An Oral History of the Portuguese Colonial War (1961–1974)*. Diss. University of Sussex, Brighton, United Kingdom, 2014. Print.
Dawson, Graham. "Trauma, Memory, Politics: The Irish Troubles." *Trauma: Life Stories of Survivors*. Eds. Kim Lacy Rogers and Selma Leydesdorff. New Brunswick, NJ: Transaction Press, 2004. 180–204.
———. *Making Peace with the Past? Memories, Trauma and the Irish Troubles*. Manchester: Manchester University Press, 2007. Print.
Evans, Martin. "Rehabilitating the Traumatized War Veteran: The Case of French Conscripts from the Algerian War, 1954–1962." *War and Memory in the Twentieth Century*. Ed. Martin Evans and Kenneth Lunn. Oxford: Berg, 1997. 73–85.
Medeiros, Paulo de. "Hauntings: Memory, Fiction and the Portuguese Colonial Wars." *Commemorating War: The Politics of Memory*. Eds. Timothy Ashplant et al. New Brunswick, NJ: Transaction, 2004.
Portelli, Alessandro. "Memory as Process." Master Class. 16th International Oral History Association Conference. Prague, July 7, 2010.
"Portugal Ainda Vive Mal com a Guerra Colonial." Governo de Portugal: Ministerio da Defesa Nacional. December 19, 2011. Web.
Quintais, Luis. "Memória e Trauma numa Unidade Psiquiátrica." *Análise Social* 34 (2000): 673–684.
Rogers, Kim Lacy and Selma Leydesdorff, eds. *Trauma: Life Stories of Survivors*. New Brunswick, NJ: Transaction, 2004.
Teixeira, Nuno Severiano. "Portugal e as Guerras da Descolonização." *Nova História Militar de Portugal* (volume 4). Eds. Manuel Barata and Nuno Teixeira. Lisbon: Círculo de Leitores, 2004. 68–92.
Thomson, Alistair. *Anzac Memories: Living with the Legend*. Melbourne: Oxford University Press, 1994.
———. "Memory and Remembering in Oral History." *The Oxford Handbook of Oral History*. Ed. Donald Ritchie. New York: Oxford University Press, 2011. 77–95.
Winter, Jay. "Forms of Kinship and Remembrance in the Aftermath of the Great War." *War and Remembrance in the Twentieth Century*. Eds. Jay Winter and Emmanuel Sivan. Cambridge: Cambridge University Press, 1999.

CHAPTER 2

Voices of Spanish Socialist Trade Unionism during the End of the Franco Regime and the Transition to Democracy

Pilar Domínguez Prats

The labor movement was the primary hotbed of social protest against the dictatorship that held sway in Spain from the end of the Civil War in 1939 to General Franco's death in 1975. Under Franco's regime, Spaniards were forced to relinquish their civil and political rights. The lack of trade union freedom and the widespread repression of democratic unions hampered efforts to organize workers within Spain for many years. At the time, the only legal means of organizing labor was under the auspices of the Confederación Nacional de Sindicatos (CNS) or National Labor Union, also known as the Vertical Union. This organization was "a copy of the Italian corporate fascist model in which workers and employers were brought together by the paternalistic state to share one institution" (Cazorla 43) and the only legal trade union in Spain until the end of the dictatorship. The authorities did make a minor concession; in 1958, the new Collective Bargaining Act allowed workers to choose their own union representatives—albeit within the state-sanctioned CNS—and collectively negotiate labor conditions and agreements in companies with 50 or more employees. However, workers' rights remained very limited. Workers were not free to hold meetings in the workplace or associate with other workers outside the CNS (Cazorla 40).

In the 1960s, during the later years of Franco's rule, Spain's economy began to grow and labor protests multiplied exponentially. Worker mobilization was considerably less intense in the south, in Andalusia, and the Canary Islands, than in the more industrialized northern regions of Catalonia, the Basque Country, Madrid, and Asturias. Socialist trade unionism, specifically that of the General Union of Workers, or UGT,[1] played a fairly minor role in anti-Franco social protests until the 1970s, when the dictatorship was on its last legs and the union began to step up its activity. Despite its long history, the UGT had little power to influence the labor movement because it refused to operate within the legal framework of the CNS and participate in CNS-organized union elections.

Using oral sources to examine the history of trade unions in Spain during the Franco era and the transition to democracy[2] has gained ground over the last decade thanks to the creation of oral history archives within the leading trade unions, especially the Comisiones Obreras, or Workers' Commissions (CCOO).[3] The official history of socialist trade unionism has largely been shaped by written documents held in the archives of unions that were banned under Franco, including the UGT, which relocated to Toulouse, France, along with its leaders, during the dictatorship. Since the establishment of democracy, the organization's archives have been located in Madrid[4] and used to write the official history of the socialist trade union, drawing heavily on the writings of its national and regional leaders.

The opportunity to pursue oral history projects came in 2007 when Spain passed the Historical Memory Act,[5] a law that proposed to "recover the historical memory" of the victims of Franco's dictatorship, including those persecuted for political opposition to the regime or trade union activities. This recovery effort entailed, among other measures, collecting the oral stories of key players in trade union opposition, particularly leaders and members of the UGT. As part of a larger research project titled "The Oral History of Socialist Trade Unionism," funded by the government through the Largo Caballero Foundation, I interviewed a group of working-class union leaders who had held important positions in the UGT in Andalusia and the Canary Islands during the 1970s and 1980s, during Spain's transition to democracy (Domínguez 2012). In this chapter, I focus on the personal and political trajectories of five union workers: Emilio Fernández Cruz (born in Córdoba, 1941), Justo Fernández Rodríguez (born in La Palma, 1936), Anastasio Travieso (born in Las Palmas de Gran Canaria, 1942), Miguel Guillén (born in Sevilla, 1940), and Juan Ramón Troncoso (born in Cádiz, 1950).

Many oral historians (Portelli 1998; Llona 2007) have criticized the concept of "recovering memory" on the grounds that memory is not an inert object. Memories cannot be filed away for future reference or retrieval like documents; rather, they are living things, which are activated by stimuli in the present and questions posed by the interviewer. Perhaps it would be more productive to consider the retrieval of stories long hidden and silenced as an expression of the "culture of remembrance" in civil society (Froidevaux 230), which refers to the social memory of a group and the importance of its conmemoration.[6]

In addition, my analytical point of departure is Maurice Halbwachs's idea (2004) that it is the individual who remembers, but that the process of remembering takes place in a social framework influenced by the group to which that individual belongs. This context not only shapes individual memory but also creates a collective memory that is clearly conveyed in oral narratives. In this respect, gender identity—male in this case—is a fundamental factor in these life stories. The respect and dignity derived from work were key elements in the dominant model of masculinity during this period, and, as such, were involved in the construction of the worker's biography before the advent of postmodern society (Roca 2012).

This research project, commissioned by an institution associated with the UGT, was conducted in circumstances that also influenced the course of the interviews. As the questions focused on the public arena, labor, unions, and political activity, there was little opportunity to discuss aspects of the interviewees' private lives, which account for only a fraction of the narratives if we exclude memories of their childhood and youth. Even so, in this kind of open-ended interview, the subject chooses a narrative identity, a form of self-representation that unwittingly reveals things about his individual identity and brings us closer to the personal dimension of historical events (Portelli 2006).

Nonetheless, the interviewed leaders are more frequently seen as part of a collective—the socialist trade union. Their personal recollections reveal the identifying traits of the UGT workers' culture, marked by certain conceptions of politics, society, and the individual, a set of deeply held ideas and values to which they feel both a subliminal and conscious emotional attachment. For, subjects will only embrace discourses that strike an emotional chord within them (Aresti 20; Romeo & Sierra 2014; Llona 2012).

This chapter is divided into two parts, representing the period before and after the national elections of June 15, 1977, a major turning point for social and political movements in Spain, as these elections introduced a new framework of civil rights and freedoms. The two sections also cover different phases of the interviewees' political careers. The first part unfolds against the backdrop of the Franco regime. The union activists that were interviewed belong to the postwar generation born in the 1940s and 1950s. While they did not live through the Spanish Civil War (1936–1939), they did suffer its consequences. In Andalusia and the Canary Islands, these were years of hunger, poverty, and meager financial resources. This situation frequently forced poorer families to send their children to orphanages or religious boarding schools, as these were often the only educational possibilities open to them. At such institutions, education was generally oriented toward early entry into the workforce, at a time when the minimum working age was 14. Thus, the first part of the chapter analyzes the subjects' introduction to and early experience of union activism in this particular context, while the second part explores their view of socialist trade unionism during Spain's transition to democracy.

The Genealogy of Activism and Stories of Resistance

The life story of Emilio Fernández Cruz began as a tale of poverty. Born into a humble working-class family in Córdoba, Emilio was separated from his widowed mother when he was two-and-a-half-years old and spent his childhood and adolescence far from home. As his mother was unable to provide for all her children, Emilio was placed in a "social relief" orphanage, a state institution created by Franco's regime to take in poor and orphaned children as well as the offspring of the "reds." Ángela Cenarro (4), who interviewed a group of these children, suggests that they share a common trait stemming from the "arbitrary and brutal treatment, which instilled in them not a sense of loyalty but a desire to betray the regime."

Throughout the interview, Emilio was very reluctant to relive this experience, and yet he began his story by speaking about it. In his words, the truth was stranger than—or at least as strange as—the fiction narrated in films about children's experiences at the social relief schools. He begins his oral account as follows:

> I was born in April and, when I was two and a half, I was put in a boarding school until I was fourteen, the age when I finished an apprenticeship.

> [I have] sad memories of... of the boarding school... I think that everyone has memories, but I think that anyone who was at an orphanage had it worse because, well, we were nothing, we were beaten, which was normal in those times. What they put in films about orphanages was the reality that I lived in my orphanage, which was also the same for my brothers and sisters.

Emilio also speaks of how his years at the social relief school fuelled his later rebellion against the regime and predisposed him to take part in workers' struggles and protests, which emerged through union activism after he was hired at the Westinghouse factory:

> The orphanage left a mark on you, to, to be a rebel, because, of course, as a kid you had to put up with the slaps and the kicks in the ribs, not to mention the times when they made you sing and dance to entertain them. This made me rebel, and being a rebel, in the factory, well, when the worker's movements began I decided to revolt.

His rebellion at the orphanage cultivated a rebellious spirit in his adult life, as he later remarks:

> *Emilio*: In fact, I was taken down [to the police station] several times because of my record or my, my rebellion, because I know I was very rebellious.
> *Pilar*: But why did they take you? Can you give me an example?
> *Emilio*: I'd be talking in the bar and the secret police would show up and cart you off to the station again.... They'd go looking for you at the factory and take you to the station.

This self-representation as a "rebel" from childhood is frequently found in the life stories of activists, as Luisa Passerini (1984) notes in her pioneering study of Turin's working classes. In the course of the interview, individual memories are tailored to fit certain narrative forms, revealing the existence of different aspects in the identity of a single individual that are associated with his or her political culture.

Miguel Guillén is another union leader with humble roots. In his life story, he locates his desire to rebel against social conditions in his first job as an electrician in a small metallurgical company. The hard reality inside the company and the abuse that the workers received collided with his worldview of Franco as the "head and savior of the motherland" that had been drilled into him in the Salesian Catholic School. He says:

> What worried me most was the tremendous brutality in the way they treated the workers, how they lived, the humiliation.... A supervisor who was there treated people like animals, people were terrified of him.... That caught my attention. It left an impression on me because of the difference between this and the country that they had described in school, with "Franco as head of state, saving the motherland".... I don't know what or how much we owed to this man, but the idyllic country that they had described to me was very different from the country I found, which had gone through such a brutal experience.

This opposition was also part of the wide-scale Christian activism that played an important role in the labor movement during those years. Miguel was a member of HOAC, the Catholic Action Workers' Brotherhood, which instilled in him a sense of solidarity and the determination to fight social injustice. Meanwhile, his job experience at Construcciones Aeronáuticas, one of the largest metalworks in Seville, served to cement his opposition to the regime. He says:

> The only thing that makes me want to rebel against all of this is a human sense of solidarity with those I see suffering there in such a humiliating way... And I've known priests who, without removing their cassocks, ran circles around many of us in the struggle against the regime, and that's a fact.

The Christian socialism promoted by a new generation of Roman Catholics played a pivotal role in the culture of protest and worker mobilization. Progressive Catholics took action by organizing cultural events in working-class neighborhoods, allowing assemblies on church property, and actively supporting mobilization efforts.

In his interview, Juan Ramón Troncoso, from Andalusia, describes the anti-Franco protest culture:

> After '67, '68, '69, with the state of emergency,[7] a movement finally began to emerge in Cádiz, a movement with no particular political affiliation because there were old-school anarchists, people from the Workers' Commissions, people from the USO[8]... A lot of workers gave up their

religious beliefs when they became union members, connecting with organized sectors in the fledgling union movement that existed at the time: people from the USO, a few folks from the Communist Party who were starting to set up the Workers' Commissions, some old-school anarchists. So the PCE [Spanish Communist Party] was really, really powerful then in Cádiz and the Commissions had the majority in the labor movement.

He rightly notes that, at this point, the mainstream anti-Franco movement had "no particular political affiliation," though this would change during the final years of the dictatorship. Even the socialist political culture, which included the UGT, had very little clout. Its leaders were absent, forced into exile, and it refused to go through the legal channel of the Vertical Union. Like the other interviewees, Troncoso attributes his opposition to the appalling conditions in which people were forced to work:

> We moved through a labor system in which we had, um, practically zero rights... that is to say that what we had there was exactly what the owner wanted and the way he wanted it. This is what pushed me to begin collaborating very early on with the HOAC, the Worker's Vanguard, and the Youth [Juventudes Católicas].... These groups basically were under the wing of the Church... and those of us who were beginning to consider that we were being suffocated by the Franco regime, by the dictatorship, well, we began moving in those circles... primarily through two priests, two working-class priests, who were parish priests but at the same time they were also workers: Father Pepe Asenjo, from "La Pastora," and Salvador y Sebastián, from "La Viña."

In this part of the narrative, Troncoso uses the plural "we" to indicate how strongly he identified with the leaders of the workers' protests and later with the UGT. Recalling his militancy, he makes it a point to lay claim to his family's political background:

> I remember that we all had to be screened by the *Frente de Juventudes*[9] and we all had to become card-carrying members [of the party] an obligation that, for many of us, didn't sit very well. It was a very silent time; the Civil War wasn't talked about at home, the Franco repression wasn't mentioned, no one talked about politics and there was a lot of fear. We weren't, of course, the kind of people who were moved, one way or the other, by the [national anthem] *"Cara al sol."* And while we were vetted by the Youth

> Front, well, I was fourteen and not very aware of things, but my relationship with my uncle—above all, my uncle—well, I was a little turned off by all of it... like many on the Left, my uncle was condemned to death, which was modified to a sentence which he completed at the end of around six or seven years.

Troncoso's uncle, a member of the radical Republican Party during the Second Spanish Republic was imprisoned for seven years when Franco came to power. This is the kind of publicly vetoed, officially silenced story that could only be told in the safety of the family circle or among trusted friends.

These activists were young men and women who did not suffer first-hand the traumatic events and severe reprisals that paralyzed their elders during the harsh postwar period. They were a generation less frightened by the regime's repression of democratic attempts to organize labor. The oral testimonies presented here show that many Andalusian and Canarian labor leaders joined the socialist union movement after serving as shop stewards in the Vertical Union or sitting on labor management committees.

In his interview, Justo Fernández Rodríguez, from the Canary Islands, reveals that, when he turned 16, he went to work as a clerk at a small branch office of the Banco Hispano Americano in Los Llanos de Ariadne on La Palma, the island of his birth. He soon organized a one-man protest against the bank:

> Well, there was no such thing as banker's hours there, [after working all morning]. Every afternoon you had to go back and the shift, which supposedly ended at six, would end up lasting until nine or nine-thirty. And when the end of the month rolled around... well, you could be there until one in the morning. But it pissed me off because the manager had a girlfriend and he'd go off with her and I had to wait around for him to return... I mean, that was my unionist beginning and the start of my rebellion. I just couldn't take that.

So he filed a complaint against the bank for violating the legal limit of working hours, sending letters to the labor inspection bureau. Later he went through the union's legal channel:

> Then there were elections and I ran... Mr. Solís Ruiz, who was Minister of Trade Unions, called elections with the idea of "choosing the best." He cut

us a bit of slack, and it really was choosing the best, not choosing like before, because the best couldn't run, only those the Vertical Union named.

Fernández refers to the official union elections of 1966, which marked a turning point. For the first time in years, elected officials actually represented the will of the workers. According to his story, he became the most voted shop steward in Spain because he was not affiliated with any political party and he ran on a simple program:

> Back then [my platform] was that there had to be a bargaining agreement and that the bargaining committee had to be elected by the workers, because normally that was done at a meeting of the higher-ups at the Vertical Union; they just said, "you, you, and you," and that was the committee.... Well, in '70 we really rallied the troops on a large scale and started striking... Seriously, these were bona fide strikes, not standing around for five minutes, or demonstrations and such, we took a step forward and really started organizing strikes.

Fernández Rodríguez recalled how, when he moved to Madrid after one of the conflicts, the bank initiated disciplinary proceedings against him for being a troublemaker. After that, in 1971 Justo met a well-known socialist lawyer who brought him over to the union:

> After I got in touch with Peces Barba, he introduced me to Pablo Castellanos and he started telling me that what I had to do was join an organization, because they were... you know the line: "Better defended, more protected," and all that; in an organization that had absolutely nothing, I mean, I almost walked right out when I went in—there was nothing at all!

Justo Fernández's repeated use of the first person to narrate the prolabor actions in which he participated underscores the importance of his role. How he chooses to represent himself throughout the interview reveals certain aspects of his identity. One of his most telling statements was:

> I'm a dyed-in-the-wool individualist, and that's always caused a lot of problems for me when it comes to accepting decisions and orders from someone else. I've always handled that poorly, in the UGT, in the PSOE [Socialist Workers' Party], and everywhere.... The UGT practically didn't

> exist in the banking industry; so I started to organize it and began signing up all the people who were with me.... I began signing in UGT's name and I created the banking union branch of the UGT in Madrid.

The life story of another Canarian union leader, Anastasio Travieso, also emphasizes how participating in the Vertical Union structure ultimately helped the UGT's growth, a fact not acknowledged in the organization's official history:

> I ran for the first time in my life in the shop steward elections, then I had to run against other shop stewards, the next level, the shop stewards in each category for a seat on the labor management jury[10] and the Provincial Committee of the OSE.

Travieso confessed to being "anti-establishment" since his youth, an attitude rooted in several experiences that marked him for life:

> I have to share something I've just remembered because I think it was the spark that ignited in me a spirit of rebellion against that system, not politically conscious but definitely "anti." I was still a student at the time, my father was working for that construction company; my father was a humble subordinate. And one day they did staff restructuring and my father got the boot. That was a real drama in my house.... I remember it as a traumatic experience, it was seared into my memory. For me that building, the Vertical Union, was part of the establishment, the thing that didn't work.

Nonetheless, Travieso used "the establishment" as a springboard for the union struggle and rose to occupy the highest position in the Vertical Union when he was named chairman of the Provincial Committee of the CNS in Las Palmas. After resigning in 1975, he went on to become secretary-general and cofounder of the new provincial UGT, whose first congress was held in May 1976. Other activists had recruited him for the union and the PSOE after seeing him at work in the Vertical Union. In Las Palmas, the strategy of infiltrating the state-sanctioned union with workers opposed to the regime—including independent activists and those affiliated with the Workers' Commissions—worked like a charm.

The union careers of the interviewees from Andalusia followed a similar pattern. Emilio Fernandez was elected shop steward for the Spanish Syndical

Organization in the Westinghouse factory in Córdoba. From that moment, he began to participate in the clandestine Workers' Commissions in Córdoba. These were important schools for political apprenticeship:

> At that time, my first experiences were with this group, which later started calling themselves Comisiones Obreras and almost everyone had to belong to the Communist Party, but I wasn't a communist and, well, I resisted.... There was one time, one man, who now is a doctor—Rafael Vallejo—found out through someone else that I was a steward at Westinghouse and he called me on the phone, without even knowing me, and that began my contact with the UGT.

These Workers' Commissions, led by members of the Spanish Communist Party, were very powerful in Córdoba and Seville. They managed to attract a large number of workers and formed the core of the labor movement. Their strategy of participating in union elections within companies and taking advantage of the possibility of holding legal meetings there, allowed these underground commissions to gain considerable strength from the 1960s onward. Emilio's activism in the Workers' Commissions lasted several years; however, he glosses over this period and focuses on his transition to the UGT, which in his mind was a more interesting topic for the interview. He explains how later, he was recruited by the socialist UGT. Toward the end of the Franco regime, joining the socialist union was a logical step in light of the dictatorship's rabidly anti-communist leanings.

In his narrative, Miguel Guillén described how the shop stewards worked within the legal framework on the factory floor to obtain the support of the workers. This, in turn, helped them achieve their demands. Although Guillén was forced out of the factory for being a "troublemaker," he moved on to become a union leader in another steel company, Siderúrgica Sevillana. His oral interview places considerable importance on the 1970 labor conflict in this company. During the strike, a group of workers, including Miguel, left the communist union, Comisiones Obreras, to join the UGT, at a time when the UGT in Andalusia barely had any working-class members:

> At that time there were socialists...and above all, [in the] period of the Socialist Youth—who were UGT activists...but what was happening was that no one was actually a worker because everyone was either a lawyer or school teacher.

In those days, a small number of laborers was actually considered detrimental to the creation of a "working-class union." In his narrative, Guillén eloquently sums up the political position that the trade unions adopted during the Franco years: "My struggle for decent pay...above and beyond my struggle for decent pay was my struggle against Franco." Consequently, in the context of the dictatorial regime, workers' economic demands became political stances. This would change with the arrival of democracy.

The Vision of Spain's Transition to Democracy: Between Individual and Collective Memory

Several important events shed light on the unionist and political paths taken by the interviewees during Spain's transition to democracy. Although Franco died in November 1975, the Vertical Union was not dissolved and democratic trade unions were not legalized until April 1977, two years later. However, in the interim, the as-yet illegal democratic unions were given a great deal of leeway. In April 1976, the UGT met openly for the first time in 40 years at its thirtieth Confederated Congress in Madrid. Its slogan was "Trade Unions United for Freedom" (Vega 2011). The more tolerant political atmosphere also extended to other parts of Spain. In his account, Travieso recalled "the demolition from within" of the Vertical Union of Las Palmas in the spring of 1976:

> One day we decided to leave [the Union] and we decided to do it on the first of May. So we proposed organizing a demonstration for the first of May, knowing they wouldn't let us do it. With communiqués to the press, in the papers...And they were published in "La Provincia," in "El Diario"....So we gathered and went ahead with that, knowing and being prepared to say, "We're leaving, we can't stay here, let's hit the streets already and show our faces." We were taking a risk because the Constitution hadn't been enacted yet.

After that point, all the executives on the Provincial Council of the CNS resigned, starting with Travieso himself. He went from a clandestine member of the banned socialist union to secretary-general and cofounder of the new UGT of Gran Canaria, which held its first congress in Las Palmas in May 1976 and soon had a considerable number of card-carrying members (*Informe* 1978).

The first democratic national elections were held in June 1977, and the Socialist Workers' Party (PSOE), won a large number of parliamentary seats as the second most-voted political force. The UGT benefited from this new situation, given its political affiliation with the PSOE. That year, as Justo Fernández remarked, "We had an avalanche of people wanting to join."

The vision of Spain's transition to democracy conveyed in the interviewees' narratives is strongly colored by the official or public memory of this historical period, a story written by the parties that emerged victorious from the Transition and their administrations, as the self-appointed "managers of memory" (Joutard 2013). One of them was the PSOE which governed Spain from 1982 to 1994 and ushered in a period of greater democratic stability. That official memory has been manufactured from the oral and written accounts of those who played "starring roles" in the process of democratic change, leaders like Felipe González, Alfonso Guerra, Adolfo Suárez, and Santiago Carrillo. The media in general, and television in particular, has faithfully transmitted their interpretation of Spain's recent past, impressing it upon the minds of civil society. According to this version, the principal driving forces of democratic change were those same leaders, together with the king, downplaying the influence of social movements—including the labor movement—on the transition from dictatorship to democracy.

The UGT's close ties to the socialist PSOE meant that the trade union was represented in both parliamentary houses, the Congress of Deputies and the Senate. As the Socialists had pockets of power in government institutions, a few prominent unionists were able to work their way into the state apparatus. For the unionist deputies, Congress was a place for socializing, and social interaction was a cornerstone of socialist political culture during the transition years—something they hold dear and recall with great fondness in their interviews. The interviewees' memories have been shaped by the discourses of the top union leaders in the Spanish Parliament,[11] discourses they have accepted and internalized. These snippet views of the union's collective memory are enlarged when they talk about the democratic transition process and the role they played back then.

Emilio Fernández, secretary-general of the UGT in Córdoba, was elected to the Congress in 1977. He describes this experience as a local leader in politics as fundamental to his life trajectory:

> In the Cortes [Congress], I had a wonderful experience, the truth is that I learned a lot, but, I mean, the most important step was to leave the steel stripping machine—that is, going from being a lathe operator to a member

of Congress—that was huge.... As a deputy in Congress I had more power than the civil governor of Cordoba.

Elaborating on this situation, he makes an interesting comparison based on his experience as a metal worker:

> I always said that, eh, the Transition has been like the shock absorbers of a Pegaso big rig truck. They are continually compressed by an iron plate. If you release that plate, that shock absorber begins to bounce until it stablizes. That absorber can be jumping for months. So, um, in the "consensus" something similar happened. We went from being oppressed to, to, to making every demand you can think of. But, of course, if you are always confrontational and don't have a strategy in mind, you end up drowning yourself.

These political experiences entailed the acceptance of new ideas and values that defined the socialist political culture of the transition era. Consensus, a willingness to negotiate, and compromise, stood in stark contrast to the confrontational stances typical of the anti-Franco political culture. The situation called for moderation and pragmatism. However, these concessions facilitated the triumph of the mindset and values shared by the UGT leaders at the time, which bound them together as members of the union and of the PSOE.

Looking back at the transition period, the trade unionists that were interviewed understood the purpose of labor consensus. According to Guillén:

> Spanish trade unionism had to make a concerted effort to calm the workers.... On some level, we understood that what we had to do was tranquilize and calm the situation down a little because there was one strike after another and thousands of man-hours lost in each company.

Guillén became the secretary-general of the Metalworkers' Federation. He became a Socialist Workers' Party (PSOE) candidate from Seville for the Congress of Deputies in 1977, although he was not elected.

Troncoso shares this perspective, as do other leaders interviewed. He agrees that the UGT evolved from a highly political and demanding union movement toward a union willing to negotiate with management, which was possible in the 1980s. Prioritizing dialogue with management and adopting a "pragmatic union politics" presupposed "a shift in the union's strategy betting on the politics of agreement with management" (Vega 84). This new pragmatism marked a radical shift in union practice, imposing from that point on a politics of consensus. For some of the interviewed leaders, that policy became decisive:

> I think that signing the ABI[12] is an important moment, a much discussed chapter in the inner circles of the union, because there were some who said that there was no way that we could move to a consensus model of trade unionism. That is, there was, I believe, a moment in which we came to understand that socialist trade unionism, social democratic [unionism] in Europe, is a unionism in which pressure and confrontation are a part, but in the end a union has to negotiate. As a result it has to recognize the opposing party not as an enemy but as an entity with which one has to reach an understanding, to negotiate, and establish a model of labor relations.

This union strategy clearly differentiated the UGT from communist Comisiones Obreras, the Workers' Commissions. The UGT reaffirmed with the ABI accord its position toward consensus. In the 1980 union elections, the socialist leadership received greater support from the rank and file, confirming that a significant sector of Andalusian and Canarian workers agreed with the new policy. To commit themselves to "strengthening union structures," the union asked that several of the most experienced members in union struggles be given leave from their workplaces. The majority were young local leaders, like Troncoso. Calling these workers up for union duty was a positive step in its growth, although it did lead to a more bureaucratic model. This model replaced the traditional "struggle and fight" approach, which characterized the late Franco period, when the militants were still underground and connected with workers on the shop floor.

Conclusion

In analyzing these interviews, it is clear that the narrators follow certain patterns of self-representation. Some unionists, like E. Fernández Cruz, identify with the stereotype of the lifelong rebel. The rest of the interviewees represent themselves as fighters combating the rampant injustice they experienced or witnessed in the workplace. The working world is the central theme of their life stories and the setting of the main social conflicts in their oral accounts.

These oral testimonies also shed light on the political attitudes of trade union members during those historical periods. What makes these accounts particularly valuable is the fact that they explain, from a personal perspective, the origins and evolution of union activism and the labor movement during those years. These narratives often challenge academic historiography on the development of trade unions, which tends to focus on the role played by professionals rather than on the rank and file.

The narrators, all from working-class backgrounds, demanded to be recognized as key actors in the reconstruction of the socialist union. The oral accounts of grassroots activists illustrate certain aspects of the socialist trade union's internal history. One is the fact that, when deciding what type of political actions to pursue during the underground years, unionists enjoyed a considerable degree of autonomy, and their activities often strayed from the official "party line" drawn by their leaders in exile. A case in point was the elections for representatives to the state-sanctioned Vertical Union, in which the interviewees decided to participate even though the UGT Executive Committee was against the idea. From the interviewees' perspective, this was a smart decision because it allowed closer contact between elected union representatives and the factory floor rank and file. In addition, the interviews reveal other aspects of union activism, like the powerful influence of the grassroots Christian movement led by "worker priests" in working-class neighborhoods.

These oral narratives are also a testament to the power of collective memory. This is particularly noticeable during the years of Spain's transition to democracy, told by people who still belong to the union and are more concerned about their present-day position. The socialist political culture that emerged in the early years of the Transition gradually gave the union leaders a strong collective identity that has kept the organization united. In those years, this culture was characterized by values such as moderation, pragmatism, and compromise in labor relations between workers and employers. The interviewees embraced these political notions wholeheartedly at the time, although their narratives reveal that today some of them do not fully identify with that memory, taking a more critical view of the ideas and values that characterized socialist unionism during the transition years.

However, in most cases, their memories of the UGT's actions during that period are not critical. The oral accounts of union activism are quite similar, casting the politics of consensus in a positive light. Their memories can be explained in light of two important facts: the high-ranking positions that the majority of the interviewees, with the exception of Justo Fernández (the most critical voice), held in the union during the transition period, and the favorable electoral outcome for the UGT and the Socialist Workers' Party in the early years of that transition to democracy.

Notes

1. The UGT [Unión General de Trabajadores] was the first Spanish trade union, founded in 1888.
2. The "transition to democracy" refers to the period between the end of the Franco era in December 1975 and the election of the first Socialist government.
3. CCOO Andalusia Archive, CCOO Catalonia Archive, 1st of May Foundation, Muñoz Zapico Foundation.
4. Specifically, at the "Archivos del Movimiento Obrero" [Labor Movement Archives], in Alcalá de Henares. This building is also home to the Largo Caballero Foundation. The foundation currently has two oral history projects related to this chapter: "The Reconstruction of Socialist Trade Unionism [1970–1994]" and "The International Trajectory of Spanish Social Syndicalism [1888–1986]."
5. This act, passed by the Spanish parliament in December 2007, established support for those who had suffered persecution, seizure of personal property, forced labor, or internment in concentration camps, whether in Spain or abroad. It also called for an acknowledgment of all Spanish citizens who were deprived of their homeland due to a lengthy and, in many cases, irreversible exile or due to violent acts during the Spanish Civil War and the ensuing dictatorship.
6. "Culture" is used here in a broad sense, defined as the interaction of human beings in social groups. See Assmann 1995.
7. The state of emergency was "the temporary suspension of a series of constitutional rights, though these rights were not respected by Franco's regime as a matter of course. It provided the pretext for legalizing a series of habitual police practices, such as holding detainees for more than the 72-hour maximum stipulated by law, effectively giving them license to perpetrate such violations on a massive scale" (*Euskadi* 1975).
8. The Unión Sindical Obrera, or Workers' Trade Union, was a Christian socialist union secretly founded in 1966.
9. Frente de Juventudes was the youth wing of the Falange, the only authorized political party during the Franco dictatorship.
10. Labor management juries consisted of the foreman (owner or manager of the company) and the jury members, who represented the workers. These juries have participated in negotiating collective bargaining agreements since 1958: http://www.archivoshistoricos.ccoo.es/convenios colectivos.
11. Jerónimo Saavedra was one of those top leaders in the UGT, a Socialist congressional deputy whose name often came up in the interviews.
12. ABI stands for the "*Acuerdo Básico Interconfederal*" [Basic Inter-Confederal Agreement] signed by the UGT and the country's largest employers' organization, the CEOE (Confederación Española de Organizaciones Empresariales) in 1979.

Works Cited

Aresti, Nerea. *Masculinidades en Tela de Juicio*. Madrid: Cátedra, 2010. Print.
Assmann, Jan. "Collective Memory and Cultural Identity."*New German Critique* 65 (1995): 125–133. Print.
Cazorla, José. *Fear and Progress: Ordinary Lives in Franco's Spain (1939–1975)*. Oxford: Wiley-Blackwell, 2010. Print.
Cenarro, Angela. "Memoria Oral de los Niños Acogidos en las Instituciones en la Posguerra Española." XVI Conferencia Internacional de Historia Oral. IOHA: Prague, 2010. CD.
Domínguez, Pilar. "La Reconstrucción de UGT en Andalucía, del Franquismo a la Transición." *Combates por la Democracia. Los Sindicatos de la Dictadura a la Democracia (1938–1994)*. Eds. Alvaro Soto and Manuela Aroca. Madrid: UAM, 2012. 383–404. Print.
Euskadi: El Ultimo Estado de Excepción de Franco. Paris: Ruedo Ibérico, 1975. http://www.ruedoiberico.org/libros. Web.
Fernández Cruz, Emilio. Personal interview by Pilar Domínguez. Cordoba, April 18, 2011. Archivo Oral de la Fundación Largo Caballero.
Fernández, Justo. Personal interview by Pilar Domínguez. Santa Cruz de Tenerife. May 31, 2008. Archivo Oral de la Fundación Largo Caballero.
Froidevaux, Alexandre. "Una Cultura del Recuerdo 'Desde Abajo:' La Recuperación de la Memoria Histórica en el Levante y Aragón." *Entelequia. Revista Interdisciplinar* 7 (2008): 229–246. Print.
Guillén, Miguel. Personal interview by Diego Herrera. Seville, April 23, 2008. Archivo Oral de la Fundación Largo Caballero.
Halbwachs, Maurice. *Los Marcos Sociales de la Memoria*. Barcelona: Antropos, 2004. [English: *On Collective Memory*. Chicago: University of Chicago Press, 1992]. Print.
Informe Congreso Insular de UGT [Island Congress Report]. Las Palmas: Union General de Trabajadores, 1978. Print.
Joutard, Philippe. *Histoire et Mémoires: Conflits et Alliance*. Paris: La Decouverte, 2013. Print.
Llona, Miren, ed. "Memoria e Identidades. Balance y Perspectivas de un Nuevo Enfoque Historiográfico": *La Historia de las Mujeres: Perspectivas Actuales*. Ed. Cristina Borderías. Barcelona: Icaria, 2007. 360–385. Print.
———. *Entreverse: Teoría y Metodología Práctica de las Fuentes Orales*. Bilbao: University of Pais Vasco, 2012. Print.
Passerini, Luisa. *Torino Operaria e Fascismo*. Roma: Laterza, 1984. Print.
Portelli, Alessandro. "What Makes Oral History Different." *The Oral History Reader*. Eds. Rob Perks and Alistair Thomson. 2nd ed. London: Routledge. 1998. 63–74. Print.
———. "El Uso de la Entrevista en Historia Oral." *Historia, Memoria y Pasado Reciente. Anuario* n°20. Rosario: Escuela de Historia, 2006. 35–49. Print.

Roca i Girona, Jordi and Lidia Martínez Flórez. "Mi Vida, Tu Vida, La Nuestra: Determinantes y Configuración de la Estructura Narrativa de los Relatos de Vida." Llona *Entreverse* (2012): 93–130. Print.

Romeo, María Cruz and María Sierra eds. *La España Liberal 1833–1874: Historia de las Culturas Políticas en España y Latinoamérica*. Vol. 2. Madrid: Marcial Pons, 2014. Print.

Travieso, Anastasio. Personal interview by Pilar Domínguez. Las Palmas. June 22, 2012. Archivo Oral de la Fundación Largo Caballero.

Troncoso, Juan Ramón. Personal interview by Pilar Domínguez. Sevilla. March 14, 2011. Archivo Oral de la Fundación Largo Caballero.

Vega, Rubén. *Historia de la UGT: La Reconstrucción del Sindicalismo en Democracia, 1976–1994*. Madrid: Siglo XXI, 2011. Print.

Website Comisiones Obreras: http://www.archivoshistoricos.ccoo.es/convenios colectivos. Web.

CHAPTER 3

"Gendered" Memories: Women's Narratives from the Southern Cone

Cristina Scheibe Wolff, Joana Maria Pedro, and Janine Gomes da Silva

The 1960s and 1970s in the Southern Cone were marked by authoritarian regimes, supported by the United States, that coalesced around a Cold War ideology of the threat of communism to national security. These dictatorships appeared almost simultaneously in Argentina, Bolivia, Brazil, Chile, Paraguay, and Uruguay. Despite media censorship and fierce restrictions on political activity, these decades were also marked by women's widespread participation in political, cultural, and social movements. Energized by feminism and the sexual revolution worldwide, women claimed their protagonism in political, social, and cultural debates and, hence, constructed new subject positions for themselves.

In 2005, the History and Gender Studies Laboratory (LEGH) at the Federal University of Santa Catarina (Brazil) launched a major research project titled "Gender, Feminisms and Dictatorships in the Southern Cone."[1] For ten years, a multinational team of professors and graduate students has been researching issues of gender in left wing resistance movements as well as the formation of feminist activism in the region during the period of military dictatorship. We have amassed a collection of 170 interviews, recorded in Argentina, Bolivia, Brazil, Chile, Paraguay, and Uruguay.[2] This chapter is part of our effort to analyze these interviews, calling attention to the multinational and regional dimensions of women's political activism during the 1960s and '70s.

The memories of women who participated in the resistance movements in the Southern Cone are strongly marked by gender configurations. We became particularly aware that these women structure the narratives of their memories through fundamentally gendered themes: the body, maternity, family situations, as well as feelings of resentment toward the organizations, authoritarian governments, and often toward their families and partners. The growing impact of feminism, from within the countries as well as during the narrators' exile abroad, helps explain the centrality of gender in women's accounts of their activism and life during that period.

In the effort to gather the interviews for this project, we traveled throughout the region between 2005 and 2014, and also took advantage of academic conferences and meetings to record oral histories. Initially, through previous contacts, we began to identify potential narrators who militated in left wing organizations and feminist groups during the '60s and '70s. We also searched the Internet, academic publications, and bibliographies for names and information. Our interviews followed a basic script that prioritized the narrator's militant trajectory, but the interviews were also open-ended, allowing narrators to raise other topics they felt relevant. Most of our narrators were women (150), but we also interviewed a few men (20), who participated in left wing movements and/or had become feminists. Besides interviews, our team collected data from books, journals, manuals, regulations, and other primary documents from left wing organizations and feminist groups.

As we listened to the recordings and read the transcripts, common themes seemed to jump out at us, cohering into blocks of images, figures of speech, and common topics of concern to the narrators. This led to the question: What accounts for the fact that people who participated in different left wing organizations, in different countries, in different languages, express such similar feelings and memories? In theorizing memory, Maurice Halbwachs (1992) drew attention to the collective and social character of memory, arguing that the social and group referent is always present. In our research, we were also dealing with an historical process collectively experienced across the Southern Cone. These military dictatorships began to extend their reach, at different moments and through different strategies depending on local circumstances. But they all obeyed a kind of general plan, orchestrated with the United States, to respond to the proliferation of left wing movements, to guerrilla movements inspired by the Cuban Revolution, to the protracted People's War of Mao Zedong, to the New Left groups that grew out of the established Communist and Socialists parties, to anarchist movements, and especially to university student movements that were increasingly imbued with a transformative and revolutionary role (Gandolfi 1991). In these left wing movements, as opposed to the traditional Communist and Socialist parties, women appeared to occupy an increasing role, and sometimes—although rarely—took on positions of leadership and command. Many of them took up arms (Wolff 2007). What did this mean to them? How did they feel about their participation? How was this expressed in their narratives? Were their memories differentiated by gender? These were some of our research questions.

Do Memories Have Gender?

In an article titled "Práticas de memória femenina," Michelle Perrot asks if a feminine memory exists. She affirms that in the theater of memory, women are faint shadows. She concludes that female memory is not specifically anchored in nature or biology. However, she asserts that,

> socio-cultural practices present in the triple operation that constitutes memory—primitive accumulation, rememoration, and narrative order—overlap in actual male/female relations and, as such, are historically constructed. (18)

Therefore, she concludes that memory is deeply sexed.

We use this statement as a point of departure, focusing not on sexed memory but on gender relations, arguing that memory is "gendered," as it is constituted by and in gender. If memory is social and referenced in the collective, it is also marked by social constructs: class, gender, race/ethnicity, generation, and many other social categories. Gender is an aspect of social relations that is especially implicated in hierarchies and relations of power (Scott 1988). In addition, memories constitute narratives, constructed and reconstructed discourses that can be considered "performances" in which gender plays a key role (Butler 1990). Oral history interviews are performances in which narrators are legitimized to speak on certain subjects, in particular places of locution, about events that mark the time of the narrative.

Based on this relationship between gender and memory and on the importance of women's testimonies in post-dictatorship Argentina, Alejandra Oberti offers an important insight:

> Unrest over the loss of loved ones, stupor in the face of defeated ideals, but also awareness of the limits to these ideals, shape a memory that allows one to distance oneself from established versions; it also offers new ways to understand the past and redefine the tools we use to analyze the recent past in order to develop a critical memory... We discover new connections between the public and the private, the personal and the political, through a movement that inscribes the general in the singular, the political in the private. We don't try to rescue the women who took part in these struggles from oblivion by placing them in a pantheon with the "heroes." Instead we recover their more subtle gestures, what cannot be so easily represented. (28–29)

According to Oberti, it is not simply a matter of including women's testimonies in the historical record, giving them the recognition previously denied. Women's testimonies, she argues, emphasize aspects often overlooked by male witnesses who are more rooted in public space and politics. In this sense, women's testimonies bring different aspects into focus and produce a different understanding of history.

Consequently, our research has tried to capture women's memories not just to include them in a history of the dictatorships in the Southern Cone, as participants in the movements of resistance, in human rights organizations, and eventually in forces of repression.[3] We also want to understand how the discourses of resistance and armed struggle used gender and notions of masculinity and femininity. We want to understand how personal relationships became politicized, especially in the recruitment of women and men into political organizations, where they often established relationships that went beyond party or institutional affiliations. These relationships often turned into love affairs, friendships, even families. In their narratives, emotions also tell a story that moves the listener. As Miriam Suárez, a feminist activist from Bolivia who was part of the resistance movement in the 1970s—and remains active today—reflects:

> Time had passed and I've kept silent, not wanting to remember the pain and the saddest moments of my life, perhaps thinking that silence helps us protect our loved ones. Many of the women who were victims of dictatorships

speak little or never about being deprived of their most basic rights, like the right to move freely throughout the city, to express ideas without fear, to get together with friends, and get information. The story of these women has yet to be fully told. This is the first time I share a piece of my soul. (64)

Miriam Suárez spoke about her time in prison, about encounters with the police, on the one hand, and on the other, with comrades who treated women as second-class militants in the movement. She told about the birth of her daughter Libertad, in a dark prison of La Paz, about her time in exile and discovering feminist groups and feminism. In speaking with us about the time of the dictatorship, she was sharing "a piece of her soul," sharing feelings that have the power to move us.

Memories of Discrimination

In our interviews, we often heard left wing militant women claim that they did not feel discrimination, at least not at the beginning of their activism. This is often made as a peremptory statement. As Margarita Iglesias Saldaña, who was from the MIR [Revolutionary Left Movement] in Chile and still a leftist today put it:

> What happens is that in the places where I was operating I never saw a big difference, and only many years later did I notice differences between men and women within the MIR. But at that time, there was not a lot, nor was there a big numerical difference [between men and women]. Of course, afterwards, when you begin to look back from another perspective, you realize that in higher decision-making positions, there were fewer women. But at my level, I was the person in charge in many places, and I never had problems because I was a woman.

So, while she tells us she did not feel discrimination, in retrospect she admits that there were fewer women in leadership positions. At the time, however, this was not perceived as prejudice. M., from Argentina, who belonged to ERP [People's Revolutionary Army] says:

> There was a hierarchy, and the hierarchy had levels of command that could be occupied by men or women. But the party leadership was male. The truth is that the top leadership was male, as far as I remember. But at the

[middle] level of command, there were as many men as women, and in the small groups I frequented, there was no problem with men not respecting an order given by a woman. I never saw that. If that happened, it was pretty hidden. I didn't notice it.

In Uruguay, Bolivia, and Brazil we find a similar discourse. The accounts are always colored by the present and by the researchers' questions, which did allude to the possibility of differences in how organizations treated men and women. Interestingly, those who espoused gender neutrality at the time, tended to be women who are still left wing militants but who never embraced the feminist movement. Some among them, however, reported that they felt a nagging discomfort but could not put their finger on it. Alejandra López Gómez, who militated in the Communist Youth in Uruguay, recounted:

> That system had been bothering me for some time. I saw it but couldn't name it. But at that time, the patriarchal structure clearly bothered me, women's participation was... in the words of an Argentinean writer, "We all learned how to speak, but not all of us were given the chance to speak." Compared to male comrades, the words of women comrades were less respected.

Clearly, there were differences between men and women rooted in society at the time. In the case of Paraguay, for example, we found very few women who had participated in armed movements. One of them, Guillermina Kanonnikoff Flores, did not come to say that there was no distinction between men and women, but she attributed all the weight of this difference to her condition as a woman in Paraguayan society, rather than to the directives or practices of the OPM [Political Military Organization], the organization she joined. Her situation was further complicated because she became pregnant during her militant years and had to work to support her family, leaving just a few hours to devote to militancy. She was considered "petty bourgeois," unlike her partner who was a full-time militant. As she says:

> As a woman, I often had the added burden of having to go back and forth [between home and the organization], and because I was pregnant, I had to take another type of care. It was hard for me to advance beyond this level, to get promoted, and so I stayed on the fringes....Therefore, my involvement was limited in multiple ways, by being a woman, being pregnant, and being petty-bourgeois.

The '60s are always remembered by the rise of the Women's Revolution and the Sexual Revolution. Although it is difficult to speak about a feminist movement in the Southern Cone in those years, the impact of the US and European feminist movements were felt, especially in big cities like São Paulo, Rio de Janeiro, Buenos Aires, Santiago, and Montevideo (Pedro 2010). One such impact was the feminization of the universities. In Brazil, female enrollments in universities grew from 26 to 40 percent between 1956 and 1971 (Barroso and Mello 52). In Uruguay, women comprised 40 percent of the student body in 1963 (Sapriza 42). These figures should be understood in the context of the overall expansion of universities throughout the region. These were years of urban expansion and growth of the middle classes. The sons and daughters of urban workers, service workers, and even rural workers were given access to universities. The expansion of public education and the rise of student movements became an important source of militancy for left wing political movements and parties.

Like many of the women we interviewed, Silvia Escobar (2008), from Bolivia, described how her activism began at the university. At the time, majoring in sociology was a kind of passport into the Left, and she said that many of her male colleagues went into the guerilla movement to fight with Che, and later went to Teoponte. The women usually stayed in supporting roles often very important ones.

The main complaint made by many of those interviewed across the different countries was that a woman would rarely be found in leadership or combat roles. They were placed mainly in support functions that were always seen as inferior to armed combat and leadership. Che Guevara espoused this himself in his manual of guerrilla combat, *Guerrilla Warfare* (1961). Although he also said that "A woman is capable of doing the most difficult tasks, of fighting alongside a man and, despite current belief, she does not create conflicts of a sexual nature among the troops." He goes on to say that women are especially important as messengers, cooks, seamstresses, and above all, as nurses:

> The woman plays an important part in medical matters as nurse, and even as doctor, with a gentleness infinitely superior to that of her rude companions in arms, a gentleness that is so much appreciated at moments when a man is helpless, without comforts, perhaps suffering severe pain and exposed to the many dangers of all classes that are a part of this type of war. (112)

It is interesting to note that he chooses to contrast the rudeness of men with the gentleness of women.

Despite their absence in leadership, never before had so many women joined left wing political organizations as during this period in South America. In the traditional Communist and Socialist parties, for example, women represented less than 10 percent of militants.[4] In the armed organizations of the New Left in the Southern Cone, the proportion of women was between 20 and 30 percent. These numbers were based on data from government security forces that, as a rule, underestimated the number of women involved in support and informal roles. What we are arguing is that these organizations offered a chance for many women to become involved in politics, a rare opportunity in those times. It is no coincidence that three women from this generation would go on to become elected presidents of Brazil, Argentina, and Chile.[5]

This may explain why many women do not recall this period as a time of exclusion and discrimination. From today's vantage point, we can see that they were relegated to carrying out secondary tasks, and very rarely did they reach positions of decision-making or command. But they experienced that time as a moment of inclusion, a time in which it was new for women to become involved in politics. Organizations were recognizing women as militants side by side with their male comrades.

Memories of the Female Body

The body appears in women's memories in different ways. It also appears in the memories of men, especially around the subject of torture (Tavares 1999). Women sometimes narrate the female body as a limitation to militancy and armed struggle. At other times, it presents possibilities that a male body cannot accomplish. Of course, the capacity to bear children is a realm inaccessible to men and can be used to either explain or justify nearly everything, from militancy that goes to extremes to save a child or recover its body, to abandoning the struggle in order to care for a child. The female body poses a problem, because left wing militancy, even general political militancy, is constructed as a male space. In the politics of the polis, those men who are "free" to conduct politics are those who are liberated from work and family demands—they can go to meetings at any time; they can move freely throughout the city, even late at night; they do not need to give explanations to anyone, they do not need to be concerned with children, husbands, the home, making dinner on time, or taking the clothes off the line before it rains.

Gloria Ardaya, militant of the Bolivian Movimiento de Izquierda Revolucionario [Revolutionary Left Movement], recalls how difficult it was to attend meetings, being a woman and a divorced mother:

> We had the clear idea that as a woman, the double shift issue was a fact of life. For example, the male comrades who...I already was divorced then and of course, meetings went until 1, 2, or 3 in the morning. Then of course they said, "And why do you have to leave?" There were over 30 of us in leadership and I told them, "Damn it, because I have children and I don't have a wife to take care of my children like you do!"

Walking the streets at night, alone, was something that women of certain social classes did not do at that time. In addition, how could a woman escape the responsibilities of maternity or marriage? For women, this meant a constant concern for children. Gladys Díaz (2008), a Chilean journalist who became one of the few women national leaders of the MIR, said that when she was arrested, the father of her five-year-old son filed for custody of their child. She then adopted the following strategy. She had someone from the resistance infiltrate her son's father's house. When the boy fell sick, this person arranged for a doctor on behalf of the boy's mother. She would write threatening letters to the boy's father when she found out that he had punished the boy. In this way, she maintained effective oversight of the boy. When she was expelled from the country, she threatened to call the international press if the father did not return her son to her. In the end, she was able to take her son with her into exile. This case shows, on the one hand, Gladys's determination to maintain her role as a mother, and on the other, how children rendered such strong women vulnerable. Cases were quite frequent of women and even some men, whose torture included threats to and abuse of their children. Torture was very present in experiences of militant women and men. Those who were not tortured certainly lived in constant fear of it. Those who escaped alive or were physically unharmed, lived with guilt. For all those involved, it was traumatic. For women, torture was nearly always cloaked in sexual violence. The first act was to strip the female prisoner naked in front of several men. Sexual insults, such as whore, slut, cow, bitch, were commonly used. Olívia Joffily (231) cites Gilse Cosenza's testimony:

> They put me in the pau-de-arara[6]...I had given birth to a baby girl shortly before and the suture marks were still quite visible. Leo [the torturer] ran

his hand over the stitches and said: "This is truly the *puta que pariu* [the bitch who gave birth]! Look here, all stitched up!"

According to Graciela Sapriza, "Torture was the extreme expression of the asymmetry of power between men and women. It was a gross example of sexual abuse, a violation of the body. Seduction was practiced as a form of subjugation, the conquest of a trophy" (104). This does not mean that men did not also suffer sexual abuse. Many narratives speak of torture of the male genitalia, but the main difference is that men rarely speak of these events.

Masculinization

Another quite common discourse that appears in the interviews we conducted, and also in the literature on the subject, is that to be accepted and respected in left wing organizations, militant women had to assume male attitudes and even dress like men. One interviewee, who was one of the few women leaders in her organization says, "I dressed like a man. I adopted male attitudes... I was determined, strong, I knew how to shoot [a gun]... and many women knew all this... I also slept with various men" (Oliveira).

Similarly, Adriana Boria, who was a militant in student organizations in Cordoba, Argentina, speaks of "masculinization": "We women looked just like the men. We abandoned the positive elements of womanhood and assumed a series of behaviors that were male. Anything connected to affection, passion... all these were frowned upon."

Gladys Díaz also draws attention to this dimension in her militant trajectory:

> *Gladys*: I say, "I moved in a world of men so that I could gain decision-making power. And along the way, I lost part of my femininity." Then came a moment when I wanted to regain my femininity. And that's what I do, until today.
> *Cristina*: What do you mean by losing your femininity?
> *Gladys*: I believe, let's say, that the woman has a number of characteristics that are particular to her, of high value: intuition, the ability to persuade, to use, say, a mountain of qualities that involve the emotions. I transformed myself into a person who banged on the table, who was insistent. I came "head to head" with men as an equal, I used their same methods, which are not those of a woman. A woman is very "clear,"

very transparent, women don't have to boast. In politics, when you are with men, boasting is unavoidable. If you don't, you lose face, they don't respect you.

Many of the women that researcher Ana Maria Colling (1997) interviewed in Brazil also needed to renounce their condition as women in order to be recognized in organizations. Violeta, one of her narrators, remembers that:

We had a hard time being considered normal, ordinary women. If we thought, if we engaged in politics, if we had our own ideas, if we did not accept being restrained like a dog, which we did not accept at all, it was hard to believe you were a woman. (70)

Moriana Hernández, who was a member of the Communist Party and the Communist Youth of Uruguay, and is today a militant of CLADEM [Latin American and Caribbean Committee for the Defense of Women's Rights], said that at a certain moment in time, she came to the conclusion that she was a man! That is to say that the leftists of the '60s took up militancy as if it had been handed to them. And of course, militancy was male militancy.

Like other militants, she also talked about clothing and cosmetics, which if too feminine, were highly criticized within the organizations:

Moriana: It's very funny, because I remember being criticized within the Communist Youth, for the way I dressed, too feminine...
Cristina: What did you wear? Skirts?
Moriana: I wore the most scandalous miniskirts (laughs). The militants' uniform was jeans, but I say this anecdotally to show how all behavior was... male, I can't find another word to express it.

Nélida Auger, better known as Pola, recounted to interviewer Marta Diana how she was admitted into the PRT [Workers Revolutionary Party] in Argentina. On her first meeting with the leader, her entry was put off: "I arrived on time. Seventeen years old, long straight hair down to my waist, a tiny miniskirt, a low-cut blouse, and my heart pounding furiously because I was about to meet the 'Leader'!" She left that meeting deflated, but for her second interview she changed her tactics: "I arrived before he did. I cut my hair short, like a man's; wearing loafers, blue jeans, a man's shirt" (Auger in Diana 88). She had to introduce herself, as the leader didn't recognize her. Along with her change in appearance, Pola changed her attitude as well. She was sure of herself, she asserted herself. And, she was accepted into the party. Analyzing reports from women in the Argentine guerrilla, Alejandra Oberti (2006) calls attention to the fact that this male-ness in appearance coexisted with the representation of women as "mother." Oberti quotes an interview with a militant nicknamed Gringa, recorded by Marta Diana:

> The gun became an extension, a way to externalize the struggle in which women participated...and we women were there...and we proved we were capable of taking care of our children, doing the housework, and grabbing a weapon to fight an oppressor that deprived us of justice or of the ability to feed our children. (32)

According to Oberti (2006), masculinity did not appear as taking the place of femininity, but as sharing the same space—a single body—an added dimension that did not necessarily contradict being a woman. As Judith Butler points out:

> If one "is" a woman, that is certainly not all one is; the term fails to be exhaustive, not because a pre-gendered "person" transcends the specific paraphernalia of its gender, but because gender is not always constituted coherently or consistently in different historical contexts and because gender intersects with racial, class, ethnic, sexual, and regional modalities of discursively constituted identities. (20)

Left wing militants needed to transform themselves in the context of the political struggle and underground life. As Alejandra Ciriza affirms they were in search of the new man, who would be the subject in the revolution and in the new world that they intended to build. Upon entering the underground and choosing the path of armed struggle, militants lost many things, and in losing them would be transformed: they would lose their names, their families, their childhood friends, they often moved to other cities, lost their professions, jobs, pleasures, obsessions, all in the name of the revolution (Fernandes Junior; Paz). But they did not lose their gender, which in the case of men was reinforced and mirrored in the virile image of Che Guevara. The story was quite different for women. Even though Uruguayan Daniel Viglietti's (1971) song "Muchacha" called her the "complete woman," a guerrilla woman needed to completely reconstruct herself, including her gender. Only then would she come to be accepted as a "compañera," as women "comrades" were called.

Conclusion

The discourses of left wing militant women in the various countries of the Southern Cone emphasize themes, practices, trajectories, and discussions that are common to left wing organizations. All of these women and men experienced organizations, struggle, and resistance that mobilized a considerable number of people. Many were young people and university students. Each one of these movements developed under particular national contexts and circumstances. Each organization had its ideological line (which also changed over time), its own type of structure and hierarchy, its own position regarding the participation of women and men, its own form of recruitment, regulations, and positions on secrecy.

At the same time, there were many shared aspects across the movements. Gender was not the only commonality. These organizations, with all their differences, were the result of an historic movement that caused people to believe that revolution was indeed possible. The movements used common manuals, common images, heroes, and sources. In the journals and bulletins produced by organizations in each country, the same passages of Che are quoted; the star and the rifle appear in red, white, and black; and courage and audacity are emphasized as great qualities of a guerrilla warrior. Feminism and the sexual revolution arrived through various routes, in various ways. The narratives about this time were "framed" (Pollak) by new relations of gender. Along with their desire to bring about a socialist revolution, and the impact of new feminism and other new social movements, militants experienced and experimented with new relations of gender. Clearly, the "experience" that constructed the memory of this time was "gendered."

However, we should also remember that our narrators' memories are constructions in the present, resignifying their pasts, and thus bringing into the present moment a new—or different—understanding of their actions in either the feminist or revolutionary movements—or both.

In these present rearrangements of memory, many of our narrators express feminist perspectives and the importance of studying gender and/or gender relations. Our research shows that many women throughout the Southern Cone were already cognizant at the beginning of their militancy of the differences between being a man and being a woman in the movement, and that they used gender as a way to stand up against repression and to fight for human rights. In some cases, militant women's groups gave birth to feminist groups. Therefore the experience of "being a woman in the movement" also served to "genderize" the memory of the dictatorships. In this regard, the "dialogue" that Luisa Passerini establishes with Joan Scott's classic text (1988) on gender as a category of historical analysis is worth remembering. Passerini remarks:

> In the meeting between History and oral history, gender had a role to play, but not as a central and dominant category. Its role was apparently more modest. It was used in its verbal form, "gendering," that could be translated as *genderizar*. That is, as a procedure to modify or redefine existing historical approaches. Therefore, in many cases, oral history contributes significantly to the "gendering" of History. (2011: 99)

Passerini is referring to her own and others' research, proving that, little by little, other interpretive categories began acquiring importance. "Oral history played a role in another shift, the need to combine gender with other categories of difference, more often and more carefully, as a category of historical analysis" (101). Therefore, beginning an analysis from the relationship between gender and memory, but also paying attention to other components of a gendered memory (workers and peasants, indigenous peoples, blacks and whites, some religions, labor unionists), we begin to comprehend women's experiences in the dictatorships of the Southern Cone.

At the time of this writing, the National Truth Commission report is being released in Brazil. The commission investigates allegations of deaths and disappearances of people as well as the use of torture by agents of the state in Brazil, between 1945 and 1985. In Argentina, trials of torturers and assassins who took part in the Dirty War continue. The memory of this period of dictatorship plays an important and decisive role in all the countries in the region. Increasingly, the role of women as protagonists in the resistance movements becomes known and valued, to the extent that women today also make claims for greater political participation, calling for an end to violence against women, and for the right to make choices about their own bodies. In this sense, hearing their accounts and listening to what women have to say about their histories of resistance acquires current political significance. This act of listening connects younger generations with the past, producing an encounter between generations, and forges a political link between resistance and transformation.

Notes

1. The three projects that comprise this research were funded by the Conselho Nacional de Desenvolvimento Científico e Tecnológico [National Council for Scientific and Technological Development]. The three projects are: "Clandestine Lives, Underground Gender Relations: A Comparative Study in the Southern Cone Countries on Appropriations of Feminist Theories (1960–2008)," coordinated by Joana Maria Pedro; "Tears as Flag: Emotions and Gender in the Rhetoric of Resistance in the Southern Cone Countries," coordinated by Cristina Scheibe Wolff; and "Memory Spaces: Files and Documentary Sources on the Meaning of Military Dictatorships (Brazil and Paraguay)," coordinated by Janine Gomes da Silva.
2. All the personal interviews referenced in this chapter are archived in the Laboratorio de Estudos de Genero e Historia (LEGH), at the Universidade Federal de Santa Catarina: http://www.legh.cfh.ufsc.br/acervo/entrevistas/We wish to acknowledge the many students who transcribed and reviewed the interviews included in this chapter: Lílian Back. Joana Borges, Priscila Carboneri de Sena, Yarssan Dambrós, Larissa Viegas de Mello Freitas, Cristina Hentz, Luciana Fornazari Klanovicz, Andrei Martin San Pablo Kotchergenko, Luana Lopes, Paolo Andrés Mondino, Vivian Barbosa Moretti, Gisele Maria da Silva, Juliano Malinverni da Silveira, and Maria Laura Osta Vázquez.
3. In Brazil, women participated in the repression as police officers (Moreira and Wolff), and, in Argentina, as nuns and police officers.
4. Marcelo Ridenti, in "As Mulheres...," provides numbers for Brazil.
5. Other Southern Cone countries also had presidents that came from resistance movements. In Uruguay, José Mujica was a former Tupamaro; in Paraguay, Fernando Lugo was a theology of liberation priest; and in Bolivia, Evo Morales was active in the Tupac Katari movement of the '80s.
6. *Pau de arará* is a pole that extends horizontally and used to hang people by their wrists and ankles.

Works Cited

Ardaya, Gloria. Personal interview by Cristina Scheibe Wolff and Joana Maria Pedro, La Paz, Bolivia. October 27, 2006. Digital. LEGH/UFSC Collection.

Barroso, Carmen and Guiomar Namo de Mello. "O Acesso da Mulher ao Ensino Superior Brasileiro." *Cadernos de Pesquisa* 15 (1975): 47–77. Print.

Boria, Adriana. Personal interview by Cristina Scheibe Wolff, Córdoba, Argentina. October 27, 2006. Digital. LEGH/UFSC Collection.

Butler, Judith. *Gender Trouble: Feminism and the Subversion of Identity*. New York: Routledge, 1990. Print.

Ciriza Jofre, Alejandra. "Genealogías Feministas: Sobre Mujeres, Revoluciones e Ilustración: Una Mirada Desde el Sur." *Estudos Feministas* 20.3 (2012): 613–633. Print and Web.

Colling, Ana Maria. *A Resistência da Mulher à Ditadura Militar no Brasil*. Rio de Janeiro: Rosa dos Ventos, 1997. Print.

Diana, Marta. *Mujeres Guerrilleras: La Militância de los Setenta em el Testimonio de sus Protagonistas Femininas*. 2nd ed. Buenos Aires: Planeta, 1997. Print.

Díaz, Gladys. Personal interview by Joana Maria Pedro and Cristina Scheibe Wolff. Chile, September 2008. Digital. LEGH/UFSC Collection.

Escobar, Silvia. Personal interview by Cristina Scheibe Wolff and Joana Maria Pedro. La Paz, Bolivia. 2008. Digital. LEGH/UFSC Collection.

Fernandes Junior, Ottoni. *O Baú do Guerrilheiro. Memórias da Luta Armada Urbana no Brasil*. Rio de Janeiro: Record, 2004. Print.

Flores, Guillermina Kanonnikoff. Personal interview by Cristina Scheibe Wolff. Asunción, Paraguay, February 22, 2008. Digital. LEGH/UFSC Collection.

Gandolfi, A. *Les Luttes Armées en Amérique Latine*. Paris: PUF, 1991. Print.

Gómez, Alejandra López. Personal interview by Cristina Scheibe Wolff. Montevideo, 2007. Digital. LEGH/UFSC Collection.

Guevara, Ernesto Che. *Guerrilla Warfare*. 3.ed. University of Nebraska Press, 1985. Web.

Halbwachs, Maurice. *On Collective Memory*. Chicago: University of Chicago, 1992. Print.

Hernández, Moriana. Personal interview by Cristina Scheibe Wolff. March 24, 2008. Montevideo, Uruguay. Digital. LEGH/UFSC Collection.

Joffily, Olívia. "O Corpo como Campo de Batalha." *Gênero, Feminismos e Ditaduras no Cone Sul*. Eds. Joana M. Pedro and Cristina S. Wolff. Florianópolis: Mulheres, 2010. 225–245.

LEGH [Laboratório de Estudos de Genero e História], Universidade Federal de Santa Catarina, Brazil.

M. Personal interview by Cristina Scheibe Wolff. October 27, 2006. Córdoba, Argentina. LEGH/UFSC Collection.

Moreira, Rosemeri and Cristina Scheibe Wolff. "A Ditadura Militar e a Face Maternal da Repressão." *Espaço Plural* X.21 (2º Semestre 2009): 56–65. Web.

Oberti, Alejandra. "Contarse a Si Mismas: La Dimensión Biográfica en los Relatos de Mujeres que Participaron en las Organizaciones Político-Militares de los '70." *Historia, Memória y Fuentes Orales*. Eds. Vera Carnovale, Federico Lorenz, and Roberto Pittaluga. Buenos Aires: CeDinCI, 2006. 45–62. Print.

———. "Qué Hace el Género a la Memória?" *Gênero, Feminismos e Ditaduras no Cone Sul*. Eds. Joana M. Pedro and Cristina S. Wolff. Florianópolis: Mulheres, 2010. 13–30. Print and Web.

Oliveira, Eleonora Menicucci. Personal interview by Joana Maria Pedro. Cáceres, Brazil. October 14, 2004. Digital. LEGH/UFSC Collection.

Passerini, Luisa. *A Memória entre Política e Emoção*. São Paulo: Letra e Voz, 2011. Print.

Paz, Carlos Eugênio. *Nas Trilhas da ALN: Memórias Romanceadas*. Rio de Janeiro: Bertrand Brasil, 1997. Print.

Pedro, Joana Maria. "Narrativas do Feminismo em Países do Cone Sul (1960–1989)." *Gênero, Feminismos e Ditaduras no Cone Sul*. Eds. Joana M. Pedro and Cristina S. Wolff. Florianópolis: Mulheres, 2010. 115–137.

Pedro, Joana M. and Cristina S. Wolff, eds. *Gênero, Feminismos e Ditaduras no Cone Sul*. Florianópolis: Mulheres, 2010. Print and Web.

Perrot, Michelle. "Práticas da Memória Feminina." *Revista Brasileira de História* 9.18 (1989): 9–18. Print and Web.

Pollak, Michel. "Memória, Esquecimento, Silêncio." *Estudos Históricos* 2.3 (1989): 3–15. Print.

Ridenti, Marcelo Siqueira. "As Mulheres na Política Brasileira: Os Anos de Chumbo." *Tempo Social* 2.2 (1990): 120–128.

Saldaña, Margarita Iglesias. Personal interview by Cristina Scheibe Wolff and Joana Maria Pedro. June 2007, Santiago, Chile. Digital. LEGH/UFSC Collection.

Sapriza, Graciela. "Memórias del Cuerpo." *Historia, Género y Política en los '70*. Eds. Andrea Andujar, Débora D'Antonio, Nora Domínguez, et al. Buenos Aires: Feminaria, 2005. 39–60. Print.

———. "Memoria y Memorias de Mujeres en el Relato de la Ditadura (Uruguay, 1973–1985)." *Gênero, Feminismos e Ditaduras no Cone Sul*. Eds. Joana M. Wolff Pedro and Cristina S. Wolff. Florianópolis: Mulheres, 2010. 94–114. Print and Web.

Scott, Joan. W. *Gender and the Politics of History*. New York: Columbia University Press, 1988. 28–50.

Suarez, Miriam. "Recordar Pensando el Passado para Repensar el Presente." *Gênero, Feminismos e Ditaduras no Cone Sul*. Eds. Joana M. Wolff Pedro and Cristina S. Wolff. Florianópolis: Mulheres, 2010. 264–275.

Tavares, Flávio. *Memórias do Esquecimento*. São Paulo: Globo, 1999. Print.

Viglietti, Daniel. "Muchacha." *Canciones Chuecas*, Orfeo. 1971. LP.

Wolff, Cristina Scheibe. "Feminismo e Configurações de Gênero na Guerrilha: Perspectivas Comparativas no Cone Sul 1968–1985." *Revista Brasileira de História* 27.54 (2007): 19–38. Web.

PART II

Subjectivity and Identity Construction

CHAPTER 4

The Healing Effect of Discourses: Body, Emotions, and Gender Subjectivity in Basque Nationalism

Miren Llona

This chapter addresses the role that emotions play in the construction of gender nationalist subjectivity. Oral narratives transmit people's feelings, likes, and frustrations, revealing the emotional imprint that lived experience stamps into memory. I would argue that the fact that memory is a process of continual evaluation does not imply that all the meanings and resonances of the past are distorted. In my experience, I have observed that there are certain types of accounts in memory that, even if not immune to the intersubjective character of the interview and to the passage of time, have a deep emotional charge. This charge enables the account to remain quite faithful to the experience and the emotions felt in the past that provoked the memory in the first place.[1] My purpose is to demonstrate that in human experience, emotions are intertwined with discourses and comprise a significant component of memory. The emotional imprint plays a fundamental role in recording a memory, but I also insist on the materiality of emotional experience. Consequently, we are both relating individual and social memory and inscribing emotion and feeling on a body that experiences and positions itself in the world.

Introduction and Historical Context

I argue that those emotions that have left an indelible imprint in memory are fundamental pieces in the construction of subjectivity.[2] National identities, gender identities, class identities, and so on, constitute meanings that enable the subject to define her/himself and to speak about her/himself, as well as to distinguish the self from the other and to recognize difference. It is through identity that we identify the limits between what is legitimate and what is not. I believe that the establishment of these boundaries is related to the imperishable nature of emotions written on the body.[3] From my point of view, those emotions seared in memory, together with available discourses of nationalism, contribute decisively to "naturalizing" these identities, to our considering them as part of our being rather than as the result of concrete experiences and learning.[4]

In this chapter I focus on the process of constructing national identities and will start from the concept of "shame,"[5] a feeling that can be brought on by the confrontation between hegemonic cultures and belonging to a subordinated community. I analyze this experience of embarrassment and connect it to the emotional incorporation of nationalist discourses. I attempt to show that there is a tight connection between these two emotional experiences and that, to a large degree, the ability of nationalist discourses to offer a sense of dignity to people who previously experienced the feeling of shame contributes to their success. I will also propose that the emotional politics of the nationalist movements are fundamental to the design of national projects—learning to differentiate oneself from the other.

To understand this, we go back to the first third of the twentieth century when the Basque nationalist movement began to expand.[6] I draw on an interview that I conducted in 1997, with Polixene Trabudúa, a woman propagandist of the Basque nationalist movement in the 1930s. She was born in 1912 in Sondika, a town not far from Bilbao.[7] Polixene Trabudúa's testimony narrates her rural origins, her discovery of Basque nationalism, and her embrace of the new patriotic discourses produced by this movement in the context of the Second Spanish Republic (1931–1939). It also lets us explore how the lived experience of subordination can lead to the acceptance and embrace of nationalist projects.

My interest in the construction of national identities stems from the fact that, like gender, national identities are one of the most essentialized forms of lived experience. This is also true of Basque national identity, a complex issue that has a genealogy, an evolution, and an historical trajectory.[8] My argument further introduces subjectivity into the analysis of the attractiveness of nationalist ideas. As Barbara Rosenwein proposes, the nation is above all an emotional community (2010: 12). From a research perspective, this idea of emotional community offers a way to "uncover systems of feeling, to establish what these communities (and the individuals within them) define and assess as valuable or harmful to them" (Rosenwein 2002: 842). This perspective leads us to pose questions about the emotional economy and the feelings that were present during the process of constructing Basque nationalism (Díaz Freire 2001: 86).

Basque nationalism was one of the three political cultures, along with liberalism and socialism that formed the backbone of contemporary Basque society from the late nineteenth through the early twentieth centuries. The origins of Basque nationalism are intimately connected to the figure of its founder, Sabino Arana.[9] Although Arana didn't start from scratch, we can consider him the motive force behind the "invention of tradition," that constructs Basque nationalism and the "imagined community" of the Basque nation. Arana's brand of nationalism, like other nineteenth-century nationalist discourses, was essentialist.[10]

The narrative I present here illustrates the emotional effectiveness of this type of discourse and its potential to foster feelings of national belonging. During the first three decades of the twentieth century, the time frame of Polixene Trabudúa's narrative, Arana's Basque Nationalist Party developed a nationalist ideology around the concept of a collective Basque people and their political independence from the rest of Spain. Expanding industrialization and rapid economic transformations in the Basque Country during the last quarter of the nineteenth century and the beginning of the twentieth century were decisive factors in the emergence of this new ideology. Basque nationalism confronted this modernization process with a steadfast defense of tradition and a reaffirmation of Basque uniqueness. The arrival of massive numbers of immigrants and workers attracted by industrial development was seen by a part of the local population as a potential danger. The new nationalist discourses responded to this feeling by stigmatizing the new arrivals in defense of the supposed "native" population (Díaz Freire 2003: 90). The same process of modernization had favored the development of an urban culture in the city of Bilbao. This produced a sharp dichotomy between two universes that ended up opposing one another: one side included lifestyles linked to the cultivation of land, the Basque hamlet, the figure of the villager, and *Euskara* (the Basque language), representing all these dimensions; the other side included urban life associated with liberalism, the middle classes, and the Spanish language (Juaristi 156). In this cultural polarization, urban culture came to represent civilization and progress, and the rural community came to be associated with nature. From a symbolic standpoint, the relationship between the two became hierarchical, in which the Basque cultural universe became subordinated.

In this complex context, Basque nationalism constituted a paradoxical political and social movement that mixed modernity with traditionalism. On the one hand, it made the defense of tradition and the particularities of the rural world the core for constructing its distinguishing national identity. In this way, the new imaginary cultural nationalism reevaluated the cultural aspects associated with rural life, the Basque hamlet, and the Basque language, all of which had suffered an affront by the urban context of Bilbao, and turned them into iconic pawns for the "reinvention of tradition" (Juaristi 34). On the other hand, the national movement found another instrument associated with modernity—the political party. It also used mass propaganda, a clear indicator of modernity, to achieve its expansion and become an active agent of social promotion and cultural change in Bilbao in the first three decades of the century.

The Story of Polixene Trabudúa

This very process of modernization and adaptation and the Basque Nationalist Party's mass politics saw the restoration and reevaluation of traditional Basque culture. Thus, people who had felt subordinated found in the new nationalist discourses a possible path to dignity. An effect of these nationalist discourses, at least in theory, was that those who belonged to a formerly marginalized universe now had the chance to become part of urban middle-class culture. This was a complex process, but I will try to show how middle-class identity and national identity ended up reinforcing one other.

Now we turn to analyzing Polixene Trabudúa's life narrative. I have chosen four moments in her account that have particular emotional importance. In my view, these are deeply felt moments, or "enclaves of memory." These are segments in which Polixene Trabudúa recurrently uses the word "feel," where she uses anecdotes about the past to try to convey the sensation or impression of what she experienced, and in which her tone of voice becomes exultant. Along with "feel," she uses other emotional words, such as "crying," "pride," "shame," "frustration," and "admiration." The narrative segments transmit emotional exaltation, and are sometimes interspersed with laughter or inflections and modulations of tone. The first segment refers to the cultural contradiction in Polixene's family universe: the influence and power of Spanish culture over the subaltern culture of the "hamlet." The second describes the liberating effect of nationalist discourses and the way in which they were able to repair the shame she suffered in the condition of subalternity. The third shows the close relationship between middle-class identity, urban culture, and construction of new national identities. Finally, the fourth segment suggests that cultural nationalist teachings were effective to the degree that they were bodily, not just mental or ideological experiences.

Polixene Trabudúa belonged to the rural culture of the Basque hamlet, which as previously mentioned, was subordinate to urban middle-class culture. She was born in 1912 in Sondika, a rural town near the city of Bilbao. Her family was economically comfortable since her father chose not to work the land and instead became a successful builder. Their economic position and liberal attitude toward the education of women enabled Polixene to go to school with the daughter of the town doctor. They were the only girls in town who were sent to school in Bilbao. Her education with the Sisters of the Cross, and later in the Vizcaya Normal High School for Teachers, founded in October 1902, taught her how to move in an urban environment. Thus, Polixene could measure in cultural and class terms the distance between the rural environment she came from and the culture of the urban, middle class, Spanish-speaking city. She says:

> [It was] an education entirely in Spanish...studying about all the kings of Spain...the dates of all their reigns....An absurd education, but it was that way everywhere. That is, there were no indications of nationalism among the nuns, none. It was totally Spanish. But to me this was entirely normal because in my house, my father was a monarchist...completely Spanish insofar as education was concerned. That's why when I discovered nationalism it had a huge impact on me. Because I had felt a contradiction in my life, between my grandparents who didn't speak Spanish, the life of the hamlet, so pure, healthy, so, so, different...but there was a huge contradiction because in Bilbao, for instance, when my father would go to get my grades from the nuns, I didn't want my father to go. He made me ashamed because he spoke Spanish so badly so I would ask my uncle

>   Aureliano, who was the Mayor of Sondika, a big boss... to go to the school and get my grades.

In this account, we see that Spanish cultural hegemony had penetrated the rural domestic world. Spanish was not just the language of culture and education in the urban world but also part of the daily lives of families like the Trabudúas in the surrounding rural towns. To them, Spanish language and culture signified being EDUCATED, in capital letters, in the face of a Basque culture that was more domestic, folkloric, and lacking in social prestige. In any case, despite her father's privileged economic situation, his Basque accent, difficult to disguise, gave away his village origins and this made Polixene feel ashamed. In the civic and urban environment of her school, she tried to camouflage herself and escape the country stigma of her rural origins. This account shows the value assigned to cultural signifiers, "the sticky association between signs, figures and objects" to use Ahmed's words, is critical to the process of social stratification and the establishment of social barriers ("Affective..." 120). It also implies that although economic power might be necessary, it was not sufficient to guarantee belonging to the urban middle class.

In formal terms, this recollection enables us to observe how subjective meanings are transmitted through anecdotes, simple accounts that often start with a "for instance," as in this case, and then present a brief story that seeks to reproduce the reality of the past. Such narratives allow the subject to return to that past, describe the situation, and give a name to the lived experience. "I was ashamed," is the feeling that runs through Polixene's narration of the cultural subordination she experienced.

Yet, in turn, the narrative reveals the complexity of memory, given that recognizing the feeling of shame is already a reinterpretation of the experience, performed by the subject in the heat of discovering nationalism, a fact that as Polixene acknowledges, made a real emotional "impact" on her. Nationalist discourses are those that allow the subordination of their history to be rewritten and turned into a beautiful tale: "my grandparents did not speak Spanish... life in the hamlet, so pure, so healthy, so different." This embellishment of history helps transform the feeling of shame into other type of emotions, "frustration," "tremendous contradiction," that are proactive, and to a certain extent into restorative feelings that enable the subject to recount her/his experience. The narrative, thus, reveals a full emotional evolution, from the reality of a lived experience and the feelings it aroused, to the transformation of that emotion, by means of a discourse, into another, more complex feeling which, in this case, is dignifying for the subject.

So, in the nationalist imaginary, elements like rural origins or the Basque language became principal sources of social prestige, opening opportunities to experience change and to subvert in practice the inequality inherent in particular binary conflicts. In fact, Polixene describes her encounter with Basque nationalism as a new baptism, an event that could bring emotional healing to her frustrations. As we will see, the account is complex and simultaneously includes a counternarrative in which Polixene reviews and evaluates her own past. This is one of the beauties of oral narrative and its analysis. It enables the subject to tap into the emotional memory of events that caused deep impact while at the same time offering an opportunity for evaluation, self-reflection, and self-criticism from the present standpoint. Polixene affirms:

> It liberated me. No, it was more than a liberation, it was the discovery of something new, something huge in my roots, that now that I didn't have to be ashamed of but instead could be proud of those roots, of those traditional wooden shoes behind the door, of that farmhouse with its hearth, of that field work and all of it. To feel, perhaps, a little too proud, maybe that was the sin of those times, perhaps...That nationalism, so pure, so fiery, so, so, so strong. That raising of the Basque race, of light eyes, of four surnames, and all that. Because we felt, they made us feel too proud of our roots [she nods]. That too is not good.

The key feeling in this account is the liberating effect, the "unveiling of the truth" that essentialist nationalisms provoke. The power of these discourses resides precisely in their ability to make the present seem like it is part of a preexisting reality, an authentic nature that otherwise was hidden. Recognizing this marks the beginning of a new era of liberation. The eternal nature of this type of conception situates the present as part of a long past and transforms ordinary cultural elements into "roots," that is, into elements of significance. Thus, the very elements that previously formed the basis of stigma acquire new meaning in light of this new truth. From the point of view of emotions, this change is important in that it makes it possible to perceive the effect of this process in healing past humiliations. This narrative, then, reveals the capacity of nationalist discourses to restore dignity. The attributes of the rural Basque universe acquire new meaning as part of a quintessential nationalist iconography. They became a source of identity and admiration within the national community.

These new social and cultural conditions of remembrance allow the narrator, immersed in the present, to reevaluate the past. So, Polixene's recognition of an excess of pride and vainglory in being Basque suggests that there have been fundamental changes in her way of understanding Basque nationalism and national identity that differ from those she held before. The substance of her evaluation suggests that the racial and ethnic arguments of Basque nationalism have lost legitimacy.

I would also like to point out that this narrative is an example of how discourses interpellate their subjects and the way in which an individual's coming-to-consciousness takes place. We can see the back and forth movement inherent in the process of reappropriating collective discourses, as expressed by "we made ourselves," or "they made me feel." The "them," the "us," the "self," all those subjects are involved in this awareness process. At the same time, we are speaking about feelings. What we normally consider to be ideological conviction is really an empathetic, emotional issue. The change occurs in the conversion of the feeling of shame into pride. The narrative allows us to verify that the success or failure of the rhetorical interpellation does not come out of nowhere. Anthony Smith suggests that nationalist discourses are successful and attract a strong social following in the degree to which they connect with the feelings and emotions of the people who share a collective memory prior to the creation of these nationalist narratives (13). Without turning Smith's argument into a teleological one, I do consider it important to pay attention to the genealogy of the elements that play a role in the acceptance/expansion of nationalism. From my point of view, the emotional conditions of reception are relevant to understanding the appeal of national discourses. In our case study, the situation of subordination, codified as shame, provided the emotional foundation upon which Basque nationalism built a sense of dignity.

Polixene's close identification with the nationalist movement led her to join the Emakume Abertzale Batza (The Association of Nationalist Women) at the beginning of the Second Republic in 1931. She was part of the Propaganda Commission, working to spread the nationalist platform, and serving as a female icon of Basque nationalism, representing the "new woman" of the 1930s.[11] Moreover, making a name for herself in the nationalist universe also led to upward mobility. Class and national identities were inextricably intertwined, so that the acquisition of one meant the strengthening of the other, and vice versa. As Polixene recognizes:

> Look, my mother with a scarf tied around her head! [women in the hamlets wore headscarves]. What a contradiction, right?! And me with a hat! I started wearing hats when I became active in the Basque Nationalist Party, when I was 19 or 20 years old, but we didn't know what hats were.

Rising to a renowned political position in the Basque Nationalist Party signified full entry into a middle-class environment, requiring adoption of its class symbols. Consequently, as Basque nationalism exalted the peasant world and its traditions, it also brought about the assimilation of working-class people into the urban middle class, who identified themselves as nationalists. In the urban world of the 1920s and '30s, the signs of distinction associated with middle-class status were automatically linked to wealth and social wellbeing. In her next account, Polixene talks about being attracted in her youth to middle class life. She recalls:

> As students, we were fascinated by two people—I'm referring to the students in my class—Presentación Pescador y de la Cruz, a member of the Nationalist Party. We all noticed her. She wore red nail polish, silk stockings, something incredible in those days. The other was Lolita Ferrer who was driven from Neguri by a chauffeur. The chauffeur dropped her off and picked her up.... The chauffeur in his uniform opened the rear door for her. And for us, these were the most marvelous examples [she laughs] to aspire to.... We knew that there was a better world than ours, where you could paint your nails, which for us was unthinkable, and wear silk stockings.

These associations of meanings that were engraved in Polixene's memory lead us to wonder about the relationship between the body and adornments as external signs of social status, a link that in itself generates undeniable feelings and meanings. In this case, a connection is made between the bodies of young middle class women and wellbeing, wealth, and superiority.[12] Not only that, it may be that related to the use of modern women's accoutrements is the idea of women's emancipation. Associating female social distinction with material prosperity and progress, along with the possibility of achieving greater measures of independence as women, could be very seductive and convert the prototype of the middle-class *señorita* into a future prospect for Polixene.[13]

At the same time, this narrative suggests another interpretation—that Polixene's self perception belongs to a different world, socially and culturally separate from the "higher civilization" of the urban middle classes. In this context, Basque nationalism could create great expectations: at one and the same time, it constituted a movement that was firmly anchored in a middle class culture and it brought a new language that rehabilitated the cultural dimensions of traditional Basque culture. That is why Polixene could reaffirm her desire to become a *señorita* and a nationalist. They constituted two acts that were not just contradictory, but also mutually reinforcing.

Polixene recounted one last event about her attending the nationalist play called "Pedro Mari." When Basque nationalism tried to become a party of the masses and construct a wider multiclass base, it put in motion an active politics of feeling, with the goal of nationalizing the masses of people. The emotional policies of nationalist movements facilitate a fundamental experience in the design of national projects: embracing difference. As Sara Ahmed argues, "*Emotions do things* and they align individuals with communities... through the very intensity of their attachments" ("Affective..." 119).[14] "Pedro Mari" is an educational play whose main plot seeks to show that Basques are neither Spanish nor French, thus teaching audiences how to define and differentiate the specific nature of the Basque identity from other national identities.[15] The format of the play ensures that difference is learned emotionally and not intellectually. This was done through sentimental exaltation of the cultural past and through repetition, which resulted in a shift in subjectivity. As Judith Butler argues, it is through the repetition of norms that the world becomes material to us (12–13). The play worked precisely in these ways, extolling sentimentality, and reinforcing through repetition a political transformation in subjectivity.

Political discourse and nationalist ideology were enacted frequently through public events in which folklore, tradition, and esthetics created an atmosphere conducive to patriotic communion. Polixene affirms:

> The pledge of allegiance... as in party militancy, there's a moment in which you feel some kind of truly powerful force. Watching the play "Pedro Mari"... I don't really remember the story... I don't remember what the conflict was. But you clearly felt that we Basques were neither French nor Spanish, but Basques [she nods]. That play really had an impact on me. I remember that I left the Arriaga Theater crying, crying, crying! And José [her boyfriend] says to me "What's the matter, Polixene?" [She replies] "Leave me alone, leave me alone, leave me alone!" I was hysterical, right? [She nods].

There was a clear didactic and performative purpose to those mass-oriented nationalist theatrical productions, in which the plots raised all kinds of feelings. Their meanings became permanently etched in peoples' memories. The emotional impact translated into foundational lessons that unquestionably affirmed the existence of the Basque nation and confirmed the desire to belong to it. The account is a clear example of what Cherríe Moraga has called "theory in the flesh" (23). This theory argues that the construction of identity cannot be divorced from the emotional imprint of bodily experience. In this way, the basic lesson—to be able to differentiate Basques from the French and the Spanish—became an emotion, the feeling that Basques were neither Spanish nor French, as evidenced in the nervous excitement that Polixene describes feeling. The narrative allows us to see how the emotional impact of experience on the body enables ideological discourses to be transformed into definitions of being, in this way converting social identities into natural essences.

In Polixene Trabudúa's biography, embracing nationalism was a crucial episode that took place when she was 19 years old. Her first contact with Basque nationalism fully determined her whole life. Her commitment to the Basque Nationalist Party led her to political activism. Once the Civil War ended, Polixene left Spain, beginning a long exile first in France and then in Venezuela with her husband and four children. She returned from Venezuela to the Basque Country in 1990 and lived the last years of her life with her son Unai. During those years, she devoted herself to remembering her past, writing the story of her eventful life, and staying actively involved in Basque nationalism and politics in general until 2004, when she passed away.

Conclusion

"Emotions," as Sara Ahmed argues, "do things." In this case study, we have seen how emotions and feelings prepare the terrain for nationalist ideologies: learning to differentiate oneself from others. Often, these teachings end up becoming definitions of the self and are lived as natural phenomena. However, the analysis of an individual memory allows us to trace the process of its construction. In this sense, the inherent subjectivity of oral history narratives becomes a valuable and necessary resource, since it is the subjectivity of the narrative itself that allows us to understand this process of identity construction.

Through the analysis of a single life story, I have tried to show that the emotional foundation of Basque nationalist discourses in the 1920s and '30s is complex. The narrative invited us to explore feelings like shame, provoked by the experience of subordination, and to link this to the expansion of nationalist discourses. This has also allowed us to explore ways in which middle class and nationalist identity could be mutually reinforcing—with class identity insuring the primacy of belonging to a national community and national identity insuring social and class mobility. Finally, Polixene Trabudúa's narrative reveals how ideological messages become inscribed on the body, in this instance through emotional strategies espoused by the Basque nationalist movement in the twentieth century.

Notes

1. These indelible imprints, associated with exaltations, anxieties, or deep impressions on the body are what I call "enclaves of memory." I propose that these enclaves are related to mental spaces, to personal images intimately connected to the body and to the configuration of identity resulting from the emotional impact of lived experiences. I have suggested that these narratives are especially important to the historian, because within these enclaves we can find important keys to the individual and collective experiences in a particular period of time (see Llona 2012: 19, 50–51).
2. I use existential phenomenology's notion of subjectivity (Vattimo 47–55; Overgaard 45–63; Kirby 22–38). Luisa Passerini's work is a source of inspiration for my approach to memory and subjectivity (1988: 105–153; and 2006: 65–89).
3. I ascribe to a nondualistic concept of the body, in which mind and body constitute one related whole. (Damasio 2001: 68; and 2004: 110). In Spanish historiography, this holistic idea of the body has been developed by Díaz Freire (2003: 5–29).
4. For the state of the historiography of emotions, see Matt 117–124; Reddy 302–315. In the Spanish context, regarding the state of the debates on the history of emotions, see Medina Doménech 161–199.
5. I echo the definition of shame offered by Norbert Elias: "The feeling of shame is a specific excitation, a kind of anxiety which is automatically reproduced in the individual on certain occasions by force of habit.... it is a fear of social degradation or, more generally, of other people's gestures of superiority.... This defenselessness against the superiority of others" (292).
6. The Basque people are an ethnic group mainly inhabiting the Basque Country (adjacent areas of Spain and France) that speaks *Euskara* (Basque language). This language is the only pre-Indo-European language that is still extant in contemporary Europe. The Basques have therefore long been supposed to be a remnant of a pre-Indo-European population in Europe. This fact has historically underscored a separation between Basque, Spanish, and French cultures. The protection and promotion of *Euskara* has been at the heart of the Basque national identity. Large numbers of Basques have left the Basque Country for other parts of the world in different historical periods, often for economic or political reasons. Historically, the Basques were

often employed in sheepherding and ranching, maritime fisheries, and as merchants around the world. A large wave of Basques emigrated to Latin America. The largest of several important Basque communities in the United States is in the area around Boise, Idaho. All the same, Basques have a close attachment to their home, the "Basque hamlet," especially when this consists of the traditional self-sufficient, family-run farm or *baserri(a)*. Home in this context is synonymous with family roots. Traditionally Basques have been mostly Roman Catholics. In the nineteenth century and well into the twentieth, Basques as a group remained notably devout and church-going. The Basque Nationalist Party in the 1890s constructed a nationalist ideology that defended the notion of a distinctive Basque people, and of its political independence from the Spanish State.

7. Bilbao is a commercial port city of the Basque Country that experienced an accelerated process of industrial development and urban and cultural modernization in the late nineteenth and early twentieth centuries. As a consequence, Bilbao is an outstanding laboratory for studying the formation of contemporary identities. The narrative of Polixene Trabudúa (1912–2004) is part of a collection of 26 interviews conducted by Miren Llona: *Polixene Trabudúa, Mujeres de las Clases Medias*, archived in Ahoa, Ahozko Historiaren Artxiboa (http://www.ahoaweb.org/coleccion.php?col=7), part of a broader research project on middle-class women's identity in the first three decades of the twentieth century.

8. As is evident in this discussion, my argument is constructivist and so-called modernist, aligning with philosophers like Anderson, Hobsbawm, Gellner, and Balibar, all of whom made important contributions in the 1980s to our understanding of nations and nationalisms. Smith's ethno-symbolic arguments also form part of my theoretical toolkit.

9. Although Sabino Arana may not have been the sine qua non of the rise of nationalism, most agree that he was the principal designer and author of the symbolic imaginary and of the political project that gave rise to Basque nationalism. In fact, during the last decade of the nineteenth century, Sabino Arana spread his political program founded on three pillars: religion, the old laws, and the Basque language. In 1893 he founded Bizkaitarra, the main newspaper, in which the essential elements of Basque identification repeatedly appeared: the flag, the anthem, and the geographical boundaries of a new national project called Euzkadi (consisting of four territories in Spain and three in France). Finally, in 1895, Sabino Arana founded the Partido Nacionalista Vasco (Basque Nationalist Party). For a history of Basque nationalism, see Corcuera, Fusi; De la Granja; and De Pablo, Mees, and Ranz.

10. The Basque nation was conceived as an eternal entity whose life cycle Arana described as a primordial narrative: paradise, fall, revelation, and rebirth. This organic nature of the nation gave it an origin in the remote past, and the resurgence of nationalism in the present takes the form of a revelation.

11. For a study of Basque nationalist women as pioneers of the "new woman," see Llona 2002; 2010; 2014.
12. In this regard, Sara Ahmed understands that the work of emotion involves the "sticking of signs to bodies" (*The Cultural*...13).
13. On the expectations raised by the ideal of middle-class *señorita* and the boundaries in redefining this stereotype during the twenties and the thirties in the Basque Country, see Llona 2002.
14. Jo Labanyi (2010) also defends the materiality of emotions and links them to a subject's practices in his/her relationship with the world.
15. The story takes place in 1793 during the Guerra de la Convención (War of the Convention) between France and Spain. The plot is as follows: Pedro Mari, a young Basque man from Navarra, travels to the Spanish port of Cádiz to leave for America. En route, he is arrested by Spanish troops and sent to the battlefront. One night, while on patrol, he hears someone singing in *Euskara* (Basque). He abandons his post and crosses over to the enemy troops where he finds a group of French Navarre Basques singing in Basque. Later, he is captured by Spanish soldiers and accused of desertion. He is convicted and shot. A study of this play can be found in López Antón 177–194.

Works Cited

Ahmed, Sara. "Affective Economies." *Social Text* 79, 22.2 (2004): 117–139. Print.
——. *The Cultural Politics of Emotion*. Edinburgh: Edinburgh University Press, 2004. Print.
AHOA, Ahozko Historiaren Artxiboa [Archivo de la Memoria]. http://www.ahoaweb.org/
Anderson, Benedict. *Comunidades Imaginadas: Reflexiones Sobre el Origen y la Difusión del Nacionalismo*. [English title: *Imagined Communities*]. México: Fondo de Cultura Económica, 1993. Print.
Arana, Sabino. "El Juramento de Larrazabal." *Obras Completas, Sabino Arana*. Bayona: Partido Nacionalista Vasco, 1948. Print.
Balibar, Etienne and Immanuel Wallerstein. *Raza, Nación y Clase*. Madrid: IEPALA, 1991. Print.
Butler, Judith. *Bodies that Matter: On the Discursive Limits of "Sex."* New York: Routledge, 1993. Print.
Corcuera, Javier. *La Patria de los Vascos. Orígenes, Ideología y Organización del Nacionalismo Vasco, 1876–1903*. Madrid: Taurus, 2001. Print.
Damasio, Antonio. *La Sensación de lo que Ocurre. Cuerpo y Emoción en la Construcción de la Conciencia*. Madrid: Debate, 2001. Print.
——. *El Error de Descartes*. Barcelona: Crítica, 2004. Print.
De la Granja, José Luis. *El Nacionalismo Vasco (1876–1975)*. Madrid: Arco Libros, 2000. Print.

De Pablo, Santiago, Ludger Mees, and José Antonio Rodríguez Ranz. *El Péndulo Patriótico. Historia del Partido Nacionalista Vasco*. Barcelona: Crítica, 2005. Print.

Díaz Freire José Javier. "El Cuerpo de Aitor: Emoción y Discurso en la Creación de la Comunidad Nacional Vasca." *Historia Social* 40 (2001): 79–97. Print.

———. "Cuerpos en Conflicto: La Construcción de la Identidad y la Diferencias en el País Vasco a Finales del Siglo XIX." *El Desafío de la Diferencia: Representaciones Culturales e Identidades de Género, Raza y Clase*. Eds. Mary Nash and Diana Marre. Bilbao: Universidad del País Vasco, 2003. 61–94. Print.

———. "Cuerpo a Cuerpo con el Giro Lingüístico." *Arenal* 14.1 (2007): 5–29. Print.

Elias, Norbert. *The History of Manners: The Civilizing Process*. Vol. 1. New York: Pantheon Books, 1978. Print.

Fusi, Juan Pablo. *El País Vasco. Pluralismo y Nacionalidad*. Madrid: Alianza, 1984. Print.

Gellner, Ernst. *Nacionalismo*. Barcelona: Destino, 1998. Print.

Hobsbawm, Eric and Terence Ranger. *La Invención de la Tradición*. Barcelona: Crítica, 2002. Print.

Juaristi, Jon. *El Chimbo Expiatorio. La Invención de la Tradición Bilbaína, 1876–1939*. Bilbao: El Tilo, 1994. Print.

Kirby, Kenneth R. "Phenomenology and the Problems of Oral History." *The Oral History Review* 35.1 (2008): 22–38. Print.

Labanyi, Jo. "Doing Things: Emotion, Affect and Materiality." *Journal of Spanish Cultural Studies* 11.3–4 (2010): 223–233. Print.

Llona, Miren. *Entre Señorita y Garçonne. Historia Oral de las Mujeres Bilbaínas de Clase Media*. Málaga: Universidad de Málaga, 2002. Print.

———. "Patriotic Mothers of Basque Nationalism: Women's Action during the Spanish Second Republic in the Basque Country." *Feminist Challenges in the Social Sciences. Gender Studies in the Basque Country*. Eds. Mari Luz Esteban and Mila Amurrio. Reno: University of Nevada Press, 2010. 85–101. Print.

———. "Historia Oral: La Exploración de las Identidades a Través de la Historia de Vida." *Entreverse. Teoría y Metodología Práctica de las Fuentes Orales*. Ed. Miren Llona. Bilbao: Universidad del País Vasco/Euskal Herriko Unibertsitatea, 2012. 15–61. Print.

———. "From Militia Women to Emakume: Myths Regarding Femininity during the Civil War in the Basque Country." *Memory and Cultural History of the Spanish Civil War*. Ed. Aurora G. Morcillo. Leiden and Boston, MA: Brill, 2014. 179–213. Print.

López Antón, José J. "El Imaginario Pesimista de Vasconia en Arturo Campión." *Vasconia, IV Jornadas de Estudios Histórico Locales: Formas de Transmisión Social de la Cultura* 27 (1998): 177–194. Print.

Matt, Susan J. "Current Emotion Research in History: Or Doing History from the Inside Out." *Emotion Review* 3.1 (2011): 117–124. Print.

Medina Doménech, Rosa María. "Sentir la Historia. Propuestas para una Agenda de Investigación Feminista en la Historia de las Emociones." *Arenal* 19.1 (2012): 161–199. Print.

Moraga, Cherríe and Gloria Anzaldúa. *This Bridge Called My Back: Writings of Radical Women of Color.* New York: Kitchen Table, Women of Color Press, 1983. Print.
Overgaard, Sore. *Wittgenstein and Other Minds: Rethinking Subjectivity and Intersubjectivity with Wittgenstein, Levinas and Husserl.* New York and London: Routledge, 2007. Print.
Passerini, Luisa. "Per una Critica Storica dell'Oralità." *Storia e Soggetività, Le Fonti Orali, la Memoria.* Firenze: La Nuova Italia, 1988. 105–153. Print.
———. *Memoria y Utopía, La Primacía de la Intersubjetividad.* Granada: Universidad de Granada, 2006. Print.
Reddy, William M. "Historical Research on the Self and Emotions." *Emotion Review* 1.4 (2009): 302–315. Print.
Rosenwein, Barbara. "Worrying about Emotions in History." *American Historical Review* 107.3 (2002): 821–845. Print.
———. "Problems and Methods in the History of Emotions." *Passions in Context* 1 (2010): 2–32. Print.
Smith, Anthony D. *La Identidad Nacional.* Madrid: Trama, 1997. Print.
Trabudúa, Polixene. *Polixene. Crónicas de Amama.* Bilbao: Sabino Arana Kultur Elkargoa, 1997. Print.
———. Personal interview with Miren Llona. October 10, 1998.
Vattimo, Gianni. *Introducción a Heidegger.* Barcelona: Gedisa, 1998. Print.

CHAPTER 5

Lola's Story: The Struggle to Build a Professional Identity with No Good Jobs in Sight

María Eugenia Cardenal de la Nuez

> Life stories are not just material for the researcher; they are also productions of the subjects, who construct themselves in the telling.
> (Claude Dubar. *La Crisis de las Identidades*)

This chapter brings a key aspect of personal identity into focus: professional identity. I look at how young Spanish university graduates construct their professional identities under highly adverse socioeconomic conditions. For the last eight years, Spain has been caught in an economic depression, with shrinking employment and a rollback in worker's rights. Insecurity and lower wages have pervaded the entire employment structure, including jobs for graduates (Ministerio 96–105). How do university graduates adjust their work, professional, and personal expectations to the reality of a declining and progressively insecure job market? And in doing so, what "forms of identity" (Dubar 2000: 185)[1] do they develop in the face of precarious employment? What is the role of the family, the educational system, and peers in the construction of these forms of identity? These were the main questions that guided the project.[2]

The study of autobiographical narratives allows us to identify the ways in which people handle crises, how they weave and unravel social ties with the "others" they encounter along the way, and how they construct meaning from their life stories. I examine these issues through the narrative of a young woman—Lola—using Wengraf and Chamberlayne's Biographical Narrative Interpretive Method (BNIM). The method is a psychosocial approach to biography focused on narrative as a source of evidence for the understanding of subjectivity. To do so, rather than using a more or less structured guide, the interview is improvised, starting with a single, very open-ended question that aims to stimulate a narrative ("Please, tell me the story of..."). This question is followed by an uninterrupted answer. The interview continues with a series of narrative questions, formulated exclusively from the topics that are brought up in the initial answer and using the interviewee's own words. By doing so, subjective meanings can be induced from the implicit, unconscious frames of reference embedded in the experiences told, rather than from the explicit statements and beliefs expressed (Wengraf 2001: 112–151).

The BNIM interpretation is also very specific. It requires the development of two tracks of information, namely the biographical facts of the story (the "lived life") and the narrative (the "told story"). Both tracks are analyzed separately in an inductive way, focusing in each case on the shape and flow of the data. The interpretation process is often carried out in teams, called "panels," after which a meaningful interpretation of the case is proposed.[3]

BNIM's in-depth approach is particularly suitable for case studies like Lola's story. It aims to understand the inner structure of the narrative, in order to build a case that allows a deeper understanding of the general research question. Representativeness, thus, is not achieved by accumulation—or, to quote Bertaux (33), by saturation—but by building connections between the different cases in order to detect patterns (Rosenthal 207). As Roseneil and Budgeon put it, "Each individual story is interesting in its uniqueness, but these stories are not exceptional; they speak of patterns of transformation in general life" (144).

The BNIM interview and research procedure has much in common with oral history methods, especially those interested in accessing the interviewees' subjectivity, not just the "hard facts." It requires the interviewer, as Anderson and Jack have noted, to remain "suspended and attentive" (169) during the interview, letting the narrator take the lead in determining its structure. Interpretation entails paying close attention to subtle details, such as evidence of emotion in the narrative or its internal logic, and to speech patterns and silences, what Williams calls "Voice with a capital V" (43). The analytical process, on the other hand, is much more formal than in most oral history approaches or even in conventional methods of qualitative analysis used in sociology, such as speech analysis (Conde).

I found Dubar's distinction between predicative and attributed identities particularly helpful in analyzing Lola's narrative. According to Dubar, attributed identity is inherited: it comes from the identifications we receive in our environment. Predicative identity, on the other hand, is actively constructed: it is a product of what we do and the significance with which those actions are charged (2002: 105–106). That predicative identity is the focus of my research, and in this case I discovered that my subject's predicative identity is not only found in Lola's statements about herself but is also implicit in the actions and decisions she made when facing obstacles and opportunities, and in the "narrative production" (110) Lola creates by telling her story a certain way.

This chapter is divided into four parts. In the first, I describe the circumstances in which I met Lola, the reasons why I decided to analyze her life story, and the conditions under which I interviewed her. The part that follows is a brief summary of Lola's lived life. The third section characterizes Lola's narrative based on the structure, narrative flow, and main topics of her story, and offers my interpretation of the case. Finally, in the conclusions, I sum up the key insights into professional identity that Lola's case offers for consideration/discussion. I also point out the advantages of an emergent and interpretive methodology like BNIM for understanding subjectivities in the process of being formed.

An Encounter with Lola

I met Lola when she was studying for a master's degree in family mediation and intervention at the ULPGC (University of Las Palmas de Gran Canaria). I was teaching a course on social research methods, and she was one of my most participatory and thoughtful students. At the end of my last class, as I usually do, I handed out registration forms to be completed by any students interested in participating as informants in my research on job market integration processes.[4] Months later, when I reviewed them to prepare the new project's preliminary interviews, Lola's immediately caught my eye. Most of the forms I receive from students are incomplete or provide only the minimum required details. Not only had Lola supplied all the requested information, but she had also written two additional paragraphs in the "comments" box I always include on these forms. In them, she explained that she had previously been employed as a clinical social worker at a juvenile treatment center and was now working with families of children with severe psychological disorders. She also indicated her monthly income at the time (€200), the number of families she had worked with (three) and that she was presently working with one.

Lola was clearly making a case for me to interview her, and she had several points in her favor. In a few short lines, she had outlined a patently precarious career history and claimed to have a job, which from what I could tell, seemed quite unusual. After comparing her profile with that of other potential informants, I decided to begin my research with her. She was a logical choice because she was eager and willing to participate, but also because, after finding that her current occupation did not exist in the formal job market, I thought her case might reveal some interesting dimensions of the relationship between precarious employment and professional identity. What exactly did Lola's job entail? How had she made the transition from formal to informal employment? How had this change affected her sense of professional identity? Was she content with what she was doing, or was she longing to get out of that situation? These were some of the questions that struck me about Lola as a specific case of the general problem I was researching.

I interviewed Lola in my office at the university three months later, in June 2012, once the final grading period had ended and she was no longer my student. In class, Lola had shown herself to be an independent, critical thinker, so I had no fear that our former student-teacher relationship would significantly bias the data. I contacted her by email, and she promptly replied that she would be happy to come in for an interview. I chose to interview her using the BNIM technique which, as mentioned above, begins by asking a Single Question aimed at Inducing Narrative (SQUIN). My question was as follows:

> **As you know, I'm researching**[5] *the experience of young university graduates and their transition to the working world, the expectations they originally had and the realities they encounter, the decisions they've made, the resources that have been available to them, and their assessment of this experience.* **So, please, tell me the story of** *how you entered the working world, from the moment you first considered entering the profession you studied for up to the*

present day. **All the events and experiences that were important for you personally. Begin wherever you like; please take all the time you need. I'll listen first; I won't interrupt; I'll just take some notes in case I have any further questions for after you've finished telling me about it all. So please, tell me the story of how you entered the working world.**

After the opening question, Lola talked for twelve minutes without interruption. The interview then continued with narrative questions phrased using her exact words. It lasted for a total of three hours. After that initial encounter, Lola and I exchanged several emails to confirm specific details of her life story. Her replies to my queries were always prompt and meticulously precise.

Lola's Lived Life

The following is a presentation of what the BNIM method calls the lived life: a summary of key events in the interviewee's life, in the order in which they occurred, omitting—as dictated by the BNIM rules of analysis—the person's narrative of those events. In this first approach to Lola's life story, the goal is to interpret the characteristics and sequence of past events in order to identify the pattern of the life she has lived up until now (Wengraf 2014).

Lola's professional identity began to take shape at an early age (ten years old) when she became a volunteer at her school, a commitment she continued to pursue in her teen years by volunteering at increasingly larger and more important institutions (her local maternity and children's hospital and the Red Cross). She then enrolled to study for a degree in child and family social work. As an undergraduate, Lola tried to embark on her first professional adventure and got her papers in order to travel to Latin America as an aid worker. However, her mother vetoed the plan, saying, "What will I do if you leave?"

After graduating in 2008—when the Great Recession had already begun to rear its ugly head in Spain—she received two job offers but turned them both down. She accepted the third—although it meant paying for her own training—and became a clinical social worker at a juvenile treatment center—a secure facility for underage mental patients. She moved steadily up the ladder at this institution until discrepancies over corrective measures used on the young patients brought her into conflict with the facility's new management. Two months later, she suffered a panic attack and was fired while on sick leave. Lola sued her employer, won, and could have been reinstated, but she decided against it, despite not having any other job prospects at the time. In 2010, with the financial crisis in full swing, Lola was 23 years old. She registered with the unemployment office and spent a year looking for work and educational opportunities in vain.

After that "lost" year, in 2011 Lola was accepted into a master's program in family intervention. Around that time, the psychiatrist at her former place of work contacted Lola and asked if she would like to work privately with families of children with mental illnesses. Lola thus embarked on an activity with no official recognition in the working world, no clear definition of her professional status, duties, or rights, and no guaranteed clients. The interviewee negotiated the terms, set her rates, and tried—unsuccessfully—to obtain a contract. In this respect, she accepted a job with all the responsibilities of a normal profession, but without the protection and security afforded to those who work under the aegis of an institution or professional association: her job did not exist as a legally regulated occupation in Spain. In 2012, when I interviewed her, she was still in the same situation.

Upon analyzing the events in her educational and employment history, it becomes clear that Lola's trajectory is one of thwarted progress: though promising at first, the upward trend is eventually broken and her path takes a downward turn. However, this opportunity was cut short by her termination and subsequent inability to find work in her field in the formal economy. Now let us hear how Lola tells the story of her relationship with work.

Lola's Narrative

Lola's Self-Presentation

Lola's first words after hearing the opening question are forceful: "Right! Let's see, so I should start with when I graduated." Her initial reaction is a statement, not a question. The interviewee sets the ground rules for how she will answer; at most, she seeks confirmation of her choice, but she does not subordinate herself to the interviewer. From the outset, Lola presents herself as a decisive person, one who plays the cards she has been dealt and freely applies the criteria she considers relevant to her history.

After that emphatic "Right!" she launches into a chronologically ordered narrative that follows a regular pattern as it moves forward in time: after briefly describing each event, Lola adds a series of arguments and explanations about why she made certain decisions and/or acted a certain way. Each event leads to a conclusion, after which she introduces a new mini-narrative and fleshes it out in similar fashion. Lola's account of her first job interviews and her decision to accept the third offer clearly illustrates this structure:

> I had my first interview about a month after finishing [my degree]. It was...for doing something that didn't really interest me. I mean, even though they wanted me, I said no. Because it was something I'd already done before, for free, because back then I was a volunteer. So I'd already done that, and what I really wanted was to grow. So I turned that job down, and they called me for another one with an association for drug addicts. But it was the same deal, it was for an internship, and I'd already done internships and I wanted something more. So I turned that down, too. Then later they called me up for an interview, for a job that I thought, "Hmmm, I don't have the training for this, but it sounds really interesting." So I went to the interview. I loved the idea: it was a new project they were going to do here, there was nothing like it at the time, and I loved it. Apparently the girl felt the same about me, and she proposed that I, um...go on a trip to Tenerife, for a training course...It was voluntary, and I had to pay my own way. So it was like..."Only if you want to," and they didn't promise me anything. I went. Because it seemed so interesting, I said [to myself], "This should count for something, and if not at least I'll have learned something new." So anyway, I went, and the following month they called to say that I'd made it through the first round of the recruitment process. "This is interesting," I thought, so I went back for another interview. That also went pretty well.

Lola presents herself as a proactive person, someone who decides, chooses, and refuses. Her first story is also remarkable for its linearity and homogeneity, which contrast sharply with the pattern of her lived life. As I have already pointed out, the trajectory of her life can be described as a slow, steady upward climb followed by a sudden and dramatic drop from which she has yet to fully recover. Her self-presentation reflects these facts, but they are narrated dispassionately, without evidence of a break or change in either her tone or her language. Lola's account of her dismissal and her year of unemployment is a case in point.

> In the end I was with them [at the juvenile center] for two, I think three months, and then they fired me. Ever since then, well, I started looking for

work, but I found that by then the job market had changed, that things weren't so easy anymore. So I said to myself, "While I'm looking for a job, I'm going to see what... what kind of training options are out there." But there weren't any, there was nothing because all the courses, either they'd already started or they were too expensive and I couldn't afford them. So that was that. I didn't get anywhere until I started the master's program [She goes on to talk about her experience in the master's degree program].

The detached, matter-of-fact tone used to narrate this extremely difficult period of her life is quite suggestive. It may be an indication of how painful this particular episode was: her decision to merely report the facts might be a way of including it in the narrative without being forced to relive it. On the other hand, from the perspective of identity construction, it might imply that Lola is developing a narrative (and thereby narrating an identity) that hinges on looking forward, without dwelling on the more negative experiences of the past.

One might conclude that such a flat, concise self-presentation, rather than denoting a specific process of identity construction, is merely a way of efficiently answering the initial question, which asked for nothing more and nothing less than "the story of her relationship with work." However, the coda to Lola's initial presentation confirms and simultaneously qualifies my interpretation. Following the BNIM interview structure, when Lola concluded her first account I asked if she had anything to add. The following interaction ensued:

[min. 8.44] *Lola*: Now I'll let you ask me whatever you want [6s pause]
María Eugenia: **Thank you very much. Is there anything you'd like to add? Anything at all, whatever comes to mind...**
Lola: For me, my experience was really rich, Eugenia. Oh, the things I could tell! But of course they'd all just be trivial anecdotes.
María Eugenia: **Whatever you feel like telling me is fine.**

Encouraged to continue talking, Lola returns to the topic of the juvenile treatment center to criticize the educational shortcomings she perceived at the time.

Lola: Well look, when I started working, if there was one thing that impressed me it was that I didn't have even the most basic tools. I didn't... I mean, I didn't have a clue when I started working. I mean, if you hadn't done volunteering before, you felt a bit like you'd been cut loose. Um... not even... A report, they'd never even showed us how to write up a report... You know? You start working, and even though you think you've got what it takes, you say, "Yes, I can do this, but *I'm really going to have to make my own way here because the thing is I don't have a clue.*" It's something that... Of course, in the beginning, you expect to leave college.... "I can get in, I can get started, 'cause I've got the basics." But when you see *you don't even have the basics*, [it's] like, "Well, now what am I supposed to do?" The truth [is] that it [the experience at the juvenile center] was... an incredible opportunity for growth [emphasis added].

Lola's reasoning is highly critical. Her language expresses the acute sense of helplessness and fear she felt at the time. It also significantly discredits the university as a place for acquiring useful skills that prepare students to face their first job. Yet Lola does not mention its shortcomings merely to illustrate how helpless she felt as a first-time worker, criticizing the university's inefficiency. As she continues, her focus shifts to the present and she brings a new factor into the equation: "the others," specifically those classmates who have been unable to find employment as child and family social workers since graduation.

Lola: [Continuation of the previous statement] The truth [is] that it was... an incredible opportunity for growth. I'm struck by that realization when I look at my classmates who never had a chance to start working...
***María Eugenia*: Uh-huh.**
Lola: You can really tell the difference. With people who are just as worthy, and who don't get the chance, and the thing is, they get left behind. Because I think about it... And I mean, now that we're twenty-five years old, twenty-six, twenty-seven, whatever... I, who was able to get a foot in... Of course! I started out volunteering for a lot of years, [I was] working two years. As soon as I left, I started the master's program, I started to try and find something on my own. In a way, *I've always been on the move. Those who lagged behind, well, they're behind.* That's how important it can be to have that first job experience. And you can tell that it's getting harder every day. But of those who studied with me, only a few of us started to work (28s pause). Done, done, done [end of Lola's self-presentation at 12m 12s] [Emphasis added].

This shift in chronological perspective—what Portelli calls "shuttlework" in his analysis of the use of time in stories (65)—is highly telling in such a linear narrative. A more contemplative Lola emerges here, a Lola who voices her current concerns and how she interprets her own experience from a present-day vantage point. At the time of the interview, she was in a similar position to that of her classmates: no official job, out of work for quite some time, and struggling to find stability in her life through further education. However, although she sympathizes with them, Lola sees her case as distinctive and separate from theirs given the nature of her trajectory, a history she traces from her volunteering days to the present, in which the fundamental milestone is her job at the juvenile treatment center and the least important chapter is her time at the university. Lola describes herself as someone who has moved beyond the stage of "incompetence"—reserved for those who only have a degree—and attained the status of experienced worker. In discrediting her university education as a genuine professional learning experience, she credits work as an experience that *did* allow her to construct her identity as a child social worker, thereby validating her "hands-on" professional learning process. Comparing herself with the others, she sums up the comparative benefits of her professional career, which she achieved by taking risks—as she "didn't even have the basics"—and which, in her view, gave her an advantage over the rest. In this way, the interviewee implicitly defines herself as someone who has a better chance of succeeding than the rest, thanks to her early vocation and constant pursuit of new challenges. The narrative identity hinted at in her self-presentation is thus reinforced and revealed as a "trajectory-identity," whose center of gravity is the sum of experiences rather than the track record of specific professional achievements.

The Second Part of the Interview: Lola's "Voices"

In this second part of Lola's story, the interviewee responds to my requests to tell me *more* about the topics mentioned in her self-presentation. Here there is a remarkable contrast between the topics the interviewee talks about readily, enthusiastically, and in great detail, and those she mentions briefly and with apparent reluctance. The analysis that follows focuses on the difference between what I have termed Lola's "Voices."

First of all, I feel I should briefly explain the sense in which I use the concept of "Voice" here. As Williams notes, the Voice with a capital V "embraces different types of articulation: the utterances as well as non-vocal expressions such as a gesticulating body or a silent moment" (43). By interpreting these expressions, we can uncover the meanings implicit in the narrative.

In this story, we can distinguish between Lola's restrained Voice and her passionate Voice. The restrained Voice is manifested in terse, often single-phrase replies, requiring multiple interventions on my part to get the interviewee to elaborate on her initial answer. This Voice is also perceptible in the frequent, lengthy pauses (in some cases, between 6 and 21 seconds long) that pepper her answers, which the narrator resorts to when reliving a highly emotional situation in which she felt powerless. These are the times when the restrained Voice surfaces: when speaking of her period of unemployment or, as in the following passage, when remembering the moment her mother asked her not to go abroad as an aid worker, saying, "What will I do if you leave?"

> *Lola*: She didn't really come out and ask me to stay, not in so many words, but that phrase was a plea. [17s pause]
>
> ***María Eugenia*: You said that phrase was a plea. Do you remember anything else about that particular moment?**
>
> *Lola*: Yes, the need I saw in another person. I tell you, that...Me, when it's for something I really want, that I feel I need and think will turn out well...We almost always have to leave something behind. At that moment my family, even though things weren't great at the time, you count on them being resilient. I mean...well, even if I'm not there, they'll make it. But, in saying that to me, not anymore. Because I could see the face [sic]. And I know at that time, that person was really depending on me. [21s pause]
>
> ***María Eugenia*: You said you could see the face, do you remember anything else about that situation?**
>
> *Lola*: No, I think it was especially that, the expression on that person's face, and my feelings. [7s pause] And, well, you know, you have to leave something you really love behind, and you say, "Hey, you're an adult, too, and you can get through this. Whether I'm here or not, you can do it." But you have to decide, and since the family is going to be there, and Latin America is going to be way over there, well....
>
> ***María Eugenia*: Uh-huh. [13s pause] You said that you remember your feelings. Do you remember anything more? Do you remember an image associated with those feelings?**
>
> *Lola*: Frustration. Not an image, I remember my frustration.
>
> ***María Eugenia*: Uh-huh.**

> *Lola*: Like, I can't believe all the things I'd tried, I joined the Red Cross as a volunteer, because I knew the Red Cross also did overseas aid work. They told me it wasn't possible, so OK, let's try somewhere else. Like, really? Now that I finally have it? Now that I have it… [6s pause] Of course, later, their gratification [*sic*, probably gratitude] when I told them I wasn't going.
> **María Eugenia: Uh-huh.**
> *Lola*: For them it was a relief… [8s pause]

This was one of the tensest, most difficult moments of the interview. The interviewee never refused to answer my questions, but her replies were succinct. There were long pauses, and the conversation was awkward and stilted. At times it seemed she was about to lose that restraint and relive the experience, but another pause always stopped her. Moreover, in this excerpt the restraint is underscored by Lola's detachment in referring to her mother as "that person," and her mother's face as "the face." Above all, Lola's restrained Voice reflects a desire to play down, if not an outright effort to suppress, the negative emotions linked to moments of helplessness.

Lola's passionate Voice, in contrast, revels in rich narratives, provides gushing descriptions, fleshes out the story with details and anecdotes, shows enthusiasm, and often uses direct speech. The interviewee relives her experiences; she is in the moment, and her words flow freely. This Voice surfaces when the narrator speaks of experiences and situations that she associates with "growth." Although Lola never actually defines what she means by this word, she uses it frequently when recalling very specific moments and experiences: when she had to face challenges that made her a more competent professional, when she sensed that she could make a difference, or when she felt appreciated in the performance of a certain task. This is the case of her volunteering experiences and the accounts of her work at the juvenile treatment center. In earlier excerpts we have already seen that, for Lola, this job was a pivotal moment in her development as a professional. During this part of the interview, it is also revealed as a fundamental turning point in Lola's relationship with her closest friends. Up until then, she says, they saw her as a "hippie" who had chosen an easy major—a degree in "playing games," according to Lola—and whose opinions in debates on social issues carried less weight than those of her friends studying economics or engineering. Everything changed when one of those friends visited the center to repair an alarm. He saw Lola on the floor, holding down a youth, and he was amazed because he had always been terrified to go there when they called him in to do repairs. Lola recounts:

> That day was... the day started out, already with a case of physical restraint, the kids were in bad shape from the day before, and the day got off to a really rough start. So there I was on the floor, with one of the kids, the door opens and I see him [the friend] appear there. It was the first day I'd seen him around there, me there with a boy, and the two of us were like, "Hey, how's it going?" [Laughter] The boy on the floor, and it was, like, so funny. And later, when we saw each other outside, he said, "Lola, I never would have imagined, that you were that person." And the thing is that work brought out a totally different attitude in me, especially in that moment of crisis, right? I mean, I'm a pretty mousy kind of person, and at times like those I would get, I don't know, this attitude.... Then some people in the group started asking me questions. And I saw that their attitude toward me changed a bit, in the sense that, they started to see me as a strong person, and that now there was some substance, some merit in what I had to say. 'Cause before they were like... "Oh, the opinions of this nutcase..." Really, I was always the hippie in the group, the one who was kind of out there, doing her own thing, so my opinion didn't really count. And since they started to see that other side, they began to take me a bit more seriously, and I liked that.

For Lola, the experience at the juvenile treatment center meant that her efforts and pursuit of excellence were rewarded with the acknowledgment and respect of other professionals and of her peers. That acknowledgment, that "being for others" (Dubar 2000: 100), confirmed her sense of being a true professional, someone whose opinion mattered. That feeling, in turn, was a catalyst that continued to drive her actions, like when Lola received the call from the psychiatrist who offered her the chance to take up her current occupation. Lola continues:

> I felt valued and appreciated, when I had already left that center and the psychiatrist who worked there called to offer me the job with the families. The fact that this person, who has years of experience and has seen a lot of professionals at work, would call me, well, there must have been something about me she liked. And that a psychiatrist would see child and family work as worthwhile, and offer that resource to the families, really thrilled me, because let me tell you I've run into some psychiatrists and they don't, they don't even know what a child social worker is.[6]

Despite the importance of her time at the juvenile treatment center, Lola's story is not nostalgic. When she talks about her current job situation, near the end of the interview, Lola speaks with the same intensity, richness, and prolific detail used when narrating other "growth" experiences. The narrator is openly critical of the poor employment terms, the lack of protection she feels, and her invisible legal status. Even so, she recounts her experiences in great detail, especially her relationships with clients and the "fun" situations in which she finds herself as a result of their problems.

> One of them [her patients] who I'm still working with, it's constant, with him there's a new story every day. Things like, we're at the gym—of course, I go to the gym with him!—and he suddenly gets all these ideas. He asks a lot of personal questions, and he needs you to answer them, because if you don't, he starts to get nervous like you wouldn't believe.... Well, I remember one day when he got to the gym, cornered a trainer, and started asking him, "Do you have kids? What are their names? How old are they? How did you have them? How did you have them? I mean, were they conceived in love or was it loveless?" [Laughter]. "And how were you? What position do you think you were in when you made your kid?" And you're behind him, like, "Oh, my god." And he needs to know the answer. So, of course, with this kid, people don't know what to do, whether to laugh, step in, or what to do! And he pulls stuff like that every day!

The contrasting Voices that Lola uses in her story allow us to see the invisible threads that weave her identity. If we follow the thread of her restrained Voice, we find the experiences of helplessness that the interviewee prefers to ignore or avoid, probably because they threaten her perception of herself as the independent woman capable of surmounting difficulties. If we follow the thread of her passionate Voice, we find the growth experiences that give Lola a sense of continuity in her path through life. In this way, Lola can construct a professional identity based not on a specific job but on the sum of her experience.

Conclusion

In the 1950s, Becker and Carper stated that the four key elements of developing an occupational identity were: personal acceptance of an ideology, commitment to task, adherence to particular labor organizations, and significance of one's occupation in the status system. These elements emerge in the context of institutions and organizations: social forms which, by definition, are stable structures in which it is possible to pursue some kind of "career" (1970). Today, in the USA, in Europe, and certainly in Spain, this "typical" formula for developing a professional identity is becoming increasingly rare. Labor relations have been destandardized: contract terms are shorter, and social and workers' rights have been curtailed. Unemployment, job insecurity, and discontinuity are now the norm rather than the exception in the professional and work experience of thousands of young people, including university graduates.

As a result, it is increasingly difficult and complicated to develop elements of identification with an occupation. If identity, by definition, implies adherence to some recognizable social norm (Dubar 2002: 50), how can it be established within a context and based on an experience characterized by constant fluctuation? What are the possible elements of reference?

To analyze the problem, I thought that the biographical case study was a highly attractive option. As Portelli puts it, "Narrative is not a mere representation of the events of the story;... it is something that people do in the course of time and has effects on individual and collective behavior" (34). The BNIM interview method, based on openness and listening, yielded a narrative charged with explicit and underlying meanings. The interviewee expressed her "Voice" with as little interference as possible. Consequently, I was able to analyze both the form and content of her narrative, revealing different levels of meaning embedded in her identity construction. As Williams points out, "By being aware of Voice as we conduct and translate interviews and by probing performative elements, we can unveil layers of knowing" (45).

Lola's narrated identity is highly individualistic, emphasizing aspects of personal achievement and action and downplaying, ignoring, or burying aspects of helplessness or suffering. The stable core of her self is constructed around a story that highlights her worth, effort, and competence.

I analyzed Lola's narrative in an entirely inductive way, theorizing based on the facts and looking for an internal consistency between those facts. When I compared her case with the available literature on the subject, I found that her identity construction was analogous to that characterized in other studies on similar topics. Soto and Gaete's research, also based on narrative interviews, points to the emergence of what they call "character" identity types, in which interviewees make an active effort to project a positive self-image and embrace the ideology of the "possibilities" open to them, glossing over their suffering. These types coexist with other more nostalgic, self-vindicating identities, and they tend to be highly developed in interviewees who are self-employed or have very flexible contracts (1176). Workers with character identity, according to Soto and Gaete, have an idealized view of themselves as "agents in a permanent state of decision" who ignore the obstacles that condition their actions (1178).

In short, Lola's story shows us that, as institutions retreat, individuals end up taking charge of their own identity construction processes. Today the pressure to individualize is pervasive and hard to resist: the pressure to make and be oneself, bearing up under adversity, and defending one's self-worth against the constant onslaught of changes and fluctuations.

Notes

1. In this chapter, the concepts borrowed from Dubar are translated from the Spanish version of his writings, as the author's work has not yet been translated into English.
2. An earlier version of this essay was presented at the European Sociological Association midterm conference, RN03 (Biographical Perspectives on European Societies), in Durham (UK), September 2014, with the title: "Passion and Engagement in Informal Work? Lola's Commitment to 'Be' a Social Care Worker."
3. Wengraf, *BNIM Short Guide Bound with the BNIM Detailed Manual.*
4. This gives me a permanent database of potential informants for my research.
5. The parts highlighted in bold are standard elements of any opening question, according to Wengraf and Chamberlayne's BNIM format. The parts in cursive were added in order to achieve the specific aims of my research.
6. We must bear in mind that the child and family social work degree program was not introduced in Spain until 1998.

Works Cited

Anderson, Kathryn and Dana Jack. "Learning to Listen: Interview Techniques and Analyses." *Women's Words: The Feminist Practice of Oral History*. Eds. Sherna Berger Gluck and Daphne Patai. London: Routledge, 1991. 11–26. Print.

Becker, Harold and James Carper. "The Elements of Identification with an Occupation." *Sociological Work: Method and Substance*. Ed. Harold Becker. London: Penguin, 1970. 189–201. Print. [First published in 1956 in the *American Sociological Review*.]

Bertaux, Daniel. *Los Relatos de Vida. Perspectiva Etnosociológica* [original title: *Les Récits de Vie*]. Barcelona: Edicions Bellaterra, 2005. Print.
Conde, Fernando. *Análisis Sociológico del Sistema de Discursos*. Madrid: CIS, 2009. Print.
Dubar, Claude. *La Socialisation*. Paris: Armand Colin, 2000. Print.
———. *La Crisis de las Identidades: La Interpretación de una Mutación* [original title: *La Crise des Identités. L'Interpretation d'une Mutation*]. Barcelona: Bellaterra, 2002. Print.
Lola [pseudonym]. Personal interview by María Eugenia Cardenal de la Nuez. June 20, 2012.
Ministerio de Educación y Cultura (2014). *Datos y Cifras del Sistema Universitario Español 2013–2014*. Web.
Portelli, Alessandro. "The Time of My Life: Functions of Time in Oral History." *The Death of Luigi Trastulli and other Stories: Form and Meaning in Oral History*. New York: SUNY, 1991. Print.
———. "El Uso de la Entrevista en la Historia Oral." *Historia, Memoria y Pasado Reciente. Anuario* 20. Escuela de Historia Universidad Nacional de Rosario (2005): 35–47. Print.
Roseneil, Sasha and Shelley Budgeon. "Cultures of Intimacy and Care Beyond 'the Family': Personal Life and Social Change in the Early 21st Century." *Current Sociology* 52 (2004): 135–159. *JSTOR*. Web.
Rosenthal, Gabriele. *Interpretative Sozialforschung: Eine Einführung*. Weinheim [u.a.]: Juventa, 2011. Print.
Soto Roy, Á. and T. Gaete Altamirano. "Tensiones en la Construcción Individualizada en el Trabajo Flexible." *Universitas Psychologica* 12.4 (October–December 2013): 1167–1180. Web.
Wengraf, Tom. *Qualitative Research Interviewing: Biographic Narrative and Semi-Structured Methods*. London: SAGE, 2001. Print.
———. *BNIM Short Guide Bound with the BNIM Detailed Manual. Interviewing for Life-Histories, Lived Periods and Situations, and Ongoing Personal Experiencing Using the Biographic-Narrative Interpretive Method (BNIM)*. 2014. Available online by request to: tom@tomwengraf.com
Williams, Rhonda. "'I'm a Keeper of Information': History Telling and Voice." *The Oral History Review* 28.1 (2001): 41–43. *JSTOR*. Web.

CHAPTER 6

"Getting Ahead": The American Dream in the California Agricultural Fields

Magdalena Villarreal

By the beginning of this millennium, the development of prime agriculture[1] had shaped California in many ways. On the one hand, it generated important economic growth, but on the other, it required a great deal of manpower, largely provided in the way of undocumented immigrants from different countries, particularly Mexico.[2] Foremen and contractors played an important role in making such workers available.

María, a 38-year-old Mexican from the state of Guerrero, was one of these workers. She proudly claimed to be *mayordoma* (foreman, or rather, forewoman) working for prime agriculture in the United States. Despite the fact that she had no legal documents to live and work in this country, she had taken on this position on several occasions, explaining that she could have as many as 25 workers in her squad. In fact, she had so many contacts that she could put together four or five such groups within a day, especially when the freeze damaged the orange crop and many were left without work.[3]

This chapter focuses on María and her composite family (including her brother, sister, and niece but also very close friends that she considered almost kin). All of them migrated to the United States between 1995 and 2006, and they were all at different stages in their attempt to become documented, although none had achieved "legal" status. My aim is to show how "the American Dream" is portrayed in their everyday lives, discussing how it is construed within particular frames that enable certain aspirations while restricting others, particularly regarding migration and citizenship. Here, I am referring to the socially constructed boundaries within which people construe significations and the social tools they are able to draw upon in so doing. What people expect from their migration enterprise has everything to do with their histories, their class and gender constraints, and the knowledge and information available to them, among many other issues. These contribute to frame their possibilities to carry out certain calculations and formulate assessments. Such framing excludes certain conducts, expectations, and dreams as much as it includes others. María, for example, finds it difficult to access social and cultural devices that would allow her to transgress particular gender norms. She is proud to be a forewoman, a position that is generally attributed to men, yet she is eager to portray herself as a good mother and dutiful woman who follows the rules of American society. Frameworks such as these enclose considerations as to what is to be perceived as accessible, what is risky, and what is promising. These are assessed according to specific social and cultural criteria wherein certain rules and regulations make sense.

María is one of the 12 in-depth cases I followed during my fieldwork in the Central Valley of California, which comprised a corpus of ethnographic accounts[4] collected in 2007. My research was part of a larger binational collective project carried out by CIESAS and the University of California at Santa Barbara, of which I was co-principal director with Dr. Juan Vicente Palerm. The project involved two other senior researchers as well as 12 PhD students from both institutions. The aim of the study was to document the ways in which Mexicans build community in the United States. We argued that Latino communities were not, as was often claimed in academic literature, simply bedroom communities. Rather, they were vibrant societies wherein diverse modes of citizenship were wielded.

Having carried out research in Mexico, including the regions of origin of many of the people I interacted with during my fieldwork in California (Villarreal 1994, 2000, 2008, 2012), I was keen to come to grips with the ways in which they managed their everyday lives in the United States. Stories and literature on migrants gave me quite a good idea of what life was like on this side of the border, but I was still shocked to find two room buildings housing 16 people, homes inhabited by three families and people sleeping in their cars, particularly since I knew some of these families owned a house of their own in Mexico. I was also surprised at how much they resorted to "reverse remittances" from Mexico (Villarreal, Guerin, and Morvant-Roux). Those who had engaged in the process of buying a house often needed a bit extra to "pull through" to pay their mortgages, as did those who were, for one reason or another, forced to return to their home country. Money was also sent to support young people in college and those pursuing higher education—particularly from middle classes, who, it is important to mention, also form an important part of the (at times undocumented) immigrant population—or as part of the yields from a joint enterprise. This knowledge made their perceptions of the American Dream and their notions of citizenship all the more intriguing for me.

I selected María's case for this chapter because she was particularly articulate with regards to citizenship. Her case not only illustrates the workings of agricultural life in this part of the world, but also helps introduce the reader to the ways in which Mexicans in California perform citizenship in different scenarios (Rosaldo 27–38). They take on civic responsibilities, develop a sense of belonging, and share norms and values related to the national collectivity. They also claim space, in what William V. Flores describes as a characteristic of cultural citizenship: "Cultural citizenship includes how groups form, define themselves, define their membership, claim rights, and develop a vision of the type of society that they want to live in" (Flores and Benmayor 263).

María also narrated what life was like for workers who had crossed the border illegally and yet, as she said, contributed significantly to the American nation. Her stories describe the work situations of Mexican immigrants and the vicissitudes of their everyday life, including their fear of the border patrol, their efforts to adapt to American normativity and ways of life, and their pleasure at being able to feel money in their pockets. She also spoke openly concerning her rights and obligations as an immigrant in the United States.

In seeking to document the stories of migrants with precision, I tape recorded most of the interviews, and took careful notes after informal conversations, and dialogues. I actively participated in parties, helping set up chairs and tables and serve and distribute plates of food. I also shared moments of leisure and visited them at work. The narratives show what the American Dream meant to Mexican undocumented migrants and how they viewed their mother country in the light of new experiences. Most importantly, they reveal the frameworks within which they forge social, cultural, and financial assessments in making a living in the United States. It would be problematic to single out which assessments constitute rational calculations and which are basically desires, dreams, or impulses. Yet, I contend that all were framed in some way by underlying ideas, values, norms, socially held scripts and beliefs, which, accurate or not, were drawn upon in formulating such dreams or calculations.

María's stories were often vague, contradictory, fragmented. Although I do not have the space to present them fully, her narratives reveal how her hopes and expectations of the future are forged through life events, in encounters with others, and in maneuvering within situations. In our conversations, her stories would change somewhat depending on the circumstances and the issue she wanted to stress.

This shows how difficult it is to pin down and spell out precise codes and frameworks. But once one has embedded oneself in the relationship, it becomes clear that the structure itself is forever experiencing shifts. Its boundaries are porous and fluctuating. What we can more clearly observe are processes of *framing* and *structuring*. We see social actors busy building frames, defining boundaries, and negotiating definitions to conform to such frames. Actors are not free to impose or change frames, being as they are produced in social interaction. They can, however, rework meanings and interpretations to a degree, in such a way as to influence the process of framing. Thus, what is of interest to us is not so much to list or classify the boundaries and the frames, but to come to an understanding of the processes by which they are assigned and operated. The only way to make sense of them is to understand them in the context of people's lifeworlds (Long 2001)—in this case María's—and situate them in a particular context at a particular historical time. And, as Jorge Aceves states in the foreword to his *Historia Oral: Ensayos y Aportes de Investigación,* oral history is a resource that allows us to "re-create spaces of communication and rehearse modes of interpretation concerning the sense and meanings of life and human experience" (20–21).[5]

María

I met María in the tangerine fields, perched on a ladder, selecting good fruit to be carefully cut and then placed in the large canvas bag she carried, kangaroo style. Like the rest of the workers, she placed her knee below the bag to help support the heavy weight, while balancing herself on the ladder. Later she would climb down and dump her load cautiously—so as to not damage the fruit—into a large box placed between the rows of trees.

She came down when she saw us (that day I had gone to the field with a student) walking down the rows, wondering what we were up to. She wanted to know who we were and what we were doing. She thought we had come to help workers affected by the freeze that had crippled the citrus industry and put thousands out of work. The region had received emergency funds to allocate to counties in need. Checks and boxes of food were distributed to laid-off farm workers, particularly those having trouble paying their mortgages.[6] She asked whether we had come with help.

But later she confessed that she also came down because she was bored, particularly since the harvest was not very good and she would not be able to earn a decent wage that day. They had been asked to select the fruit by size and color. This meant they could not pick all the fruit quickly from one tree. It would take a lot more time to fill the bag. Furthermore, in this field she was not the foreman, but a laborer.

We asked whether we could visit her at home, so as to not take up more of her work time, and this was the beginning of my interaction with her. María appeared to be satisfied with her achievements in the United States, although she was striving to do better. In one of the interviews she told me the story of her childhood, which she seemed to downplay in stressing her success in her host country.

> As a kid I was different. When there were six of us in the family I told my dad that we were too many. I was mother and woman of the house. I was the eldest. I was given my dad's trousers to wash in the river, and they were heavy. I have not married because I was already married, I was mother to my brothers and sisters: making tortillas, grinding maize in the *metate*. I do not wish to get married. In my country I suffered. I shared tortillas with my brothers and sisters...coffee without sugar...more bean broth than beans.... But I have always operated with the aim of getting ahead...working, not to become rich...I had a mill and a shop, all acquired with my work. But in Mexico you cannot own a cell phone, a microwave oven. It is a provincial life. In the city you might study, but in the rural areas people don't because they don't think of the future. They are living the present. They only have more and more children...such is life in the rural areas. People don't know how to talk, they don't have education, they don't know how to dress. They say "God made me poor," but I say God made us rich from the moment we were born, by giving us life, by

giving us hands. God gave us the instruments and we should know how to use them.... We come here to obtain what we did not have in Mexico. I did not have a car, I did not have a bed... I slept on the floor. If at the time I sat on a rock, now I have a chair, if I ate with my fingers now I have enough to buy a spoon. Poverty threw us out. Here in this country... the country has all you might want. Now I give myself little pleasures (*me doy mis gustitos*). For example, when there is no work I eat at a restaurant, I don't care how much food costs because now I have the money to do so. I put my hand in my pocket... An American Dream to modernize my life, to give myself the luxury of travelling, knowing new places" [7]

"Getting ahead" is a frequent phrase in María's narratives. As an observer, one might not think that she is better off in the United States than in Mexico, but she makes her points strongly, using rhetorical devices to frame her status as a successful immigrant vis-à-vis her relatives who are poor and who have stayed behind in Mexico. Having owned a small shop and a mill, she must have had a chair and at least one or two spoons. Later she told us that she had owned an old truck in Mexico, which she used to transport grain for her shop, so she must have also had a bed, although she might have shared it with some of her brothers and sisters. And interestingly, since her arrival in the United States, María has not travelled a great deal. She was in Los Angeles for a short while looking for work before she came to Lamont, a small town in the Central Valley of California, where she rented a small, prefab cottage. The house, infested with cockroaches and rats, had two bedrooms, a kitchen and a living room, a corner of which served as her sleeping quarters. She had an old mattress on the floor, rumpled blankets and piles of clothes on the side. The other rooms were occupied by her sister and her small child, a cousin, and one of his friends. They paid 800 dollars a month for rent. This and the grocery bills were divided among the four adults.

Yet, for her, this situation was transient. What she told of her life in the United States was framed within what she perceived as a predictable future, considering the experiences of some of those surrounding her. Thus, for María, this was a better life than what she had had in Mexico. Having money in her pocket, being able to spend, owning a car, eating out, organizing parties... all this was worth the hard work and endless efforts. Parties were important. She bragged about how many parties she organized, because, as she explained, she was "doing well in the United States." She claimed that her parties were always a success. She often had live music and fed her guests "good things."[8] During parties, she never danced, and hardly ever ate or drank. She spent most of the time organizing, making sure the lights were working, the music was good, and people were fed. People we spoke to during these events referred to María as a generous, up-and-coming immigrant, which was an identity she repeatedly conveyed, partly through throwing good parties. María's clout stood out in these events. People looked up to her. Many Mexicans, Mexican Americans and other Central Americans attended, contributing to María's reputation as a good organizer and successful immigrant. Such achievements provided indications of what the American Dream was about.

One of the parties I was invited to was the "presentation"[9] of María's three-year-old niece. I was impressed with the live music, the amount of food and drink, not to mention the dainty dress and heeled slippers the little girl was wearing, despite the chilly weather. Her mother was also elegantly dressed, with a shiny blouse and high heels. But María was most proud of the big, double layered cake, the top part of which was sustained by sugar columns. Two photographers carrying professional equipment took pictures of the little girl posing beside the cake and the gifts, throwing kisses, and smiling to the camera.

The little girl's mother—María's sister—was beaming during the whole event. She explained that previously she would not have been able to hold such a party for her child because she lacked the means. She felt she owed it to her. But now, thanks to God, they had been able to do so. "I have always been a very positive-thinking person," she said.

> I always do my best. I have to work hard for my daughter. Not following the easy path, because the easiest is to prostitute oneself. But I want to give my daughter a good example. I will not give up. What would I do if I went back to Mexico? In Mexico there is nothing! Here I can get laid off work for a week but there is employment the next [week] to pay for my food. I told my husband (back in Mexico): Someday I will come back, but I want my daughter to study here, to learn English because speaking English she can find a job anywhere. Here she can study in good schools, unlike in Mexico. Now I feel super good. I feel that I am worth a lot.[10]

María, however, made contrasting statements when she mentioned her two boys in Mexico. Although she spoke of them as her sons (her being a good mother to them), they were really her nephews. She insisted that she would not bring them to the United States because here they were in danger of joining gangs. She sent money for their upkeep, but said that in Mexico they could live on next to nothing, everything was so cheap, and they always had maize to survive.[11] This contradicted, of course, her own stories about what life was like for her as a child in Mexico.

On the other hand, she agreed with her sister concerning the need for women to "get ahead." There are many women working in the fields, she said. "Half of the workers are women." Her comments show what it means for her as a woman to be able to earn a wage:

> This is something that we have here. There is equality, there is no discrimination on the job. Bosses want the work done, they don't care about color or sex. Some women are more productive than men, because a woman that has grown up working is one that succeeds here, one that gets ahead, one that can dress well and can do what she wants.

She turned to the woman sitting next to us, further describing what the American Dream meant for her:

> Look at Lupe! She came to the United States 26 years ago, when she was only 17. She married, and now her daughter has finished a degree in Administration at Bakersfield and wants to study a Masters degree. Her youngest son wants to join the army. Lupe works in the greenhouses, weeding carrots.[12]

Lupe nodded. She said she felt accomplished because her family was "doing well." I asked whether joining the army was a good option, and she nodded again, smiling proudly. Then she added (probably sensing my surprise): "It takes them out of the (agricultural) fields." Her son was born in the US, but many Mexicans join the armed forces to acquire American citizenship. "Yes, it's dangerous," she said, "but it keeps them out of gangs and also gives them a job. It isn't easy to find good jobs in this region."[13]

The American Dream, then, is framed within particular, culturally forged conceptions of what it means to get ahead. Getting ahead does not only entail making more money. It involves class, gender, and other issues that imbue meaning and provide yardsticks by which to gauge the significance of a circumstance or event. As shown in several of our interviews and dialogues,[14] class was present in their ambitions to "get out of the agricultural fields." Joining the army, working as guards or policemen or in the county jails was considered a step in upward mobility. It was also evident that, while projecting their ideas of the American Dream, the three women showed respect for their host society. However, they were critical when talking about farm labor conditions.

El fil

María is used to working in *el fil*, she says. Like other Mexican field workers, she uses the word in English (the field), instead of *campo* in Spanish. When asked directly, she answered that *campo* and *el fil* are not the same. In Guerrero, Mexico, where she is from, agriculture is different. When prodded, she mentioned that in the United States everything is more organized. "Here they're workers. They work for a company, with managers, contractors, supervisors and foremen. They have to stick to strict rules but they also have rights. Many people don't know their rights," she says, "but there's information on the radio and they can also ask."[15]

In her part of Mexico, things are different. There she didn't work for anyone, she was her own boss. She bought an old truck and transported grain to her shop, but it was difficult to earn money. Her brother helped her but he squandered their savings. Many people resorted to *fiado* (delayed payment). The prices for agricultural products were very low. She decided to migrate to the United States because she wanted to buy a new truck and there was no way she could earn the money to do so in Mexico. "Those working as agricultural day-laborers in Mexico find it even more difficult," she said. "In Mexico it depends on who you get as a *patrón* (boss) and what crop they're harvesting. Here there's more machinery, and you know that you'll be paid at the end of the week." But she declared that even here they were exploited as workers because they were undocumented. They had no benefits and they could not claim unemployment, nor did they get health insurance.[16] Here her portrayal of the American Dream was not so positive.

Yet, expectation of "getting ahead," of "making it" in the United States, pushed her forward. She complained about exploitation and unfair pay, but there was something to look forward to. In addition to being able to consume "good things" and allow herself small privileges, she could aspire to social mobility. In California, María had been mayordoma for four years. When she was not called upon to organize a squad, she took on work with someone else, like she did in the tangerine harvest. But she had been in charge of workers in the cherry and orange groves, in parsley and other vegetables, as well as in pruning grapes. She worked in pomegranate fields but did not like it because the trees were spiky and they were not paid so well. She loved working in the tomato fields, but said that there they no longer contracted people, only when it was for *la marketa* (the market). She says they harvest them mostly for puree, explaining that they use machinery to pull the plant and then take only the fruit, which the workers sort later.

The week we met her she had been working in the tangerine groves. She complained that they could only fill one box per person, because the supervisors were demanding only color and size, and this made the process slower. Sometimes they needed to pick eight trees to fill a box. And then, she said, there were sneaky workers who were constantly *barbeando* (trimming beards), jumping ahead, and picking all the easy-to-cut low hanging fruit. It was much more difficult to *escalerear* (work with the ladder). When she worked with a partner, one would cut the fruit from the lower branches and the other would work from the ladder. Then they would trade places, because working from below was always easier. She did not like the foreman she was working for at this time, but there was not a lot of other work available because of the freeze.

> Many people are *parados* (temporarily laid off). Sometimes there's no work, not even for one person, this is why they go to the tangerine fields, where the pay is not so good. Most men prefer to go to other crops. Many of the workers in tangerines are indigenous people from Oaxaca, and/or women.[17]

That day they stopped early because it started to rain. Her earning was thus even lower than she expected. She did not know whether they would work the next day. They would be called at eight in the morning. "This is the way it is in the fil, she grumbled, "You might or might not work. February's a hard month, but with the freeze it's even worse." She was not sure, but someone had told her that in the orange groves they were only paying workers two dollars an hour, since all they did was cut the oranges and throw them to the ground. Two dollars, she said, is way too little. "People have to save in order to make do during the weeks when there's no work or the pay is lower."[18]

She liked working in the grape fields the best. Workers there got a bonus of 35 cents per box, and that added up. But oranges and tangerines were the most difficult. There were other jobs that were very good, that paid per hour, but you had to be on your knees. This was the case in the *pellizco* (pinching) of organic carrots. They had to pull out the weeds with the tips of their fingers, this is why they called it pellizco.

María's appraisal of work in the agricultural sphere included considerations concerning gender and national identity, but also income. "The American Dream is to have dollars. All that you can't have in Mexico. I came with the dream of buying a truck, and till today I haven't been able to return."[19]

She preferred to be paid in cash, because they discounted taxes and other things when they got paid by check.[20] "They take off ten percent," she said.

> If I earn, for example, 350 [dollars], they'll discount around $35 or $37 dollars, sometimes more. These are federal taxes but we don't get a penny back (*no nos dan nada pa' trás*), because of the sole fact that you are a migrant you can't have rights like the others that are residents in this country. Here we don't set the conditions for any job. They tell you, you're going to work 12 hours, and we don't ask for overtime pay. For overtime they should pay more than 10 dollars an hour, but we work for the minimum... We're paying more than residents because a resident works for three or four months and then gets unemployment benefits. But for us, when work stops we have to look elsewhere and continue working.[21]

According to her calculations, only one in 20 people working in the fields is documented. And because only a handful of workers have bank accounts, they find it difficult to cash checks. They get 1 percent knocked off when they cash their checks in the nearby shops. Her status as undocumented thus restricts María's chances of getting ahead in terms of money. Yet the hope of one day obtaining documents allows her to keep going.

Migration and Citizenship

María has lived eleven years in the Central Valley. "Thanks to my merciful father in heaven," she said, "we had the opportunity to come to this land after five days of crossing the desert." It was not easy. In Lamont, the group of immigrants she came with was mistreated. She was called "*esa pinche india*" (that damned Indian) or, "*esa Oaxaca*" (that Oaxaca).[22] Sometimes, she says, it was Mexicans who mistreated them:

> Here we're even looked down upon by people of our own race... There was a time in Lamont that we didn't eat for three days. That was when we just arrived.[23]

But she stressed the fact that she was different from them. This was her way of being a good citizen, she said. Helping the needy, be they documented or not, she projected herself as a leader who looked after others and was appreciated in her community, despite the fact that Mexicans were looked down upon. She obeyed rules as far as possible. Although she could not acquire legal status and had crossed the border through the desert, she came here to earn an honest living with her work. She respected authority and believed herself a lawful inhabitant of the American territory. She worked hard and helped people find jobs, especially those that had just arrived, "Because" she said, "It's difficult here."

> You have to have contacts to find a job, and sometimes these aren't easy. Also, we have to beware of the "*migra*" (border patrol). We've learned that they can't catch you inside private land. They wait outside. They have rules. But people warn each other.[24]

They told stories of others who had made mistakes and had been picked up by the border patrol, especially for driving under the influence or being violent with their wives. Both María and her sister stressed the fact that they had to obey the law. María is careful to obey traffic laws, not drink in the streets, and, in general, follow local norms, not only because she is afraid to be thrown out, but because she thinks law is good. "This is civilization," she says.[25] She complained she sometimes found it difficult because

> [people] denigrate you because of your origin. They don't know you and they are already making judgments. But we contribute to this country. We pay taxes and don't get money back. We don't claim overtime. We only ask for work and make do with the minimum. When the "W" arrives (meaning the tax forms they have to fill in) you're following the requirements of the State of California. All individuals pay taxes. We can't apply for unemployment because only those that have "good" social security numbers can do that. We don't have MediCal or any of that. Then I ask: Why don't they acknowledge that? Why do they only criticize us as migrants? Locals can't stand the sun, the mud. We manage because we need the work.... Ok, with the freeze they brought food and some help, but that's because they don't want us to go further north to pick apples or berries. They need the workers. For the owners and contractors it's convenient that we stay. If they throw us out, who will do the work for them?[26]

The fact that they are needed as workers, that they contribute to the American nation (not only in terms of work and taxes, but because they obey laws and help the community), gives María a certain sense of participation in the country's civil society. There is an implicit claim of being a rightful inhabitant, of being subject to rights and obligations...of belonging.

Fulfilling the American Dream

I gave María a ride to pick up the van she had left at a repair shop. We stayed on a bit to chat with Tomás, the owner, who had arrived 27 years earlier from Mexico City. He said he was originally from Zacatecas, but his family migrated to the outskirts of Mexico City. He then came to California because his sister was here, working in the vineyards picking grapes, and she needed her mother to come and look after her children. They decided that he should come along, being as he was too young to stay behind. Now he worked in the mornings as a mechanic for a company that owned tractors, and in the afternoons and weekends at his own shop.

In contrast to María and her sister, he spoke with some bitterness concerning life in the United States. Despite his two jobs, he had not been able to save enough money to go back home. He was a good mechanic, but he could never get a better job in the company, which is why he opened his own shop. He married and had a family, and expenses were ever increasing and he could not keep up. He could not go back home because, as he explained: "I can't go back empty handed. It would be as if I had failed. We come to make a fortune" he said, "and end up leaving it here. This is the way we fulfill the American Dream: we get into debt."[27]

Debt is, in fact, part of the American Dream. Unlike Tomás, María did not go into debt. At least, she did not acquire formal debt. She borrowed a bit here and there from friends and relatives, but did not have a "proper" credit history, lacking, as she did, formal documentation. She did not have a bank account. Yet her financial activity was nowhere near static. She made ends meet with earnings from her job, from the rides she gave people to the work site, and from the extras she earned when she was mayordoma. But, like many other Mexicans, she was a good consumer, which contributed to keeping the economy moving, which in turn, is key to the American way of life.

Car ownership played an important role in making the American Dream real, as did the possibility of purchasing a wide range of products, from electronics to clothes, beverage, food, and particularly meat. María slept on a mattress on the floor, but she perceived that as provisional. The "real dream" would soon come, as it had for some of her friends, whose offspring had acquired good education and could now speak English. Migrants indulged in a small luxury now and then, and this contributed to a positive mindset for evaluating their experience. Negative experiences, such as lack of opportunity despite their skills, discrimination and exclusion, interrupted education, neglected health, or even the death of young Mexican soldiers in Iraq, tended to be overlooked.

At the same time, it was almost necessary for María to downplay her experiences in Mexico in order to assess the American experience in positive terms. Her social parties provided evidence of success in her migration enterprise because achievement of the American Dream was to be judged in the eyes of others as much as her own.

Framing, Valuing, and Calculating in Getting Ahead

María's initial motivation to migrate to the United States was to buy a new truck. She was frustrated with her difficulties in getting ahead as she would have liked to in Mexico. To begin with, information regarding what life was like "up North" and how easy it was to make money encouraged her. But the American Dream was reformulated along the way.

Like other migrants, María's hopes and expectations in her migration enterprise were delimited within social and cultural frames wherein not all promises are conceivable and only certain practices are deemed acceptable. What is to be considered adequate, risky, or tolerable is gauged within social scenarios wherein particular discourses and norms prevail. Here, hierarchies are acknowledged, portraying sequences of priorities: what is most important and is to be taken into consideration in a calculation and what is "coincidental noise" and is to be excluded. Unquestioned conventions—including, for example, the mechanisms by which a certain enterprise is considered attainable—are often borrowed from, and yet influence, other arenas of social life. In the process, scope for calculation is formatted. Calculation, then, is not only a rational exercise. It is made possible within particular boundaries and frames. María's calculations were limited to the information she had access to, the values she trusted, and the norms she had to adhere to. Once in the United States, these included gender roles, and other rules and regulations held within her networks in Mexico in addition to those enforced in the United States.

Her experiences in the agricultural fields, where, she felt women were treated in many ways as equals, but, as undocumented immigrants, were exploited and discriminated, influenced her views of her host society, yet she held strongly to the norms she considered were part of the civilized world she now inhabited. Her having crossed the border through the desert was classified differently. It was not so much that she was breaking the rules, since she had come in search of honest work, was paying taxes, and was in many ways behaving better than legal citizens.

Such roles, norms, and calculations are framed and reframed within certain domains of interaction. Hence the relevance of coming to grips with the processes by which they are assigned and operated. New scenarios were opened for María and her close networks, who constantly (although mostly inadvertently) reevaluated roles, norms, and values in their interactions within the United States and in their visits to Mexico. Processes of framing were thus quite dynamic. Yet, they were no less relevant in structuring their everyday lives.

In this context, getting ahead is not only a matter of money. As I hope to have shown in the case of María, there is much more to the American Dream than increasing wages. To begin with, what a decent income amounts to is gauged within these framing processes, which have to do with social and cultural aspirations, capacity and desire to consume, and class and gender considerations. But prestige, status, and self-satisfaction also play important roles, as does the sense of justice, equality, and belonging. Such everyday experiences reshape the frames within which María and her close kin revisit their past, visualize their opportunities, gauge their risks, and place their hopes. Their representation of what the American Dream amounts to colors their self-assessments of their present circumstances. It also keeps them going and motivates them to get ahead.

Notes

1. This refers to the production of top quality fruits and vegetables.
2. Although in general terms the rate of the immigrant flow had not increased, many stayed on, partly due to the fact that prime products now required specialized labor all year round.
3. María. Interviews. 22 and 24 February 2007, Lamont, CA. Taken from my notes.
4. Fieldwork comprised informal dialogues recorded in field notes, participant observation in work situations, detailed notes on social parties, taped semi-formal interviews, taped life histories, and taped collective discussions with relatives and friends on key issues.
5. My translation.
6. By then, it was clear that people were having trouble paying their mortgages (signaling what was to become a huge financial crisis). Help was distributed to both documented and undocumented workers and their families.
7. Tape-recorded interview with María, May 20, 2007. My translation.

8. Direct quotes from my notes. February 22, 2007, Lamont, CA.
9. A child's "presentation" to society is a ritual celebration, common in southeastern Mexico, that generally takes place on the child's second birthday.
10. Tape-recorded interview, April 15, 2007. My translation.
11. María. My notes. May 14, 2007. Lamont, CA.
12. María. My notes. May 20, 2007. Lamont, CA.
13. Lupe. Informal conversation. My notes. May 20, 2007, Lamont, CA.
14. For example, Hector, April 10, 2007, Lamont, CA; Angel, May 12, 2007, Delano; María 20 May, taped interview, Lamont.
15. María. Dialogue with the author. May 10, 2007, Lamont, CA. My notes.
16. Ibid.
17. María. Dialogue with the author. February 22, 2007. Fields near Lamont, CA. My notes.
18. Ibid.
19. María. Taped interview. May 19, 2007, Lamont, CA.
20. Farmers we interviewed explained that they paid unemployment and workers' compensation taxes. "Workers' comp" (as they called it) was like an insurance that they took on in case someone got hurt on the job or had some kind of accident. Laborers paid disability, but farmers had to pay 31 percent of the premium: 10 percent for worker's comp, 7.5 percent for social security, and 5 percent for unemployment. This, of course, only applied to wages paid by check. Thus, although illegal, it was convenient for farmers and contractors to pay cash instead.
21. María. Taped interview. May 19, 2007, Lamont, CA.
22. Oaxaca, a Mexican state with a large indigenous population, is used here as a derogatory label, equivalent to "Indian."
23. Direct quote from María. April 15, 2007. Taken from notes.
24. María. Taped interview. June 2, 2007, agricultural fields near Lamont, CA.
25. Ibid.
26. Ibid.
27. Tomás. Dialogue. May 19, 2007, Delano, CA. Direct quote taken from my notes.

Works Cited

Aceves Lozano, Jorge E., ed. *Historia Oral: Ensayos y Aportes de Investigación*. México, D.F.: CIESAS, 2012. Print.

Angel. Informal interview. May 12, 2007, Lamont, CA.

Dalia. Taped Personal interview by Magdalena Villarreal. Agricultural fields near Lamont. April 15, 2007.

Flores, William V. "Citizens vs. Citizenry: Undocumented Immigrants and Latino Cultural Citizenship." *Latino Cultural Citizenship: Claiming Identity, Space and Rights*. Eds. W. V. Flores and Rina Benmayor. Boston, MA: Beacon Press, 1997. 225–277. Print.

Flores, William V. and Rina Benmayor. "Constructing Cultural Citizenship." *Latino Cultural Citizenship. Claiming Identity, Space and Rights*. Eds. W. V. Flores and Rina Benmayor. Boston, MA: Beacon Press, 1997. 1–23. Print.

Hector. Informal interview. April 10, 2007, Lamont, CA.

Long, Norman. *Development Sociology. Actor Perspectives*. London: Routledge, 2001.

Lupe. Informal conversation. May 20, 2007. Lamont, CA.

María. Personal interviews by Magdalena Villarreal. February 22 and 24, April 15, May 10, May 14, 19 May, and 20 May, June 2, 2007. Lamont, CA; and June 2, 2007, agricultural fields near Lamont, CA.

Rosaldo, Renato. "Cultural Citizenship, Inequality and Multiculturalism." *Latino Cultural Citizenship. Claiming Identity, Space and Rights*. Eds. W. V. Flores and Rina Benmayor. Boston, MA: Beacon Press, 1997. 27–38. Print.

Tomás. Informal dialogue. May 19, 2007. Delano, CA.

Villarreal, Magdalena. *Wielding and Yielding: Power, Subordination and Gender Identity in the Context of a Mexican Development Project*. The Netherlands: Wageningen University Press, 1994. Print.

———. "Deudas, Drogas, Fiado y Prestado en las Tiendas de Abarrotes Rurales." *Desacatos* 3 (Spring 2000): 69–87.

———. "Sacando Cuentas: Prácticas Financieras y Marcos de Calculabilidad en el México Rural. Crítica en Desarrollo." *Revista Crítica en Desarrollo* 2 (2nd semester 2008): 131–149.

Villarreal, Magdalena, Isabelle Guerin, and Soléne Morvant-Roux, eds. *Microfinance, Debt and Overindebtedness: Juggling with Money*. London, Routledge, 2013.

Villarreal, Magdalena and Lourdes Angulo, eds. *Las Microfinanzas en los Intersticios del Desarrollo: Cálculos, Normatividades y Malabarismos*. Guadalajara: CIESAS, FOJAL y UPN, 2012.

CHAPTER 7

Migration, Sex Work, and Stigma: An Analysis in Biographical Code

Ángeles Arjona Garrido, Juan Carlos Checa Olmos, Estefanía Acién González, and Francisco Majuelos Martínez

Introduction

That wouldn't change anything, not for me...Because the S [for sex worker] is still marked on my forehead...the S of stigma. (María, Dominican Republic)

My family doesn't know about my work. How can I say such a thing? It isn't a profession anyone can know about...I was ashamed and a little afraid, I'd never done this thing before in my life...I don't want them to find out. This is a shameful thing for me and for them. (Elena, Romania)

In Spain, researchers estimate that 80 percent of women who practice prostitution are immigrants[1] and that a significant number of them are in the country illegally, having turned to sex work as a means of subsistence

(Solana 2007: 40–43). Moreover, sex work is not regulated in Spain,[2] which means that sex workers are not guaranteed access to basic social services.[3] Consequently, in addition to their vulnerability, the women suffer from a constant stigma[4] that limits and thwarts their personal ambitions and freedom of choice. Nonetheless, sex workers adopt a variety of strategies to get ahead in life. This combination of the social limitations they face and the strategies they use is precisely what makes an analysis of their discourses important.

This research project came about as a result of the Pro Human Rights Association of Andalusia (APDHA)[5] program, launched in 2002 and still active today, to help sex workers gain access to the public health care system and other social services. In the course of providing this assistance and collecting data, the topic of stigma came up repeatedly; the majority of the sex workers, regardless of their place of origin, expressed a sense of stigmatization, and we therefore decided to make stigma the focus of this chapter.

The aim of this work was twofold. First, to study the stigma attendant upon practicing prostitution and how sex workers in the province of Almería overcome it using a variety of strategies to legitimize their activity. The data collection process was, as we will explain, particularly difficult. From the outset, stigma made it hard to approach the women and earn their trust. In light of this difficulty, we decided to use a combination of qualitative methods,[6] such as participant observation, informal conversation, and recorded life stories. Thus, our second goal was to offer an effective methodological approach for understanding social discourses about stigma among sex workers.

To this end, we will begin by describing the study's methodological aspects, go on to present the results obtained from informal conversations and recorded interviews, and end with a discussion of those results and our conceptual and methodological conclusions.

The Challenges of Studying a Stigmatized Population

The goal of our research posed a methodological challenge in the choice of research techniques. Initially, we planned to use the life story method to collect information. However, the unique characteristics of our subject population and the stigma they suffer led us to combine the life story with two other qualitative techniques: participant observation and informal conversation.[7]

This mixed method of research strategies helped ensure that subjects felt comfortable with us, as we tried not to create an artificial researcher-subject situation. This allowed us to collect data in the course of everyday activities. Handing out condoms, making appointments for interviews, or escorting women to public health care facilities, therefore, became the perfect pretexts for practicing participant observation and systematizing data through informal conversations.[8]

We decided to adopt this strategy after several failed attempts to approach the women, in which we tried to conduct conventional, standardized surveys and interviews. We soon discovered that asking questions with professional detachment, positioning ourselves as researchers and the women as interviewees, created an unproductive environment, and the data we obtained was biased by distrust and the absence of a personal relationship. Therefore, we began to simply listen, observe, and converse with them.[9] In other words, we let our choice of method be guided by the depth and nature of our relationship with each woman. In the case of women who had recently arrived in Spain, we were only able to engage in an occasional informal conversation, but, as we pursued the relationship, we were eventually able to obtain a full life story.

For example, when we opted for the informal conversation technique, especially with the African women, we entered our notes in the field journal immediately after speaking to them, trying to recall and reconstruct the conversation word for word.[10] In certain cases, we also took down the subject's words during the conversation. In prearranged interviews, the researchers recorded the conversations and later transcribed them literally. Therefore, the information presented to readers is either reconstructed or direct, depending on the informant and method used in each case.

None of the sex workers reviewed their narratives, primarily due to the difficulty of contacting informants and the limited time we had to collect data during each encounter. In fact, our goal in conducting these interviews and conversations was not merely to obtain life stories but to get the subjects' perspective on different aspects of their daily lives and their work.

The fieldwork was conducted in the province of Almería, Spain,[11] primarily in the capital and the Poniente region. We made contact with the women at their places of work by handing out sanitary supplies (condoms) and escorting them to different public services (health centers and government facilities). This gave us a chance to talk with them in their everyday environments, at different times of day, and over an extended period of time.

We would like to make several observations regarding the material presented here. First of all, the data were collected in Spanish, which posed a challenge in our interactions with some of the sex workers from Africa who did not have a good grasp of the language. In such cases, when reconstructing the women's narratives we decided to adapt them to the semantic structures and rules of Spanish, preserving their meaning and context as far as possible. Second, the statements we obtained are not overly lengthy, as in many cases the information was gleaned from conversations on topics other than their profession, and also because the informants found it difficult to talk about the consequences of sex work.

This chapter focuses on the 23 informants[12] whose statements contained the most explicit references to stigma. It should also be noted that the names of the women quoted here are fictitious because all of them, except one, asked to remain anonymous.

Stigmatized Identity: The Manifestation of Stigma

> *Researcher*: If this work was regulated, you'd only have to work so many hours, you'd have Social Security, you'd be entitled to unemployment subsidies…
> *María*: Yes, but I'd still be "the prostitute."
> *Researcher*: Do you think that's the problem? Not so much the working conditions but the job itself, the stigma?
> *María*: Yes, of course. It's like you're branded.… Sometimes you go out, like, to go shopping, and they ask you, "How much do you charge?" That pisses me off, because at that moment I'm not working. Hardly anybody is on the job when they're shopping, not me and not other women.

Not all of the women who gave us their stories evaluate their profession negatively. However, they all share a negative experience of the stigma attached to it. Thus, María, with whom we spoke about the hypothetical legalization of sex work, explicitly expressed her perception of social rejection and how it is present in her life. In contrast, Blessing, from Nigeria, has very negative feelings about her work.

> This work is not [in] my blood, you know? I am not a bar girl. I do it because I have to, but I don't like it at all, it's not pleasant.

Stigma is associated with a feeling of guilt that often coexists with the desire for legitimacy (Garaizábal 36–43), something the women expressed in a number of ways. In informal conversations with Nigerian women, we frequently heard the expression "it's not [in] my blood." which Blessing summed up perfectly in reference to a strong identity conflict. María, Kate, and Nadia all expressed a sense of shame and guilt.

> When first I got into this world I just cried and cried, because I was made for just one man. (Maria, Dominican Republic)
>
> My boyfriend calls me up every day. "Leave it," he says. And I feel bad, because I can't leave it. I have to work. I have to pay rent, clothes, get money for my family... My body belongs to God, to one man, my husband. God does not want this for me or for any woman. But my boyfriend doesn't work, you know? He can't give me the money. I feel bad, but it's a living.... (Kate, Nigeria)
>
> Yes, I feel guilty, especially when we go to church. That's why I don't go very often, I'm so ashamed to go, I feel bad going in there. I know that I'm sinning, prostitution is a sin. God never said to prostitute yourself, to sell your body for money. (Nadia, Romania)

These feelings often surface in the women's stories as they recall how they wept and the fear they felt when starting out. Entering and working in the sex industry clearly takes a high toll on these women's private lives (family and friends) and social status, and the feeling of guilt is therefore most often accompanied by a sense of shame.

We also observed a tendency, motivated by shame, to deny their profession during visits to primary health care centers, despite the importance of informing doctors that they are dealing in sex work in order to ensure a proper diagnosis. Below is a brief conversation between Mariam, a Nigerian woman, and her doctor:

> *Doctor:* Do you work?
> *Mariam:* No.
> *Researcher:* You can trust her, tell her what you do.
> *Mariam:* Nothing will happen?
> *Researcher:* No.
> *Mariam:* In Nigeria you can't say so... I'm ashamed.
> *Mariam:* [leaving the health center] If I didn't feel ashamed, I would be freer.

Another illustrative case is that of Patience, a Nigerian sex worker who we persuaded to participate in a round table discussion about prostitution. As the date of the event approached, she changed her mind several times, becoming increasingly worried about the potential consequences for her and her coworkers and fellow Nigerians if she spoke openly about her profession:

> I don't want any cameras around when I'm talking, OK? It's not good for me and not good for my people. If there are cameras, I won't talk. People want to see the black whores.[13]

In the following excerpt, Olga, a Latin American woman, uses the concept of sin to identify the guilt and wrongdoing associated with sex work:

> I think I'm doing something wrong. Because you know that prostitution is a sin, and God doesn't allow it.

Here we see that guilt and shame are linked to racial stereotypes and a sense of failing to obey religious mandates. There is a contradiction between the real life the women lead and what is assumed to be socially acceptable behavior. Such is the case of, from Nigeria, and Imam, from Morocco:

> *Researcher*: Do you have a boyfriend?
> *Sofia*: Yes. That's my boyfriend over there [points to an African boy watching TV].
> *Researcher*: How long have you been going out?
> *Sofia*: He's not my fiancé. I'll marry a white man when I stop working like this.
> *Researcher*: Do you want to marry a Spaniard?
> *Sofia*: Yes, not an African. But I can't while I'm working in the bar. Get married and have children...I can't.
> *Imam*: I never thought my life would end up like this [as a sex worker]. There's no guilt, no shame or anything...I just feel like a failure in my life, looking for something better, or just normal, like everybody else.

Nevertheless, the sense of shame is also related to an inability to live up to what is expected of them as women in their home societies, particularly finding a husband and starting a family, or simply finding work in any other "respectable" profession. As Gift, a Nigerian woman, remarked:

> This is not good work for girls...for younger girls. Then they can't find a good husband. Girls can meet somebody, but Nigerian boys only look for money with bar girls. Your life can't be good, normal life. That's why I don't want Nigerian boys. But if you have a husband, nothing happens, you and your husband decide about life, and no one knows. People respect the girl.

Gift, the narrator, says that the stigma of prostitution only applies to young unmarried women. She suggests that sex workers who are already married can choose to remain in that line of work, find another job, or become full-time homemakers as long as their husbands have work.

In summary, the strong stigma attached to sex work results in the deployment of strategies to conceal or counteract its effects. "We must recall that stigmatization is what identifies these women and makes their job harder. It poses the most significant problem for prostitution and is the critical element in its definition" (Díaz Freire 90).

Therefore, women in this line of work often try to develop a coherent identity for themselves through a process of self-legitimation, explaining and justifying the circumstances that led them to earn a living as sex workers in spite of social rejection.

Controlling Personal Information

> At the club, I don't like them to know where I live. I don't give out my phone number.... (Inma, Brazil)
>
> At the bar my name is Sandra [alias], but at home, [with] my family, I don't want you to call me Sandra. If my family knew that I worked in a bar they wouldn't be able to stand it, they wouldn't. (Blessing, Nigeria)

The strategies the women use to combat stigma (or escape from it) entail controlling information about their identity and personal history, whether by directly *concealing* that information or by avoiding certain traits or habits they recognize as stigmatizing in environments unrelated to their sex work. For this reason, the first thing they do is conceal personal information. The use of a fake name or alias is a very common resource, as in Miriam's case:

> When I'm not working it's impossible to tell me apart from any other woman. I dress normally. But when I'm working and looking for clients, I dress the part so there is no doubt.

In this effort to control information, a strategy we might call *compartmentalization* is par for the course among sex workers. According to Juliano, this strategy:

> enables them to separate certain spheres of daily life from the sphere of activity regarded as shameful.... The compartmentalization strategy is widely used, especially when the place of work and the family home are at a great distance from each other, as is true for most immigrants (72).

Thus, as in Nadia's case, working in places far from home and dressing differently at work and at home are ways of separating spheres and leading a *double life*, where social actors in one space are not recognized in the other:

> It happened that one day at the Palm Beach [the club where she worked], a man came in...I said, "Hi, how's it going," and the man asked me, "Where do you live?" I told him, "Here in Almería," and he replied, "Don't you live in El Zapillo?" [a neighborhood in Almería] and I was horrified...and I told him, "Surely you understand that I have to get by somehow, I have to pay the rent on my apartment, I've got my family, I don't want you to out me." And he said, "Take it easy...don't worry, on the street I don't know you."

As we see, some women, like Nadia, pretend not to recognize people with whom they interact at their workplace outside the context of their sex work activities. Essentially, the sex worker's ability to control information about herself and her profession defines how she wants to be perceived by the rest of society; she may decide to be open as a sex worker in every social sphere and at all times, or only in certain contexts or only when she is working.

Overcoming Stigma: Common Strategies

Human beings are capable of making enormous sacrifices to earn social approval, and sex workers are no exception. As Nadia's statement reveals, they develop attenuating mechanisms that alleviate the burden of stigma:

Nadia: Sometimes people get confused and call me a whore.
Researcher: What's the difference?
Nadia: Yes, of course, there's a difference, how could there not be? [laughter] Don't you know? A whore is a woman who has a husband and cheats on him because she likes it, because she wants to. That's a whore. And a prostitute provides services in exchange for money. People say, "Where are you going?" "Whoring." I think they're wrong, they're going to prostitutes because they pay them.

First, we find strategies that attempt to change the sex worker's position in the hierarchy of values. In particular, we are talking about shifting the stigmatic burden of *whore* onto other sexual behaviors that have nothing to do with sex work. This explains why some women, like Olga, from Ecuador, believe that those who work in the sex industry, even though they have their immigration papers in order, "do it because they want to."

Olga: Honestly, if I had my papers I wouldn't spend one more day at a club, because I'm not cut out for this. When they give me my residence permit I'm quitting…I don't want to keep hooking any more.…The girls who have papers and work there, I don't know why they do it. At my club there are only two who don't have papers, the three Colombians have all their papers, it's the Romanian girls who don't have papers.
Researcher: And they want to continue?
Olga: Because they like it, because with papers they could find work doing something else. With another job and a salary of 800 euros a month, a person could get along just fine. Unless they have a man who's exploiting them. Having a husband, with both of them working they'd bring in 800 euros, I'd live well, you know? Because my husband would pay the rent and I'd buy the food and send money to my daughters.

In conversations with Nigerian women, we also detected this tendency to shift the stigma onto other women who continue sex work even though they have other options. The Nigerians find this incomprehensible. In their testimonies, the very source of their own suffering—being a hooker—resurfaces as a judgment of the behavior of other women who, in their opinion, no longer have an excuse for prostituting themselves. By putting themselves in a position of moral "superiority," as Mary does, they pass on the burden of stigma, associating other women's behavior with negative qualities or attitudes. Mary says:

> That girl doesn't pay her boss. She's not thinking about her future! If she doesn't change, she won't have a future. If I were in another line of work, I would go to the houses and talk to the girls about leaving that work.

A second set of strategies our informants commonly use to boost self-esteem and overcome the stigmatizing burden of sex work is *self-legitimation*, that is, presenting various socially accepted reasons that justify their involvement in the sex industry. The first reason is family. Juliano says,

> Some sex workers self-legitimate their activity in affective terms. They do it for their partner, out of love for a boyfriend they need to support, or, in maternal-affective terms, out of love for their children or the family they left behind, to support them or keep them from privation. (70)

As in Sofia's case, children are often presented as the strongest justification in the women's biographical narratives:

> I do it because at one time I had to do it. For example, they called to tell me that my son was sick. They've done nine blood and urine tests, and if I don't have the money, this is the way I can get it fast. I do it so my son wants for nothing and doesn't die for lack of anything. But not because I'm happy about it. I've never been happy about [that kind of work].

Another type of self-legitimation strategy we observed in the women's biographical narratives is presenting their situation as illegal immigrants in the host country as a justification for working in the sex industry, as they cannot find any other work without the proper permits. As Sonia from Nigeria puts it, "to have a normal life is to have papers." Desire, another Nigerian, expresses this in an idealized way:

> When I get my papers, I'll be happy, everything in my life will change. I'll look for a good job, a shop, a legal business, a good man and I'll study Spanish, good house, normal life! I'll never be scared again.

Even in informal conversations with Nigerian women, we often found that sex work was viewed as a phase they had to go through in order to attain a normal, legalized life. When they get their papers in order, they are that much closer to this goal.

A recurring element in the women's explanations of why they engage in this activity is the difficulty of finding a job, linked to the lack of immigration papers. Many of them, like Sofía from Venezuela, see obtaining a work and residence permit as the golden ticket that will allow them to come out of hiding, give up sex work, and find a job in something that carries less stigma. In other words, it is the key to acquiring a personal identity without the obstacles posed by the stigma of sex work:

> Having papers means showing your face, showing your face and not hiding, not being afraid. When you're illegal, your heart is always racing. I'm always looking over my shoulder in case I have to hide, because the police might catch me, because they'll send me back to my country and I haven't done what I want to do yet... to find a good job and live well.

In relation to other aspects of the migration project, we also came across justifications for sex work based on the need for survival: the need to get papers, repay debts, pay rent, and send money home to relatives are just some of these reasons. However, a variety of other motives complicate this construction. Tessy from Nigeria puts it this way: "I don't want to be rich, I just want a normal life, like the Spaniards." Sex work is part of the effort required to achieve a certain quality of life in Europe. This entails rejecting other jobs open to them in Almería, such as domestic service or, work in the greenhouses:

> My friend [a fellow sex worker] told me, "Hey, you're stupid. Let's go to the club and you'll get a good job there. That's where you'll earn more. You're not living. They're just exploiting you there [at the time I was working in domestic service]. Look how hard you work every day and you don't have anything." And she says, "Look how well I'm doing. I have my house with what I'm doing," and I decided to go to the club. (Olga)

> I can't work in a greenhouse, I'm not strong enough. Once I tried to work on a farm, but the boss was scared. The police can go there and ask to see papers. Working at a bar, you can make money without those kinds of problems. I tried warehouses, too, but it's impossible if you don't have a work permit. (Blessing)

The set of strategies we identified in the women's statements helps in valuing or empowering their perception of their profession in a way that boosts self-esteem. Miriam from Brazil says, "A lot of clients who come ask me out and just want to talk to me." The empowering strategy emphasizes the skills acquired in this line of work. Thus, the women tend to include in their narratives situations in which these skills, as in other professions, are used to benefit their clients, as a way of dignifying or elevating the social prestige of their work and overcoming stigma.

In particular, as Eufemia, a Brazilian woman, explains, they value their ability to listen to their clients' problems or satisfy their sexual desires:

> Many [clients] just need affection and for you to listen to them: they tell you about their lives, their stuff, their fantasies, everything. We're psychologists. They talk about whatever they want and know we won't say anything, we don't pry into their personal lives. I see clients around here on the street and we don't even say hello or goodbye, without that discretion it just wouldn't work.

In short, we observed that sex workers use different strategies to legitimize their work and overcome stigma depending on their personal situations and experiences. Consequently, nearly all of them agree that sex work has been a fundamental tool for achieving success, especially financial success, in the migration process. Nevertheless, in some cases, this success seems to be tied to the use of a rote discourse for overcoming stigma rather than to an actual successful experience.

The Success Story

> When I left for Turkey my mother became depressed, her spirits just plummeted; I think the whole illness she had got worse as a result of that. [On my return] when they saw me, what were they going to say? When I left I had long hair down to here... [pointing to her waist], when I came back my hair was short, a French hairstyle in vogue at the time; totally different from how I'd left. I arrived at the door of my house in a taxi, because I'd brought a huge suitcase full of clothes for everybody. (Nadia)

The success story, told in conjunction with the reasons that justified the decision to go into sex work, usually closes an expressive cycle in the women's narratives that enables them to overcome the stigma of their work and boost their self-esteem. Thus, for example, despite their dissatisfaction, the immigrants' financial success acquires overarching importance, as evidenced by the emphasis they place on this aspect of their lives when telling their stories. This success gives them a heightened sense of empowerment. The success story, as in the cases of María and Miriam, helps mitigate their initial shame and gives them a sense of accomplishment—something that is of vital importance to these stigmatized women, members of one of our society's most vulnerable groups. Miriam and María both described this feeling:

> Oh, that money! When I started out, I bought a house, where my father lives today. I worked hard to pull my family through, to help my family. (María, Dominican Republic)
>
> I don't feel ashamed because I accomplished a lot. My life, too, because I was all alone in Spain, which is a very hard country to survive in. I feel stronger, I feel like much more of a woman for going to any [foreign] country. (Miriam, Brazil)

Conclusion

In this study, we have attempted to remedy, to an extent, the empirical gap in biographical studies in Spain on the stigma of sex workers in order to give the primary actors a voice and shed light on a veiled reality. To this end, we conducted fieldwork over a two-year period, giving us time to build bonds of trust and be accepted by the sex workers. In general, sex work requires them to maintain a degree of separation between their professional lives (clients, club owners, etc.) and their private lives or inner circle (family, friends, social acquaintances outside work, etc.). In the course of our field work during those two years, we discovered that we were not able to pursue our research and obtain information that allowed us to comprehend the complex nature of their reality until we had crossed over from the outside world into their circle of trust (Acién 92–95; Acién and Majuelos 3–15).

The biographical narrative or life story, which allowed the women to express their perceptions, justifications, and resources for dealing with social stigma in their own words, was a useful method for studying this type of issue. This approach, in conjunction with other ethnographic methods such as informal conversation and participant observation, allowed us to triangulate the data to ensure veracity and reliability.

The stories of these women revealed that working in the sex industry entails stigmatization. As a constitutive element of this profession, it is not surprising that the women explicitly mentioned stigma in their testimonies. However, all women who work in the sex industry do not experience stigma the same way or with the same intensity; "on the contrary, shame, pride, fear of rejection, and self-affirmation often coexist" (Garaizábal 37).

Some sex workers, therefore, react to stigma by concealing or covering up the truth about their work, developing information control strategies such as disguising or hiding what they do from family members and neighbors. They also tend to omit certain details about their personal life, for example, by using an alias when interacting with clients or other social actors in the workplace. Other women use the compartmentalization strategy, which often involves making a distinction between work attire and normal clothes, or placing a physical distance between their place of work and place of residence.

Many of them also stated that stigma manifests itself in the form of guilt or shame for failing to live up to the expectations imposed by the dominant social ideology or conform to the moral and religious patterns in which they were socialized: "The social stigmatization of prostitution is part of what is silenced, repressed, and excluded from the official discourse" (Juliano 2007: 32).

In addition to managing stigma and concealing its visible effects, they also attempt to overcome it and boost their self-esteem by deploying various strategies. One such strategy is to redefine the concept of prostitution, justifying it as a way of making a living as respectable as any other profession and shifting the burden of stigma onto those who choose to be unfaithful or promiscuous for no financial gain. Another strategy used to overcome stigma is self-legitimation, arguing that sex work is necessary given the lack of other employment opportunities (due to their situation as illegal immigrants, for example) or jobs that pay enough to support their family or maintain their lifestyle, even arguing that sex work empowers them by equipping them with special skills, knowledge, and information.

In any case, these are elements the women use to build an identity that allows them to cope with social stigma, elements which become visible when they narrate their life stories and dare to share their experiences, feelings, frustrations, and longings.

Notes

1. In just a few short decades, Spain has gone from being a country of emigrants to a host country (however, the outward flow is now surpassing immigration

once again due to the recent financial crisis). In the mid 1990s, there were 542,314 foreign-born individuals residing in Spain; one decade later, the foreign-born population had risen to 1,370,657. According to data from January 2014, it is now at 5,000,258. Spain has therefore experienced the largest increase in foreign population in the entire European Union.
2. Under Spanish criminal law, only the exploitation of sex workers by third parties and human trafficking are considered felonies. However, offering sexual services in the public thoroughfare is a finable offense under the majority of municipal regulations governing the use of public space.
3. This chapter uses the term "sex industry" to refer to all activities related to the supply and demand of sexual services for profit. It also uses the term "sex work" to refer to the voluntary provision of sexual services in exchange for financial compensation. See, for example, Medeiros 17; Agustín 649; Solana 33; and Maqueda 75.
4. The concept of stigma was introduced in 1963 by Erving Goffman in his book *Stigma*. Goffman understands stigma as a thoroughly discrediting attribute that leads the bearer to become a person outside of the normal social stream, and at the same time establishes the limits of what can be considered "normal." He identifies three types of stigma: physical abnormalities, defects in a person's character, and belonging to or associating with a certain group. The stigma attached to prostitution falls in the third group. Even Goffman recognized prostitution as an important stigma that the individual must hide, and which is manifested in associated perceptions and feelings, which he calls the "discrediting attribute" (3). Sex industry researchers commonly recognize stigma as a constitutive element of prostitution (Acién 59–74; Juliano 55–58; Garaizábal 36–43).
5. See http://www.apdha.org.
6. The study of migrations by social scientists in Spain is more recent than the phenomenon itself. At first, in the mid-1990s, their primary focus was on "measuring" immigrants—how many came, where they came from, where they settled, their occupations, etc.—to forecast and plan for the future. Many studies used macro surveys and official statistics to collect data on immigrants. However, research and funding institutions soon began to adopt a more multidimensional perspective that required interdisciplinary approaches and mixed methods. By the year 2000, researchers were using a variety of qualitative techniques, including observation, focus groups, life stories, and informal conversations. The focus has therefore shifted to understanding migrations in "immigrant code," and emic information is no longer a supplement to numerical data but an end in itself.
7. Little research has been done at the international level, and the most common research technique for studying sex workers at the national level is the biographical method. See, for example, Negre 375–398; Jaget 10–130; Corso 39–232; Kimball 13–376; Ruth 5–136; Neira 23–141. In fact, we can find studies of different aspects of sex work that used mixed methods to construct

both biographical and ethnographic narratives. See, for example, Medeiros 29–52; Solana and Riopedre 4–44.
8. The analytical categories used in this research were not individually packaged topics but an interdependent set of experiences and events in the subjects' lives, which we outline below for a better understanding of the data compiled: First, the subjects' migration projects: reasons for emigrating, preparations for the trip, use and type of networks for entering Spain, etc. Second, their first experiences in Almería, Spain: the extent to which reality met their expectations of the migration experience, how they got into sex work, how they perceive the stigma of prostitution, etc. Third, their experiences in the area: satisfaction with their situation (housing, work, etc.), degree of involvement in networks, perception of the host society (natives, institutions, culture, etc.). And fourthly, their expectations for the future and its limitations.
9. In reality, the so-called biographical or oral history methods are not limited to a single methodological approach. Bertaux says that a life story emerges every time a subject tells another person, researcher or not, about a given episode in his or her life experience (35). He effectively warns us that this is not merely a juxtaposition of orally narrated events but a narrative sequence that is contextualized and articulated by its meanings. Oral statements alone do not provide these meanings; they must be put in context and compared with other sources. To do this, we use "data" gleaned from other narratives, whether they pertain to the same subject or other people, other documentary sources, or our own observations. Thus, biographies take shape as a result of the researcher's fieldwork.
10. In these cases, where the "voice" expressed in the narrative was reconstructed by the researcher, we considered two factors: first, how well the researcher managed to gain the subjects' trust, thereby facilitating intersubjectivity; and second, the context; in other words, during reconstruction we bore in mind the conditions and circumstances in which the interaction took place while these narratives were being shared.
11. Almería has traditionally been a province of emigrants, sending large waves of people into developed Europe and other regions of Spain. However, 146,656 foreigners live in Almería today.
12. We made contact with more than 300 sex workers. Of the total, we interviewed 24 women, obtained short biographical narratives from 29, held informal conversations with 250, and made observations in over 40 clubs (as brothels are called in Spain) and on the street.
13. As Van Dijk (23–75), Gutiérrez (823–831), and others have proven, news reports and features on immigration and prostitution fuel the stigma and self-victimization attached to this profession, portraying sex workers as objects of male domination through the violent male sexuality exhibited by their clients. For example, the daily newspaper *El País* printed the uncorroborated statistic that 95% of sex workers in Spain were forced into prostitution, entrapped by deceptive or violent means, in an editorial titled "Plaga de la prostitución" [The Plague of Prostitution] (*El País*, 13 February 2006).

Works Cited

Acién, Estefanía. "Migrantes y Trabajo Sexual. Estereotipos e Intervención Social." *Los Retos de la Prostitución. Estigmatización, Derechos y Respeto.* Ed. J. L. Solana and E. Acién. Granada: Comares, 2008. 59–74.

———. "Ethnography and Human Rights: The Experience of APDHA with Nigerian Sex Workers in Andalusia." *Citizenship, Migrant Activism, and the Politics of Movement.* Ed. P. Nyers and K. Rygiel. New York: Routledge, 2012. 92–118.

Acién, Estefanía and Francisco Majuelos. *De la Exclusión al Estigma.* Almería: APDHA, 2003. Print.

Agustín, Laura. "Mujeres Migrantes Ocupadas en Servicios Sexuales." *Mujer, Inmigración y Trabajo.* Ed. Colectivo IOÉ. Madrid: IMSERSO, 2001. 647–716. Print.

Bertaux, Daniel. *Los Relatos de Vida. Perspectiva Etnosociológica.* Barcelona: Bellaterra, 2005. Print.

Blessing (Nigeria). Informal conversation. November 5, 2005.

Corso, Carla. *Retrato de Intensos Colores.* Madrid: Talasa, 2000. Print.

Desire (Nigeria). Informal conversation. April 5, 2010.

Díaz Freire, José Javier. "Cuerpos en Conflicto: La Construcción de la Identidad y la Diferencias en el País Vasco a Finales del Siglo XIX." *El Desafío de la Diferencia: Representaciones Culturales e Identidades de Género, Raza y Clase.* Ed. Mary Nash and Diana Marre. Bilbao: Universidad del País Vasco, 2003. 61–94. Print.

Elena (Romania). Personal interview. Recorded February 12, 2012.

Eufemia (Brazil). Personal interview. Recorded November 26, 2013.

Garaizábal, Cristina. "O Estigma da Prostitución." *Andaina,* 38 (2004): 36–43. Print.

Gift (Nigeria). Informal conversation. August 18, 2007.

Goffman, Erving. *Stigma: Notes on the Management of Spoiled Identity.* New York: Simon & Schuster, 1986. Print.

Gutiérrez, Andrea. "La Actualidad del Abordaje de la Prostitución Femenina en la Prensa Diaria Española." *Estudios Sobre el Mensaje Periodístico.* 19 Num. especial. (abril 2013): 823–831. Print.

Imam (Morocco). Personal interview. Recorded December 23, 2012.

Inma (Brazil). Personal interview. Recorded April 14, 2004.

Jaget, Claude. *Una Vida de Puta.* Madrid: Júcar, 1977. Print.

Juliano, Dolores. *La Prostitución. El Espejo Oscuro.* Barcelona: Icaria, 2002. Print.

Kate (Nigeria). Informal conversation. May 14, 2008.

Kimball, Nell. *Memorias de una Madame Americana* [English title: *Nell Kimball: Her Life as an American Madam*]. Madrid: Sexto Piso, 2007. Print.

María (Dominican Republic). Personal interview. Recorded June 16, 2010.

Mariam (Nigeria). Informal conversation. July 22, 2009.

Mary (Nigeria). Informal conversation, May 11, 2011.

Miriam (Brazil). Personal interview. Recorded April 13, 2005.

Maqueda, María Luisa. *Prostitución, Feminismos y Derecho Penal.* Granada: Comares, 2009. Print.

Medeiros, Regina de Paula. *Hablan las Putas*. Barcelona: Virus, 2002. Print.
Nadia (Romania). Personal interviews. Recorded May 20, 2005, and December 26, 2010.
Neira, Montserrat. *Una Mala Mujer*. Barcelona: Plataforma, 2012. Print.
Negre, Pere. "De los Relatos de Vida al Estudio de Casos Sobre la Prostitución," *Revista Internacional de Sociología* 44.3 (1986): 375–400. Print.
Olga (Ecuador). Personal interview. Recorded October 27, 2006.
Patience (Nigeria). Informal conversation. September 26, 2005.
Ruth, Mary. *Ruth Mary, Prostituta: Memorial de los Infiernos*. Barcelona: Lector Universal, 2007. Print.
Sofia (Nigeria). Informal conversation. February 8, 2010.
Sofia (Venezuela). Personal interview. Recorded February 16, 2006.
Solana, José Luis. *Prostitución, Tráfico e Inmigración de Mujeres*. Granada: Comares, 2003. Print.
———. "Movimientos Migratorios, Trabajadoras Inmigrantes y Empleo en la Prostitución." *Documentación Social* 144 (2007): 39–57. Print.
Solana, José Luis and Estefanía Acién E. *Los Retos de la Prostitución. Estigmatización, Derechos y Respeto*. Granada: Comares, 2008. Print.
——— and José Riopedre. *Trabajando en la Prostitución. Doce Relatos de Vida*. Granada: Comares, 2012. Print.
Sonia (Nigeria). Informal Conversation. May 15, 2008.
Tessy (Nigeria). Informal Conversation. June 4, 2009.
Van Dijk, Teun. *Racismo y Análisis Crítico de los Medios* [English title: *Racism and the Press*]. Barcelona: Paidós, 1997. Print.

PART III

Memory and Public Representations

CHAPTER 8

Oral Accounts and Visual Inscriptions: Narratives under Heavily Tattooed Skin

Vitor Sérgio Ferreira

Introduction

Heavily tattooed bodies are commonly found among young people today. As João, a 24-year-old Lisbon tattooist said to me recently, "Everything, absolutely everything, has changed. From month to month and from year to year, I notice that there are more and more supporters of tattoos." One of his customers, Luis, a 23-year-old shelf stacker, went further, saying that "Society is being forced to open its doors to our scenes... And this will grow. I think it's going to reach the point of exaggeration. Even if it's not the majority, lots of people will keep getting piercings and tattoos."

Indeed, in Portugal, tattoo studios were practically nonexistent two decades ago. If in the beginning of the 1990s there were only two tattoo studios for the Lisbon clientele, today there are hundreds throughout the country. From the '90s onward, tattoo studios spread throughout the urban landscape, creating an increasingly vast and professional offering, promoted by a growing and socially diversified demand (Fortuna 69; Ferreira 2013: 55–56).

This phenomenon takes place alongside other growing body image activities. These "new hedonistic economies" are founded on the capitalistic exploitation of style and corporal experience, on the consumption of goods and services to produce and maintain one's appearance, and for bodily pleasure (Ball 281). In fact, tattooing is no longer part of a parallel or informal economy as it was in the past (Atkinson 23–50; Peixoto 22–24), but rather, part of a highly competitive industry of body design. Tattooing has been globalized and commodified clear across the western world (Bengtsson 263–265; Kosut, "An ironic..." 1035–1043). Some sociologists (Mendes de Almeida, Sweetman, Turner) enthusiastically argue that tattoos are now beautification resources and have become fashionable. At the same time, they claim, tattoos have become depleted of their traditional, subcultural, and/or native meanings, and transformed into nothing more than sign-commodities of contemporary consumerism—hyper-cool accessories that conform to current fashion trends, or ironic, playful clichés borrowed from geographically and historically distant cultures.

Although tattoos have become trendier, this is only true for relatively small body inscriptions. There are more extreme ways of tattooing oneself that go beyond the mundane and acceptable butterfly on the ankle, and that are far from being socially accepted, even among the younger generations. Such is the case of the heavily tattooed body, still socially perceived as bizarre, excessive, hyperbolic, still under suspicion.(Ferreira, 2015).

As Maria, a 32-year-old college graduate and respected high school teacher, explained, even today her family is troubled: "My mother, my parents, and perhaps my uncles and aunts and others, associate tattoos and piercing with... 'They're all druggies!' and 'They are all robbing shops!' That kind of thing." Susana, a 27-year-old designer whose body has been heavily tattooed since she was 15, has a long history of suffering discrimination:

> People talk a lot about racism in relation to the races, but I'm also a victim of that! Because no matter where I go... people are always distrustful.... And that happens all the time, in supermarkets and all that, it's common. I'm always being monitored!

The social history of these practices as deviant and pathological feeds the distrust and fear often manifested toward heavily tattooed and pierced bodies (Atkinson 53–57, Caplan 1–16). Today, a heavily tattooed young person is still at risk of being stigmatized (Goffman 2009), increasing the likelihood that he/she will suffer recrimination, incrimination, and discrimination. As some research points out, to have large portions of skin inked still evokes ideas of "madness," "perversion," "deviance," and "marginality," an abuse of the body, an unnecessary excess that subjects its practitioners to social suspicion (Favazza 4–20, Ferreira 2003: 336–340; Kosut "Mad Artists..." 80–83).

Heavily tattooing one's body, or planning to do so, is only carried out by an ultra-minority of young people. Yet, it is still considered to be an extreme and unusual decision, reviving old stereotypes of deviance and moral panic. Considering this nonfriendly social context, my initial research questions were: Why do some young people still heavily tattoo their bodies? And what does doing so mean to them? In the beginning of my fieldwork, I soon realized that these bodies had a biographical richness that needed to be uncovered.

In 2003, I conducted research in Lisbon, interviewing 15 heavily tattooed men and women in their 20s and 30s, including employees, professionals, and university students. As I detail below, my approach involved a combination of methodological strategies, including informal conversations, observation in social settings, and recorded biographical interviews.

Listening to oral accounts about their skin, it became very clear to me that narrators' bodies go beyond the mere corporal expression of a trendy and irreverent behavior traditionally attributed to youth. Instead, these body modifications were presented as result of a longstanding practice, since adolescence, of recording important identities and life courses on the skin. The surface of heavily tattooed skin acquires symbolic depth, transforming into a visual map of autobiographical memory.

My research, then, was designed to understand the identity and biographical dimensions attached to the process of body modification through tattooing. In the process, a central hypothesis started to gain theoretical ground. That is, the engagement of young people in this kind of permanent body modification project expresses an embodied struggle to conquer and maintain a desired identity, in the face of a present that they perceive as uncertain and fluid. Under such conditions, some young people permanently ink large portions of their bodies, searching for social recognition as being different, authentic, and autonomous individuals, trying to hold onto and express to the world core identities forged during key turning points in their lives.

A Comprehensive Methodological Strategy

Given that tattoos are visual inscriptions on the body, I started out thinking that the best approach to the analysis would be through visual methods.

However, I soon realized that using video or still photography would not be the best approach to document the meanings invested in this practice. Media attention to practices of extensively inking the body has led to the revival of old moral stereotypes and social panic regarding the tattooed. Public media exoticizes and sensationalizes these kinds of body modification practices (Pitts). Consequently, journalists became not so very welcome within the tattoo scene. I felt it was risky to use cameras for documentation, as this could create misunderstandings about my role in the field. I also realized that the symbolic content of tattoos would not be well captured through visual methods, as its codes have become increasingly individualized and no longer hold collective meanings, as in traditional societies (Turner 40–43). As I will demonstrate, the visual inscriptions tattooed on the skin are deeply connected to biographic accounts that go far beyond the graphic properties of each tattoo.

Analytically, I situate the heavily tattooed skin as an embodied reflexive project of nondiscursive storytelling. Tattoos are visual devices of auto-biographical expression, devices that construct a graphic narrative inscribed on a biological foundation, the skin, and used to recount and communicate a biography of selfhood. Consequently, the voice of the tattoo owners had to be heard in order to breach the silence of the skin. Through intensive and in-depth oral interviews and conversations, I acquired entry into the deeper symbolic meanings of those graphic narratives.

I conducted my fieldwork in Lisbon. I started visiting two tattoo studios. I was able to observe the social and physical process of becoming tattooed, and talk informally with many young customers and body modification professionals. Based on these informal conversations, I selected 15 young people for individual, in-depth, comprehensive interviews.[1] Rather than seeking a large sampling of cases, I wanted to gather longer and denser narratives from each individual, as a comprehensive perspective supposes (Harper). I purposely sought a diverse sampling of interviewees in order to see if the symbolic contents of the discourses on heavily tattooed body projects would be different. My first criteria were age and degree of body marking. I sought interviewees between 20 and 30 years of age, who were already tattooed over one-third of their body, and planning to ink as yet unmarked virgin skin. I also sought to diversify my "sample" in terms of gender, education, and social background. My final sample consisted of nine men and six women, out of whom six had or were completing college degrees, three were high school graduates, and the remaining six only had elementary education. In terms of social class background, they were divided evenly across the class spectrum (five upper class, five middle class, five working class). As it turned out, I did not find the diversity that I had expected. What I found instead was a very homogeneous and convergent narrative on the meanings of heavily tattooed bodies in the discourses of young people across different social backgrounds educational trajectories, and genders.

The interviews were informal and conversational, partly shaped by a preexisting interview guide, but also by issues that emerged during each interview. As with oral history open-ended interviews, my role was to both conduct and follow the discursive chain of the narrator, letting each one control her/his narrative. My position as interviewer demanded constant attention to the flow of conversation, close listening followed by active questioning, while being open and respectful toward the interviewee's narrative chain. In this kind of approach, a good question is not the one planned ahead of time, but that one found in time, occasioned by the narrator's previous response. My interview guide became fluid and cumulative, building on each interview I conducted.

The interviews were all audio-recorded and transcribed verbatim. After transcribing, I subjected the material to a qualitative content analysis (Maroy 117), which involved a meticulous, continuous, and careful reading, coding, and synthesizing of all the material. The first goal of my comprehensive qualitative approach was to produce theoretical propositions in close, continuous, and creative articulation with the data collected, a bottom-up process of hypothesis formulation.

The Heavily Tattooed Body as a Reflexive Project

"[Tattooing] is that kind of thing that it's really an addiction. To me, all this [skin] that I see empty, it's to fill in with scars," said João, the tattooist, referring to his unmarked skin. Susana, a 27-year-old designer, reported: "After the first one, it starts to be an addiction, of wanting more and more!" The interviewees frequently used the term "addiction" to characterize their pattern of consumption. However, the meaning of addiction here does not involve a physical or psychological dependence, or compulsion that generates an unmanageable anxiety (Winchel and Stanley). It signifies a patterned habit, where compulsivity is replaced by *reflexivity*, the capacity of social agents to reflect on the options and possibilities they face, to justify their choices and decisions, and to calculate their potential reactions and effects in diverse life domains.

The anxiety involved in the preparation of another tattoo is lived and enjoyed as a positive, conscious act of reflection, creativity and freedom, and not as a loss of self-control. The narrators I interviewed used the term addiction as a metaphor for a practice that they know will continue into the future, routinely, ritualistically, as long as there is a square inch of skin available. Because they are aware that their "virgin" skin is not endless, the subjects know that their future tattoos must involve careful planning and cautious reflection as to the choices and decisions they will make.

Chris Shilling, following Anthony Giddens's work (1991), has pointed out that in contemporary Western societies, there is "a tendency for the body to be seen as an entity which is in the process of becoming," subject to a "project" to be reflexively developed by the individuals, who have become responsible for the design of their own bodies (5). While the notion of "body project" is very useful to conceptualize the heavily tattooed body—as the term is used and recognized by their bearers—not all tattooed bodies can be treated as expressions of body projects. In Susana's words:

> There are those people that get a tattoo just because...And then I think that there are other kinds of people that like it, that think that it has something to do with them...They don't do one, they do tattoos, they do piercings, as a project. As a project they want for their body, they want to transform their body into something else, into a living work of art.

Miguel, a 25-year-old university student, explained the process of transition from a bodily experience to a body project of tattooing as follows:

> Each tattoo starts by being an important experience. Then, it turns into using the body as a canvas. That comes from the taste acquired from the art of tattooing.... It starts with specific things, like that small drawing that they liked. And then, after realizing that tattooing is something that gives them pleasure, they then decide to go for the true works of art.

However, most of the time, tattooing the body emerges among young people as an aesthetic and/or sensorial experience that only sometimes turns into a body project, that is, into a reflexive body design plan resulting from a succession of past and foreseeable future acts of tattooing or piercing the body.

The term addiction indicates the transition from an experimental pattern to a projectual pattern of tattooing oneself. That means that to plan a heavily tattooed body goes far beyond the mimetic, trendy, fashionable, consumerist, and impulsive act of getting a simple tattoo, as Miguel asserts:

> There are several options in terms of making a tattoo: a person who is going to get a tattoo...and makes a tattoo only at a certain point of the body. Or if a person goes to get a tattoo and considers getting another one later, I think it's better to immediately start thinking about a body part. It's better to have more or less of an idea of a project, for example, for a middle arm...Because the job will be more perfect, and aesthetically more beautiful, than having one here and another here, and after another one there [Miguel points to different parts of his own body].... Currently, I'm planning, for example, to fill parts of my arm with drawings with a certain meaning, that have a certain continuity, the drawings, right? It's better than doing everything scattered.... [My body is] a potential work of art. It's not yet. It will become...And I'm going to be my biggest critic and my biggest fan!

Luis, the shelf-stacker, also narrated the growth of his aesthetic reflexivity when he decided to keep tattooing his body:

> Now, like I said earlier, I'm arranging meanings, I'm doing things, but with a certain logic.... I think it has to do with aesthetics. I don't like to see one, two or three tattoos, like Kalkitos. It gives the impression that someone's been doing stuff without any connection. "I feel like getting a tattoo, and I just get it!" No!

Pointing to one of his tattoos, he says:

> Here a little one was born, but there will be an aesthetic framework to link here. Therefore, here everything [all the designs] will have something to do with each other. Although they have different meanings, and they are different tattoos, they will fit all together.... I like a bit of symmetry in tattoos. That's why when I did this arm I felt a bit unbalanced when I had just the left one tattooed. It's not the same type of design, it's not the same as the other side, but it's tattooed more or less the same size.... They both end up in the same area having the same width, there is a certain symmetry. I think it looks beautiful in the meanings we give them, if there's a certain symmetry.... [My body] is still not a work of art, but I'm heading that way.... Yeah, it'll have a beauty that will allow me to call it a work of art.

As these narratives clearly show, the aesthetic considerations and investment young people make in successive acts of marking the heavily tattooed body become much more sophisticated and detailed. When tattooing the body turns into a body project, the aesthetic reflexivity over what to choose intensifies, involving, for instance, the integration of designs or the size of tattoos, and aesthetic values such as coherence and symmetry. At the same time, an increasing demand for originality and quality in the embodied iconographies is strongly felt, empowering an authorial vision of the body as a work of art.

Constructing Selfhood through Tattooing

The process of reflexive densification implicit in the plan of being fully inked does not concern only the aesthetic dimension of tattooing. It also involves identity. For Tiago, a 20-year-old university student, choosing to tattoo his body

> may have been, perhaps, a... desire to be different, not to be like everyone else, and to try to have a personal thing... This was perhaps a kind of escape, perhaps it was a way of showing that there is more than one direction, just because someone dresses like that doesn't mean everybody has to.... For me, young people's lives were a cliché, that you had to grow up and be a certain way, right? I wanted to be what I wanted, not what I had to be, right?... It may also have been a way of finding myself. And perhaps I didn't identify with what other people were, at that initial stage of personality formation. It was a gradual process, it didn't happen overnight.

In Tiago's case, the process of tattoo expansion on the skin becomes a central axis in (re)constructing his social and personal identity. Tiago performs what McDonald (202) has called a struggle for subjectivity: a corporeal expression of young wearers to maintain coherently and permanently their sense of self through their transitions to adulthood, as well as to claim autonomy and sovereignty in actions and decisions about their own lives. That is the meaning beneath what Miguel calls his "personal conquests":

> [My first tattoo] It's mine! I made it. I chose it. I decided that I wanted to do.... The tattoos are mine! I can't exercise ownership over someone. But I can exercise ownership over my body. It's my body!... In spite of how we're conditioned, that is, by work, by the society in which we

live... what we do with our bodies affects only us... Nobody can tell me what to do or what not to do with my body! It's mine, above all! It's not from my mother, it's not from my father, who are responsible for me being alive. They can't control what I do or don't do with it. Just me, no one else, can tell me what I can do with my body! That's what people have to realize.... The body is an enclosure. A wrapper that represents us the whole time we've been here. And that we can use as we want!... The body is our last frontier. About our body only we know, only we decide... [My tattoos] are my personal conquests. Yes, they serve as a statement... They are mine! Mine!... I insist on this aspect of being my personal conquests. Some people do tattoos for the sake of personal affirmation. And there's no better way to feel good with ourselves than being the only ones legislating about what we are.

The process of extensively and everlastingly inking the skin becomes a metaphor for conquering a space of *subjectivity*, where young people feel they can be who they want to be and do whatever they want to do. During their adolescence, these young people start to appropriate and invest in the body as a personal display through which they can become socially recognized as an individual and emancipated person. The flesh becomes an identity canvas that creatively presents and represents a new personal identity. The heavily inked body claims "difference" and becomes a vehicle to publicly share a great feeling of personal distinctiveness and uniqueness. It is understood as a creative act of "authenticity," a strong commitment to construct a desired identity and as an act of "rebellion" that demonstrates a commitment to not follow usual and expected pathways.

João, the tattooist, stresses very clearly that he fully tattooed his body because that is: "The image that I want to have, it is the image that I created to present myself as a person. That's how I identify myself!... And that's how I want to be!" Martins, a 23-year-old unemployed young adult with an elementary education, is very enthusiastic about his tattoos as a permanent embodied device that allows him to construct and to express his "personality" as consistent, unified, and indivisible throughout time and space. He says: "Look, all this [the tattoos]. It's like being attached to my own personality! And for life!... [Today] I feel more fulfilled with my own personality and with what I've always wanted to be."

Thus, a heavily tattooed body project corresponds to a process of social construction, presentation, and representation of *oneself* as *another*, using the words of Ricoeur (1992). A selfhood that is in a process of becoming along with its embodiment, revealing the aspirations of some young people to shift into another *self*, someone they *want* to be—a selfhood that is not what they feel has been socially prescribed. This self resists the direction of sameness, choosing a pathway to otherness, expressed by a willingness to build an unconventional, singular, and extreme body.

Through the voluntary and permanent process of tattooing the skin, these young people are making public a stable, coherent, and lifelong commitment to a body and identity project, a project that intentionally escapes what they perceive as set pathways, normative social roles, and body appearances. Due to its irreversible nature, tattooing embodies a commitment that will not be threatened by the demands of what they see as an increasingly erratic, diffuse, and fragmented world, producing adaptable, permeable, and even corrupted subjectivities. These are young people who, in considering the challenges they will face throughout the course of their lives, do not want to change their self-identities, namely their embodied expression.

The Heavily Tattooed Body as a Visual Auto-Bio-Graphic Narrative

> When I did them [the tattoos] I wanted to highlight something that had happened in my life and that had influenced my life.... There are many people who, due to the death of a family member, or the birth of a son, or whatever, decide to mark their body to always remember what they went through, in the good and bad moments. A person... wants to keep that moment forever, and a tattoo is a good way of not letting things fade away.

Miguel's words show how his heavily tattooed skin displays, connects, and keeps alive in memory a system of key moments and significant experiences, tastes, values, affiliations, and/or figures that strongly define his self-identity. These topics inspire young people to visually celebrate and perpetuate their biographies through tattoos, helping them sustain a sense of temporal unity and continuity of their identities within what they perceive as a highly fragmented and labyrinthine society. Even if the subjective importance of those experiences is lost in the future—and the interviewees are conscious of this fact—their biographic value is permanently maintained on the skin, over time and space, as a map of a life course and its dilemmas.

Therefore, the heavily tattooed body is developed as embodied and nondiscursive storytelling, as a visual device of *auto-bio-graphical* expression: each tattoo intends to reflect through a drawing (graphic) on the skin (bio) a certain relevant self-identifying fact, context or emotion in the life story of its bearer (auto). In its auto-bio-graphical evocation, the tattooed body is mobilized as a canvas onto which selfhood and the threat of change are aesthetically projected and iconographically narrated.

The permanence that characterizes the tattoos lends solidity and significance to the transitional narratives that they express. Ritualistically embodied and biographically oriented, the tattoos, one after another, sustain a subjective feeling that any successive transformations of the self are made within the parameters of a chosen and coherent identity. As a result, the heavily tattooed body manifests a sense of long-lasting being, graphically transposed to an everlasting modified body. This means that a body that undergoes constant transformation keeps reproducing its sameness, as Tiago, a 20-year-old university student, articulates:

> [Each tattoo] was a drawing that I liked and that symbolized the connection to my ideals, connecting me to the earth, to those things that I love, above all.... Connecting to the earth is, perhaps, you not forgetting what you were yesterday.... And I don't want to, because now I'm feeling so good about myself, so I don't want to become a filthy pig like many people out there. People when they grow up become really hypocritical, with each other.... I'm really stuck in time, in terms of tastes. I haven't changed since I was sixteen. Nor do I want to change. I want to be like this forever.... [For me] The tattoos are an affirmation. Although we change constantly, there are some things in us that are not ephemeral; they're always there. It's not something you can change, no matter how much we age, no matter how much psychological torture and brainwashing we endure.... If I have to quit twenty jobs because of a tattoo, I will easily give them up because tattoos are something that I always wanted to have. And I can't live the present always thinking about the future, right? If that's really what I want! This one [points out his first tattoo], when I did it, it was not for the present, it was to have that present forever.

In a constant dialectic play between permanence and change, each act of modification through the inking of a new tattoo is a gesture of confirmation and celebration of the coherence and continuity of the self in its biographical singularity and authenticity. Hence, the fleshy canvas illustrates the map of routes taken, by option or accident, with its specific biographical *turning points* (Hareven and Masaoka 272), as Luis's narrative reveals:

> Each tattoo of mine has a story, from how it was done to why it was done.... There is always a sequence, a logic, along with very personal things.
>
> [Commitment] This one means a lot to me because it was on the same day that my girlfriend also did one...
>
> [Sister's death] This tattoo, for example, has my whole life until sixteen, more or less. This skull has a meaning for me. Whoever hears this thinks that this is a bizarre meaning. This skull for me is my sister that died.
>
> [Problems with drugs] I, when I was younger, I also had a problem with drugs and decided to symbolize it as a Cannabis, in tribal form, which is what is up here, without color, without the green of Cannabis, but with the leaves of Cannabis.
>
> [Accident] For example, this really small one... is an eye. The eyes, for me, in my way of thinking, have life, the eyes say what the person is.... I was a prisoner of death for one month and three days.... I won't say it was a miracle, but it merited a meaning, it deserves a mark.
>
> [Secret] This one is very personal! [the interviewee hits his arm vigorously].

Luis narrates moments of the creative destruction of his self-identity, represented by disruptive situations that give rise to moments of existential and/or relational crisis, potentially leading to transformations in his subjectivity. Each tattoo made in connection with a certain turning point speaks not to the celebration of a new collective status, as in earlier traditional societies, but the celebration of an individual overcoming the impasses of contemporary life. In this vein, each tattoo does not express an ancestral *rite of passage* anymore, but a contemporary *rite of impasse* (Ferreira 2011: 143–145). Each tattoo celebrates the capacity of resistance and survival of a personal identity in the face of critical events, integrating and recentering them within the structure of the individual's biographical narrative and subjectivity.

In the past, the perception of a tattooed body was informed by restrictive codes, collectively shared (Turner). Today, the meanings linked to tattoos are no longer related to social roles or standard life course status. Their codes are private, sometimes even secret. As Miguel explains:

> At that time, those so-called tribal tattoos had a meaning; they used to mark different steps in the development of the man towards adulthood,

within that society, within the tribe. Many of them were attributed to people according to their position, according to what the person was within the actual tribe. The hunters would have a right to a certain tattoo, the fishermen would have a right to some, and leaders would have a right to others. And now, what happens?...The tattoos that I have, when I did them, I wanted to mark anything that had happened and that had marked my life....There are many people who...For example, with regard to the death of a family member, or the birth of a son, whatever it was, decide to make a mark on the body to remember always what they've been through, through good and bad times....You want to keep that moment forever, and a tattoo is a good way of not letting things go.

Currently, dissociated from its original cultural systems, the heavily tattooed body creates a *personal mnemonic system* that leads back to biographical narratives and fuels individual mythologies. The cyclical recurrence of the tattooing ritual generates a subjective sense of identity order. It produces an individual sense of directionality and of orientation in the flow of biographical events. The ritualistic way in which the identity project is developed allows young people to build up an iconographic narrative that organizes the puzzle of their transitions into a significant and sequential order, according to a reflexive codification and an individual narrative of the self.

Conclusion

The analysis of these oral accounts highlights a convergent narrative about the meanings my narrators invest in their body projects, even though they come from very different social backgrounds, trajectories, and circumstances. What they have in common is being part of youth scenes for a long time, scenes in which tattoos occupy a central role as visual elements of bodily display. During adolescence, all the interviewees began living and constructing their identities within "alternative" or "underground" music scenes (such as rockabilly, heavy metal, black metal, punk, skinhead, gothic, hard core, straight edge, or techno), where the taste for a spectacular bodily appearance is shared (Ferreira 2009).

The socialization effects of these youth scenes, in relation to other traditional socialization contexts for young people (such as school, family, or work), are powerful. Those scenes prove to be remarkably influential, revealing the strong homogenizing effect of discourses, expectations, and values among young people from quite different social backgrounds. So the initial questions remain: Why do some young people heavily tattoo their bodies? And what does doing so mean to them? Considering their narratives, my interviewees' heavily tattooed bodies function as a visual device to express a chosen and distinctive self-identity capable of resisting a more tenuous and less certain world. Within the context of increasingly fast social changes, the heavily tattooed skin is reflexively projected as an autobiographic narrative that organizes the chaotic course of young peoples' lives in individually significant and ordered sequences. It is an ichnographically embodied device that, due to its permanence on the skin, gives its users a subjective feeling of preserving a solid and durable selfhood.

The heavily tattooed skin embodies a mnemonic system that expresses a personal identity struggling for the power, not only to recount and communicate itself to others as a biography, but also to choose and define itself in its authenticity, individuality, and stability. That is, a mnemonic system that gives a coherent and solid sense of a place in the world to one who is constantly on the move, a sense of resisting the impulse to "let go," or "go with the flow," which would mean to surrender to the structures and confinements of the expected, conventional pathways toward adulthood.

Therefore, under the heavily tattooed skin, the silence of visual inscriptions emerges as a synchronization device between the personal biographical flow and the actual historical flow. What appears subjectively invested in the expressive form of a *singularized body*, ends up reifying, objectively, a *socialized body*, revealing visual information about how body, self-identity, and social structures are interconnected, and giving resonance to a more broad cultural and social dynamics.

Indeed, the project of having a heavily tattooed body involves a struggle not only for the production of a certain kind of subjectivity, but also to maintain it when confronted with the contemporary social constraints, dilemmas, and imperatives. According to Giddens (181–208), the conventional moorings of self-identity have eroded, and traditional pathways to adulthood have become increasingly less stable sites to anchor the young people's sense of self. Less shaped by tradition, increasingly larger parts of the individual's identity and life are shaped by the variety of contexts in which young people are involved.

Ehrenberg (13–22) argues that the key to exploring contemporary social transformation lies in the emergence of the "uncertain individual," which involves an undermining and destabilization of the modern concept of a self-contained and unitary identity. The stability and coherence of the identities constructed under these social conditions are subjected to erasure, making it ever more difficult to consolidate a consistent sense of self. Thus the subjectivities among younger generations are lived as more fragmented, multiple, and elusive, not guaranteed by traditional pathways or references anymore.

In the process of figuring out who they are, or, constructing who they want to be, the successive tattooing of the body as a visual autobiography displays a struggle of young people against the potential erasure of their early chosen identity. Through inking the body permanently, their most valued symbol of the self, they strive to irrevocably embody their subjectivity as a coherent and authentic expression of a consistent unity between the self and the body. Through ritualizing the construction of the body project, they try to preserve their subjectivity as stable and durable under social conditions that portend a changing and fragmented social experience.

Therefore, beneath the visual representation of heavily tattooed skin lies not only strong feelings of personal distinctiveness, but also an auto-biographical attempt to order and unify a self-identity. The heavily tattooed body becomes a visual and silent memory device that some young people mobilize in the face of what they perceive to be a world of menacing structural conditions that promote social uncertainty, fragmentation, and discontinuity.

Note

1. The comprehensive interview (Ferreira, 2014) is a qualitative data collection technique that articulates traditional forms of semidirected interviewing with interviewing techniques of a more ethnographic nature. It was proposed by Kaufmann (1996) as an attempt to avoid the methodological formalism and the strong directivity of the open questionnaire model, very standardized in order to produce, supposedly, impersonal data. This method also attempted to overcome the laissez-faire of the nondirected interview—frequently responsible for what Back called "intrusive empiricism"(18), that is, being responsible for a cumulative, excessive, and empiricist torrent of details and curiosities, without any analytical discernment.

Works Cited

Atkinson, Michael M. *Tattooed: The Sociogenesis of a Body Art*. Toronto: University of Toronto Press, 2003. Print.

Back, Les. *The Art of Listening*. Oxford, UK: Berg, 2007. Print.

Ball, Steven J., Meg Maguire, and Sheila Macrae. "Space, Work and the New Urban Economies." *Journal of Youth Studies*, 3.3 (2000): 279–300. Print.

Bengtsson, Anders, Jacob Ostberg, and Dannie Kjeldgaard. "Prisoners in Paradise: Subcultural Resistance to the Marketization of Tattooing." *Consumption, Markets and Culture* 8.3 (September 2005): 261–274. Web.
Caplan, Jane, ed. *Written on the Body. The Tattoo in European and American History*. Princeton, NJ: Princeton University Press, 2000. Print.
Ehrenberg, Alain. *L'Individu Incertain* [The Uncertain Individual]. Paris: Calmann-Levy, 1995. Print.
Favazza, Armando R. *Bodies Under Siege: Self-Mutilation and Body Modification in Culture and Psychiatry*. Baltimore, MD: Johns Hopkins University Press, 1996. Print.
Ferreira, Vitor. S. "Atitudes dos Jovens Portugueses perante o Corpo" [Attitudes of Portuguese Young People towards the Body]. *Condutas de Risco, Práticas Culturais e Atitudes perante o Corpo*. Ed. Jose Machado Pais and Manuel Vilaverde Cabral. Lisbon: Celta, 2003. 265–366. Print.
———. "Youth Scenes, Body Marks and Bio-Sociabilities." *Young—Nordic Journal of Youth Research*, 17.3 (2009): 285–306. Web.
———. "Tatuar o Corpo Joven Hoje: Rito de Passagem ou Rito de Impasse? [Tattooing the Young Body Today: Rite of Passage or Rite of Impasse?]. *Revista Vivência* 36 (2011): 137–156. Print.
———. "Das Belas Artes à Arte de Tatuar: Dinâmicas Recentes no Mundo Português da Tatuagem" [From Fine Arts to the Art of Tattooing: Recent Dynamics in the Portuguese World of Tattoos]. *Criatividade & Profissionalização. Jovens, Subjectividades e Horizontes Profissionais*. Ed. Maria Isabel Mendes de Almeida and José Machado Pais. Lisbon: Ciências Sociais, 2013. 55–99. Print.
———. "Arts and Tricks of Comprehensive Interview. *Saúde & Sociedade* 23.3 (2014): 118–130. Web.
———. "The Tattooed Young Body: A Body Still under Suspicion? *Youth, Spaces and Times: Agoras in the Global City*. Ed. C. Feixa, C. Leccardi, and P. Nilan. Leiden: Brill, [forthcoming].
Fortuna, Carlos. *Novo Comércio, Novos Consumos* [*New Commerce, New Consumers*]. Lisbon: GEPE, Observatório do Comércio, 2002. Print.
Giddens, Anthony. *Modernity and Self-Identity. Self and Society in the Late Modern Age*. Cambridge, UK: Polity, 1991. Print.
Goffman, Erving. *Stigma: Notes on the Management of Spoiled Identity*. New York: Simon & Schuster, 2009. Print.
Hareven, Tamara. K. and Kanji Masaoka. "Turning Points and Transitions: Perceptions of the Life Course. *Journal of Family History*, 13.1 (1998): 271–289. Web.
Harper, D. "Small N's and Community Case Studies." *What Is a Case? Exploring the Foundations of Social Inquiry*. Ed. C. C. Ragin and H. S. Becker. Cambridge: Cambridge University Press, 1992. 139–158. Print.
João. Personal interview. March 30 and April 3, 2003.
Kaufmann, Jean-Claude. *L'Entretien Comprehensif* [The Comprehensive Interview]. Paris: Nathan, 1996. Print.

Kosut, Mary. "An Ironic Fad: The Commodification and Consumption of Tattoos." *Journal of Popular Culture,* 39.6 (2006): 1035–1948. Web.

———. "Mad Artists and Tattooed Perverts: Deviant Discourse and the Social Construction of Cultural Categories." *Deviant Behavior* 27.1 (2006): 73–95. Web.

Luis. Personal interview. June 27 and July 11, 2003.

Maria. Personal interview. July 13, 2003.

Maroy, C. "A Análise Qualitativa de Entrevistas" [Qualitative Analysis of Interviews]. *Práticas e Métodos de Investigação em Ciências Sociais.* Ed. L. Albarello, F. Digneffe, et al., Lisbon: Gradiva, 1997. 117–155. (Original work published 1995.) Print.

Martins. Personal interview. April 21, 2003.

McDonald, Kevin. *Struggles for Subjectivity. Identity, Action and Youth Experience.* Cambridge: Cambridge University Press, 1999. Print.

Mendes de Almeida, M. I. "Nada Além da Epiderme: A Performance Romântica da Tatuagem" [Nothing But the Epidermis: The Performance of the Romantic Tattoo]. *Psicologia Clínica,* 12.2 (2000): 100–147. Print.

Miguel. Personal interview. June 3 and 9, 2003.

Peixoto da Rocha, Antonio. "A Tatuagem em Portugal" [The Tattoo in Portugal]. *Etnografia Portuguesa.* Lisbon: Dom Quixote, 1990. 15–43. Print.

Pitts, Victoria. "Body Modification, Self-Mutilation and Agency in Media Accounts of a Subculture." *Body & Society* 5.2–3 (1999): 291–303. Web.

Ricoeur, Paul. *Oneself as Another.* Chicago: University of Chicago Press, 1992. Print.

Shilling, Chris. *The Body and Social Theory.* London: Sage, 1993. Print.

Susana. Personal interview. April 24 and 29, 2003.

Sweetman, Paul. "Anchoring the (Postmodern) Self? Body Modification, Fashion and Identity." *Body & Society,* 5.2–3 (1999): 51–76. Web.

Tiago. Personal interview. June 11 and 14, 2003.

Turner, Bryan. S. "The Possibility of Primitiveness: Towards a Sociology of Body Marks in Cool Societies." *Body & Society,* 5.2–3 (1999): 39–50. Web.

Winchel, R. M., and M. Stanley. "Self-Injurious Behavior: A Review of the Behaviour and Biology of Self-Mutilation." *American Journal of Psychiatry,* 148.3 (1991): 306–317. Web.

CHAPTER 9

The Black Movement and Race Relations in Brazil: Building New Knowledge through Online Oral History Materials

Verena Alberti and Amilcar Araujo Pereira

In 2003, under the auspices of the Center for Research and Documentation of Contemporary Brazilian History (CPDOC),[1] we embarked on an oral history project to document the black movement in Brazil. This movement had long historical underpinnings and played an important role in uncovering the persistence of racial discrimination, along with the struggles to improve social conditions for black and brown people throughout the country. We conducted 39 interviews with more than 110 hours of recordings, which are archived at the CPDOC research center of the Getulio Vargas Foundation in Rio de Janeiro. This research enabled us to learn more about the importance of this social and political movement, and to confirm persistent racism as one of the elements structuring Brazil's huge social inequality—one of the largest in the world. And, as it happens in many other parts of the world, Brazil has long avoided open discussions of race and race relations.

Our research focused on what we call the "contemporary black movement," that is, on organizations and individuals who were active since the 1970s in antiracist struggles and in efforts to improve the lives of black people. This gave us an understanding of the movement's scope, its social actors, influential texts, and the different forms of activism undertaken by those who identified with it. We also became more aware of the movement's political and cultural achievements, its relationship with the political history of the country, and how it articulated with governmental agencies and the three branches of power (executive, legislative, and judicial). The material we collected also revealed moments and frameworks for decision making, information about the rural Afro-Brazilian maroon *quilombola* movement, the black women's movement, affirmative action, and the trajectory of the different groups over time and in different regions of the country. We amassed a very rich corpus of material, and it is the CPDOC oral history collection that is most frequently consulted by researchers.

With this large body of interviews, we turned to exploring the curricular uses of oral narratives in conjunction with other forms of historical documentation on race, racism, and the black movement. These materials are available on the CPDOC website.[2] These curricular materials and accompanying lesson plan activities aim to stimulate thoughtful reflection on race relations, in accordance with the Ministry of Education's National Curricular Guidelines that value diversity and aim to promote the "reeducation of ethnic and racial relations" (501). In 2003, national legislation came into effect, mandating the teaching of Afro-Brazilian history and culture in schools throughout the country. In 2008, political action by black and indigenous social movements extended this mandate to the teaching of indigenous histories and cultures. According to the 2008 law, the national curriculum must include teaching

> the history of Africa and Africans, the struggles of Blacks and indigenous peoples in Brazil, black and indigenous cultures, and the role of Brazilian blacks and native peoples in the formation of the national society, recovering their social, economic, and political contributions to Brazil's history.[3]

As the title of this chapter suggests, our aim is not only to expand knowledge on race relations by integrating oral histories into the curriculum, but to offer students and others the opportunity to build their own new knowledge about race and racism by engaging with oral histories alongside other historical sources, just as professional historians do.

Historical Underpinnings

From the mid-nineteenth century to the first decades of the twentieth century, elite groups throughout Latin America, presumably white and inspired by racial theories that considered nonwhites as inferior, asked themselves what could be done about the enormous mass of "inferior" blacks and indigenous peoples that inhabited the newly independent countries. One of the "solutions" adopted in Brazil was to "whiten" the country by encouraging European immigration. According to the scientists who supported such strategies, the arrival of masses of white immigrants would result, some hundred years later, in a white society. The failure of this plan is evident in that today, Brazil is the country with the largest population of African origin outside of the African continent.

In the first half of the twentieth century, the whitening project gave way to a new ideological enterprise—pride in mixed racial heritage. Many Brazilian and Latin American intellectuals opposed the idea that black and indigenous peoples were a problem, proposing instead the concept of *mestizaje*—racial mixing—as a national characteristic.[4] Mestizaje went beyond biological racist theories that permanently condemned Latin American societies to backwardness. In doing so, it connected miscegenation to national pride, a strategy that triumphed in many Latin American countries, including Brazil.

Race relations became a subject of academic analysis in many countries, particularly in the aftermath of World War II. In the 1950s, the United Nations Educational, Scientific and Cultural Organization (UNESCO) sponsored a series of studies by social scientists from the most prestigious academic institutions in Brazil, among others. This project, proposed to UNESCO by Brazilian social scientist Arthur Ramos, became well known in Brazil as the UNESCO Project (Maio 2000, 2001, 2011). Its origin was linked specifically to the antiracist agenda formulated by UNESCO in the late 1940s after the impact of the Holocaust. This project began as an attempt to present Brazil to a world devastated by a racial war as an example of a country of miscegenation and "harmony among the races."

However, as Oracy Nogueira (1985), one of the social scientists responsible for the project in the state of São Paulo, pointed out, "The most striking trend in the studies sponsored by UNESCO was the recognition by the authors of the existence of racial prejudice in Brazil" (77). Comparing racial relations in Brazil to that in the United States, Nogueira developed the classical distinction between racial prejudice based on racialized physical features (in Brazil, skin color, body features, hair, gestures, language), and racial prejudice based on origins, so that even light-skinned Americans descended from blacks would be the targets of prejudice.

From the mid-1950s, a group of Brazilian intellectuals led by Florestan Fernandes, claimed that color prejudice was a legacy of the past and would eventually disappear (1965). Although functional in a society that practiced slavery, they felt that racial prejudice and discrimination would be incompatible with the competitive order established by the capitalist system. Thus, racism would disappear with the development of capitalism in Brazil, even though the whites would try to hold on to their racial privilege as much as possible. Since the 1970s, however, many other social scientists have argued the permanency of racism as being a structural element of Brazil's huge social inequality (Hasenbalg 1979).

Despite all the evidence of the persistence of racism and racial inequalities, the victory of mestizaje as an expression of national identity resulted in a practice of open avoidance of the racial question. In Brazil, it was as if the issue did not exist. Racism did not exist; privilege for the light skinned did not exist; because "we are all mixed and equal." For this reason, the history of black movements in Brazil is little known, and people are often surprised by its existence. They even discredit these movements, claiming that they are founded on ideas imported from the United States.

In each period of Brazil's history there were black movements with different characteristics that have yet to be investigated and made public. According to some (Santos 285–308), the concept of black movement remits to the struggle against slavery, which in Brazil lasted close to 350 years, until the Abolition of Slavery Act in 1888. These resistance struggles included innumerable uprisings, the formation of maroon settlements, and legal actions to liberate people illegally enslaved (Reis and Gomes 1996).

Black struggles in Brazil acquired new dimension in the post-abolition period, when important organizations were formed throughout the country. The emergence of black newspapers became a significant strategy from the late nineteenth century on. In the 1930s, the Black Brazilian Front (Frente Negra Brasileira) was founded in São Paulo, becoming the largest black organization of the twentieth century, with branches in various states. It became known among the US and Puerto Rican blacks as a true example of the struggle for civil and social rights (Pereira 2013). Thus, the notion that these ideas and values were born in the United States is incorrect. It would be more accurate to think about continual and intense circulation and exchange among different black movements in the African diaspora.

Taking into account the lack of knowledge about the histories of race, racism, and black movements, we have developed educational materials that students and teachers can access through the Internet and use in their classroom assignments. By making available these rich oral histories and other forms of documentation, our hope is to stimulate among the younger generations a deeper consideration of the black experience in Brazil. In the following sections, we detail different examples of suggested curricular uses of this material, along with accompanying critical questions. The first section focuses on the histories of race and racism. We highlight two interviews and suggest pedagogical applications to engage students in complex historical inquiry, leading to the formation of their own historical interpretations. The second section focuses on the very controversial issue of affirmative action, illustrating how oral history material can be used in a debate format.

Histories of Race and Racism

For years, blacks have fought to include the study of their African origins and for recognition of the contributions of black and indigenous peoples as nation builders, rather than as "inferior" or "second-class" citizens. As we have pointed out elsewhere (Alberti 2014), this initiative is part of a much broader effort in many countries to defend the importance of more comprehensive and inclusive historical narratives in national curricula, including, among others, the histories of different ethnic, linguistic, and religious communities. Those who research this issue unanimously affirm that, contrary to the relative ease around the mid-twentieth century in producing master national narratives, today we face a much more different global scenario that requires more substantial rethinking of how we approach the past (Stuurman and Griever 1–16). The 2005 UNESCO "Convention on the Protection and Promotion of the Diversity of Cultural Expressions" reinforced this mandate, in response to the worldwide threat of extinction of different cultural expressions.[5]

There are many benefits to integrating oral sources into educational materials. Excluding the histories of certain groups from the curriculum makes it much more difficult for members of these groups to construct a positive sense of identity. The hegemonic presence of dominant group history nourishes a feeling of superiority toward underrepresented groups, both in the curriculum and in the classroom. In both cases, feelings of inferiority and superiority jeopardize the formation of democratic perspectives during formative educational years. Providing spaces to voice differences in the curriculum and in the schools aims to generate a more democratic ethic.

Take the following interview excerpt that forms part of the section "Histories on Race and Racism."[6] Amauri Mendes Pereira, a leader of the black movement in Rio de Janeiro since the 1970s, speaks about his experience with the racial question during his own years in school. He recounts:

> The one who was interested in the racial question was my maternal grandmother, Maria Trindade. She was a slave. She was born in 1872, a year after the Law of the Free Womb was passed.[7] But she only knew of the existence of this law after the Abolition Act. She always lived as a slave to a family. She had a sharp racial consciousness. She would always say: "My child, even if you are light-skinned, one day you'll know what I mean." And then it happened. In the fourth grade, my last year of primary school, the best student of each grade would form an honor guard of the flag. And the top student in the school would hold the flag. Each grade had its flag bearer and honor guard. The second placeholder would give the salute, I think. It was a way to recognize the best students. So I really tried hard the first two months, March and April, to make good grades because in May we always had the celebration of Abolition and someone read Castro Alves.[8] I wanted to honor my grandmother who had been a slave. I wanted my grandmother to come see me. I got the top grade in April, the top grade in the whole school! I thought "I'll get to be the flagbearer!" The day before the event, the school principal called me over and said something like: "Roberto is going to be the flagbearer." Roberto was another kid. We competed in the same grade, me, Roberto, Zé Romualdo, and Celeste, who was the only girl among us. We all had the best grades for years. Roberto was white. He was going to be the flagbearer because some dignitary was coming and the principal said, "You understand, don't you, my dear?" I ran out of school and climbed the hill home, desperate, saying "Grandma, it happened!" These incidents in childhood, later on they made sense. It was clear that I wasn't going to be able to be the flagbearer because Roberto was the chosen one, because of the color of his skin. So, I ran out of school and climbed the hill and told my grandmother. She sat me on her lap and began to speak: "My child, there's nothing you can do about it. That's the way it is...I'm still so proud of you." (Alberti and Pereira "Histórias..." 37–38)

Mendes Pereira's story gives a human face to racial discrimination, as seen through the eyes of a boy and the memory of the older man. It illustrates a situation that students can understand and relate to, and use to think about the contrasts between institutionalized racism, racial prejudice, and the sense of pride that his grandmother conveys to him for his accomplishment. It is no wonder that this would be an indelible memory.

Rather than merely transmitting information acquired from our interviews and analyses, our aim is to give students the opportunity to interact with different sources and to construct their own knowledge, which we are calling "new" knowledge. To accompany the interview excerpts, we also cite analytical studies and statistical data on the issue race relations in Brazil, as illustrated in figure 9.1.

By making these sources available as pedagogical material, we accomplish certain goals. First of all, we address the importance of sources by providing information on the source: who said/wrote/photographed what, and to whom, when, and why. Along with the interview excerpts, we offer students biographical information about the narrators and about the circumstances of each interview, as figure 9.1 shows, so that they may better understand the context in which the narratives were produced.

Figure 9.1 Screen shot of video interview, with accompanying transcript, interview details, narrator biographical data, and contextual background.
Source: http://cpdoc.fgv.br/questaoracial/raca-e-racismo/amauri-mendes-1.

174 / Verena Alberti and Amilcar Araujo Pereira

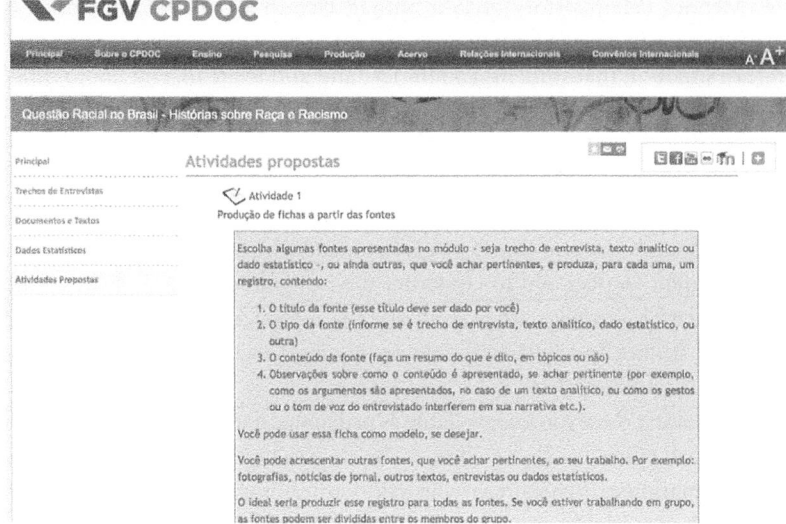

Figure 9.2 Naming and describing source files.
Source: http://cpdoc.fgv.br/questaoracial/raca-e-racismo/atividades.

The main purpose is to enable students to choose from among these sources to produce their own reflections, as proposed in "Activities" (see figure 9.2).

Once the context of the interview is explained, we pose questions about its content. The interview excerpt reproduced in figure 9.1, refers to an episode that took place in the 1950s and could lead to reflections about how the political, cultural, and ethno-racial identities were constructed in the space of that school. As a result, students might be encouraged to ask themselves: "Could a similar episode happen in a school today?" Depending on their answers, the discussion might proceed by reflecting on the existence (or absence) of racist practices in today's schools. Understanding culture as a process in which traditions and practices circulate, transform and change, forging diverse identities (Mattos 127–36), teachers might ask students, "What differences or similarities do you find between today and the 1950s?"

As with many oral history interviews, narratives from black leaders, the basis for our teaching materials, have the virtue of making the historical and social experiences concrete, offering students "stories within history," short narratives that synthesize content and meanings that are sometimes difficult to understand through other means (Alberti 2005).

Maria Raimunda Araújo's oral history offers another powerful example of the use of oral sources, in this case for understanding racial identity. Araújo has been one of the principal figures of the black movement in the state of Maranhão since the 1970s. She offered a vivid account of the prejudice she suffered on the streets of São Luís, the capital of Maranhão, toward the end of the 1960s. While vacationing in Rio de Janeiro, she found that many blacks had Afros and did not straighten their hair. The following extensive quote is rich in meaning:

Maria: It was at the end of the 1960s, the Black Rio movement was already underway: in the North Quarter everyone had these huge heads of hair, and they'd say hello when they passed by.... And that was how I came to see that I was actually part of a community. And it was really nice. Although I said to myself: "But in Maranhão..."... 'Cause I used to go to Rio and spend three months there, since as a professor I had three months of vacation. When I returned [to Maranhão], my hair was already nice and kinky. That was a shock. I became the first black woman to wear her hair natural, oh yeah....

Researchers: Everyone noticed you on the street?

Maria: Everyone noticed me, and they would hassle me. They would say: "Hey, woman, where did you get that?... Go straighten that hair!" I was very shy. Teaching had helped me speak out more freely but I was shy. I said to myself: "So, now what?" Although I never considered, not for one moment, straightening my hair. I studied at the Alliance Française, that was on Gonçalves Dias Street, there in São Luís, and I had to walk down a long street, Remedios. There was this private school, the school of São Luís. Even if there were only one student looking out the window or standing in the doorway, they would spy me way down the street. Then they would crowd around the door or the window when I walked by the school entrance, and they crowded there just to see me and boo me: "What the devil, go straighten that nest! What's that?! Is that the dog?"[9] I had to deal with that I don't know how many days a week, but I never changed my route. I could walk down another street and not have to go by the school. I thought to myself: "No. This is my hair. I'm not going to let those kids humiliate me." But it bothered me. It bothered me. Up until then I was anonymous, nobody looked at me. All of a sudden, the whole city looks at you. You would go to the movies—I'm still of the movie-going generation... And from that moment I really began to impose myself: I would walk down the middle aisle between the rows, to the end. Because when I saw that everyone was turning their heads to look at me, that's when I began to take control, I would say to myself: "I'm going to parade for them so that they can all see me." So I would pretend that I was looking for a seat, until I found one and sat down. If I went to Comercio Street and walked into a store, the salesperson would stop what they were doing and the customer... It was awful, that time! And since then some people say: "You walk right by us and don't even see us." I say: "Ever since people started harassing me in the street, I learned to keep looking straight ahead." Everyone, even the street vendors felt they had the right to harass me: "Hey, hippie!"

Then I started going to the university, and people were supportive. I joined a theater group called Laborarte. Then I'm going to get support from them: "Terrific. You look just like Angela Davis." These people were educated and they viewed my appearance as linked to the North American black movement. Although to tell the truth, I said to myself: "I was making, at the moment, my own movement." It was isolated. But already I'd started thinking "I have to make something. This is more important than people think."(Alberti and Pereira "Histórias..." 67–68)

Like Araújo's story, other interviews in the collection raise questions about the relationship between negritude and ugliness, and how a black person forms an identity, in a society that proclaims to be egalitarian but in practice bases its logic of superiority/inferiority on race and color, along with other markers of difference. These voices call attention to discriminatory processes and may shock those who consider that the racial question in Brazil has long been "resolved."

But beyond their shock value, or the emotions and sensitivities they raise, teaching materials must bring additional knowledge into the picture. How should we explore the questions that are raised by narrative excerpts like Araújo's? Once again, we start by asking about differences and similarities between the two historical contexts—the late 1960s in Maranhão and current Brazilian society. The questions include: "There are certainly many differences, but can we think of other prevalent forms of discrimination based on appearance?" "Are these forms of discrimination constructed on racist backgrounds?" "Might we establish relations between Maria Raimunda Araújo's experience and newspaper announcements from the 1940s and 1950s, such as these published in the *Jornal do Brasil,* one of Rio de Janeiro's major newspapers?"

Married couple seeks a well-behaved girl to work in a luxury apartment. Must live in and be an accomplished cook. No blacks. Experience required in all aspects of housekeeping.

*****

Seek white or light skinned, pleasant appearance, for light housekeeping in apartment from 8–11.

*****

Need white minor, under 18, as electrician-mechanic apprentice; can study and live in workplace if desired. (Damasceno 125, 142, 146)

A testimonial narrative or a newspaper announcement that strikes students as explicitly racist can be effective in identifying the racist values of the past and in asking about the continuity or changes in the present.

These narratives of ethno-racial identity formation become crucial in any attempt to deal with racism in its full complexity. By focusing on the history of how different racial identities are constituted, we suggest an alternative approach to the racial issue. Racial identities are situational and conceptions of race and racism are constantly changing in time and space, depending on historical, social, and political conditions (Bhavnani 2005; Bethencourt 2013). The same person can be black in one place and white in another. Moreover, understanding similarities and differences in relation to the past is essential in order to realize that race relations have not always been the same, nor are they necessarily the same as those encountered in the present day—implying that current race relations too may change (Alberti 2014: 201–14).

Other interview excerpts like Araújo's provide interesting possibilities for reflection on the reactions of members of the black movement to the association of blackness with ugliness, and their strategies for affirming that "black is beautiful." At different moments and in different parts of the world, militant groups found it necessary to transform the black person into a beautiful human being. Addressing the meaning of the word "race" in different moments of Western history, Francisco Bethencourt notices that the noun "has been used by African Americans to express their collective identity and turn the word's original derogatory use on its head" (7). This approach allows students to understand the contexts for declarations like "100% Black" and "Black is Beautiful." A case in point is black activist Angela Davis, cited by Araújo, who used her black Afro as a kind of revolutionary trademark.

In Brazil, the Ilê Aiyê organization, founded in Salvador, Bahia in 1974, wrote the following 1975 carnival song:

> What group is this? I want to know.
> It's the black world that has come to sing.
> Whites, if you knew how brave black people are
> You'd shower in tar and become black yourself.
> I won't reveal my mischief
> Nor my philosophy
> He who gives light to the blind is a white cane in Santa Luzia.
> We are crazy blacks and we're good people
> We have strong hair, we are Black Power.[10]

Debating Affirmative Action

Some of our interviews with Brazilian black movement leaders address the national debate over affirmative action.[11] The curricular objective is to enable student participation in this debate, by identifying recurring arguments and common misconceptions or inconsistencies in the arguments. The idea is not to convince students to adopt one opinion or another, but to equip them to reject simplistic treatments of these issues. We encourage reflection on the nature of oral sources and the central role that sources of all kinds have in expanding the knowledge of diverse human experiences.

Debates over racial issues in Brazil have become very lively, especially from 2001 on, when universities began to reserve quotas for Brazilians of African and indigenous descent. Affirmative action became a frequent topic in the media and in debates across different sectors of society. According to some, current policies that promote racial equality are actually "racializing" Brazilian society, since it would be far from easy to define who is "black," and thus entitled to an admission slot at a university (Alberti and Pereira "O movimento…").

The debate over reserving university admission slots for blacks became a political strategy of the contemporary black movement in preparing for the Third World Conference against Racism, Racial Discrimination, Xenophobia and Related Intolerance, in Durban, South Africa, September 2001 (Alberti and Pereira 2006). The phrase "quotas for blacks in universities" was inserted in the official document that the Brazilian government took to Durban, and was the part that drew the most media attention. Our research has shown that empowering members of the black movement was decisive to the inclusion of this phrase in the official document. This was possible only because the movement had achieved a degree of institutionalization, which helped the government and society at large to perceive its members as competent interlocutors. Subsequently, Rio de Janeiro's state parliament approved the country's first quota law, allotting 40 percent of state university enrollments to Brazilians of African descent.[12] The measure raised considerable controversy.

The issue of the quotas also provoked changes within the black movement. Many people feared that the upward mobility provided by access to universities only stimulated individual achievement, creating a black middle class unconcerned about the conditions of the population's most underprivileged classes. With the passing of time, however, it was recognized that the issue of quotas brought many positive outcomes. Even more important than the implementation of quotas, affirmative action stimulated public discussion about what it is like to be black. As Carlos Alberto Medeiros put it, during his interview:

> Beyond anything else affirmative action may achieve, it has already achieved a remarkable victory, which is the discussion about race. It is making Brazilians discuss race, because Brazilians don't like it, it is uncomfortable, disturbing, itchy... And we are being forced to discuss it... it is in the newspapers every day. And if we bear in mind that one cannot solve a problem unless the problem is acknowledged first, then we are moving in a positive direction. (Alberti and Pereira "Histórias..." 406)

Another positive outcome widely emphasized in our interviews was the fact that in general, the quotas and affirmative action created a single cause around which the movement could unite, displaying concrete benefits for a great portion of the black population. For some young black people, mobilization for vacancies in universities and access to jobs predominantly occupied by whites made the movement's actions more readily understandable.

Our interview excerpts present multiple points of view. They are made available to students, alongside other sources, including video and film documentaries, manifestos, newspaper articles, etc., so that students can decide which sources they consider most effective in debating affirmative action. But before analyzing the arguments and information, students are encouraged to interrogate the sources, by asking: "Where can I best find answers?"

"What do I need to know about this source?" "Which questions remain unanswered?" "Who produced the source?" "Why, when, and for what purpose?" "What does it document?" "What does it allow us to infer about the past and the present?" Before using oral history sources, teachers are encouraged to develop activities to familiarize students with the characteristics of oral history and interviewing. As Linda Shopes points out, we should always ask: "Who is the narrator? Who is the interviewer? What has been said in the interview? For what purpose has this interview been conducted? And, what are the circumstances of the interview?" (2002). In considering pedagogical strategies for the use of Holocaust testimonies, the Holocaust Educational Trust and the Shoah Foundation provide thoughtful additional questions for students to reflect on:

> Besides the interviewer, who else do you think the interviewee might be addressing? Can the interview passage be understood by itself, or does it leave the listener with unanswered questions? Is there is a narrative thread, with a beginning, a middle and an end? Which information is brought about by intonation and by the image of the interviewee? Does the interviewee provide a personal reflection on the experience? Is he delivering an opinion? Recapping a historical event? Or is he doing otherwise? Which answers could have been found in a textbook and which could not? How much of the interview contained just facts? What did you learn that could only have been told to you by this person? What made the interview different from reading the information in a book or on a website? Why do you think the selection presented contains edited extracts from interviews, instead of full length interviews? (Alberti 2011: 35)[13]

It might also be useful to suggest comparisons between the interview excerpts and interview selections in the documentary films. For instance: "How do interview passages appear in the documentary?" "What other elements besides interview passages, appear in the documentary?" "Think about the effects they create in the viewer." "Are there differences between the excerpts of interviews and the extracts that appear in the documentary?"

After having dealt with the nature of the sources and, for this very reason, the nature of the knowledge obtained through those sources, students are asked to reflect on one final question: "Can the interview excerpt/the documentary passage/the newspaper article/the manifesto extract contribute to the discussion about affirmative action? If yes, add the arguments (for or against) to your notes" (see figure 9.3).

Argumentos a favor de ações afirmativas	Argumentos contra ações afirmativas
Tome nota dos argumentos discutidos pela turma, no dia .... (preencher com a data):	Tome nota dos argumentos discutidos pela turma, no dia .... (preencher com a data):

Figure 9.3 Affirmative Action activity worksheet.
Source: http://www.arquivoestado.sp.gov.br/site/assets/difusao/pdfs/ACOES_AFIRMATIVAS_Verena_Alberti.pdf.

As atividades que empreenderemos nesse estudo incluem um debate aberto conhecido como "aquário aberto" (*fishbowl*).[4] Como funciona esse debate? Dispomos as cadeiras da sala aproximadamente como na figura abaixo. Um grupo de quatro alunos, os "peixes", ocupa cadeiras do centro, deixando uma (ou mais) cadeira livre. Um aluno (ou o professor) funciona como facilitador, propondo as questões iniciais e garantindo que cada um possa falar. Se alguém da plateia quiser participar da discussão, simplesmente sai de seu lugar e se senta na cadeira livre, como indica a seta da imagem. Nesse momento um dos quatro alunos que estavam sentados no círculo original e que já tiver contribuído com o debate deve sair para deixar sua cadeira livre.

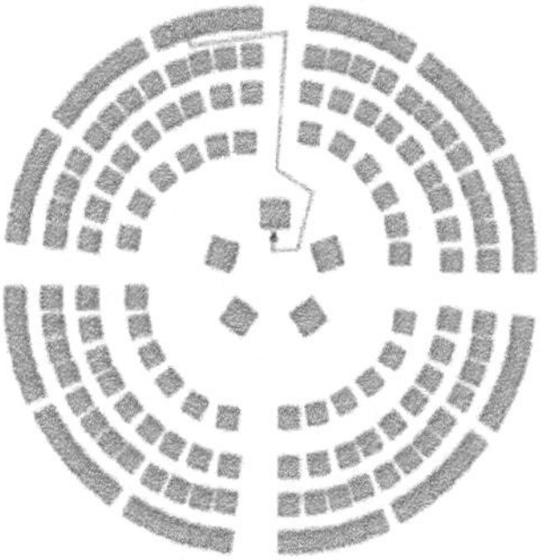

Os alunos que permanecem nos círculos de fora, o "aquário", devem ficar em silêncio e preparar questões e argumentos para quando entrarem no círculo. Todos os alunos devem ficar encarregados de anotar as principais ideias discutidas pelos "peixes", bem como os pontos fortes e fracos do debate.

Essa atividade demandará dois tempos de aula. Nos 20 minutos finais, faremos uma síntese das principais ideias e tomaremos nota das questões que ficaram em aberto.

Figure 9.4 Fishbowl activity structure.
Source: http://en.wikipedia.org/wiki/Fishbowl_%28conversation%29.

The next step is to systematize the arguments in preparation for the debate, using a "fishbowl" conversation facilitation tool as illustrated in figure 9.4, so that any member of the student audience may take a chair in the middle to enter the conversation.[14]

At the end of the activity it can be useful to ask the students to write down their impressions of the fishbowl, reflecting on its strengths and weaknesses, any questions that remain open, as well as the conclusions that the class has synthesized. Finally, as part of a self-assessment process, students are asked to record a reflection on, "What I knew/thought before studying affirmative action" and "What I now know/think about affirmative action."[15]

Conclusion

Oral history research is a considerable undertaking. It requires multiple stages of preparation, from selecting narrators, preparing interview guides, conducting the interviews, processing them for archival preservation, and making them available to others. Our project on the history of the black movement in Brazil ran from 2003 to 2007, but it continues to spark new developments. One of the most important results is its curricular relevance to the teaching of the history of racial and ethnic relations. The interviews have been open to the public for many years now, and they have nourished a good many analytical studies, our own and others. More recently, however, we have turned our attention to the potential uses of this material in pedagogical contexts.

The issue of race has been one of the most sensitive national questions throughout our history as well as today. For this reason, we feel that it needs to be addressed inside as well as outside the classroom. As with all sensitive and controversial issues, teachers and students need to approach the topic with care. Life history narratives are especially effective in dealing with sensitive and controversial issues, given their highly personal and experiential nature. To discuss the differences and similarities, between what our narrators recount of the past and race relations today, may be a good starting point for understanding the history of racial identity construction in Brazil. Oral history interviews have the advantage of bringing concrete life experiences into the debate, which become samples that help us to understand particular social contexts. These narratives have, thus, a heuristic value, as they enable us to widen our knowledge about the worlds we live in, even when they refer to particular episodes in an individual's life. In other words, Maria Raimunda Araújo's account of her experience of confronting prejudice in the 1970s with her big Afro, tells us a lot about the ideas and values in those times, but also gives us a perspective about those ideas and values today. Approaching large social issues through real life narratives is a potentially interesting strategy to break down resistance among some students and teachers in addressing these matters.

Using interview excerpts as didactic tools poses another challenge, as with other pedagogical initiatives that strive to produce rather than merely transmit knowledge. As we stated at the beginning of this chapter, our purpose has been to offer students and teachers primary sources and to propose activities so that they may design their own research pathways and produce their own new knowledge, and/or revise existing knowledge about the racial question and the history of race relations in Brazil. This implies understanding that the narrative excerpts are sources that, like any other, were purposefully produced. Consequently, oral sources must be assessed alongside other sources, asking questions like, "How and why does this source come to us? What are the contexts that produced this source? And, why has it been transmitted?"

Because our knowledge about the past and the present is always mediated by the sources that we have at our disposal, and because what we learn from these sources depends on the questions we ask, we can affirm that the intellectual process of knowledge construction is always contingent, in process, and subject to new sources and questions. Thus, the curricular materials we are producing are, by their very nature, partial and incomplete. Students at all levels—secondary, university, and teachers in training—are bringing new sources and new questions to our attention. Their own life experiences, their own ethnic/racial identities, and the diversity in their social relations all influence and impact their use and understanding of our didactic materials. And so, in each class, we professors become students and learn along with those we teach.

In sum, we have noted that once they are confronted with these life story narratives and work through the suggested activities, our students—some more, some less—experience the satisfaction of constructing new knowledge or and revising existing ideas on the racial question in Brazil. These oral sources and the inquiry process surrounding them, give students invaluable preparation for dealing with new encounters and experiences about race and racial relations in Brazil.

Notes

1. CPDOC (http://cpdoc.fgv.br), founded in 1973, is a teaching and research center focused on the social sciences and contemporary history. It houses an extensive collection of personal archives and oral history interviews that document Brazilian contemporary history. The center began recording its

first oral history interviews in 1975. Today it holds close to 2,100 interviews and more than 6,600 hours of recording.
2. See http://cpdoc.fgv.br/questaoracial/raca-e-racismo.
3. Law no. 11.645, of March 10, 2008, can be viewed at: http://legis.senado.gov.br/sicon/index.html;jsessionid=F71889B21211CBF5CE76F6F7B3B292BB#/pesquisa/lista/documentos.
4. Among the Latin American proponents of mestizaje are Fernando Ortiz, from Cuba, who in 1906 developed the concept of "transculturation" in Afro-Cuban culture; Manuel Gamio, from Mexico, who studied with Franz Boas and is considered the father of Mexican indigenism; José Vasconcelos, from Mexico, who argued for the agglomeration of all races in his book *The Cosmic Race* (1925); José Carlos Mariátegui, from Peru, author of *Siete Ensayos de Interpretación de la Realidad Peruana* (Seven Intepretative Essays on Peruvian Reality), published in 1928; and Gilberto Freyre, from Brazil, also a student of Boas, who in 1933 published *Casa Grande e Senzala* (The Masters and the Slaves), considered the founding text in what was to become known as "racial democracy" for harmonious race relations in Brazil.
5. See http://portal.unesco.org/en/ev.php-URL_ID=31038&URL_DO=DO_TOPIC&URL_SECTION=201.html, for the English text.
6. (http://cpdoc.fgv.br/questaoracial/raca-e-racismo/amauri-mendes-1).
7. Law no. 2.040, September 28, 1871, is known as the Law of the Free Womb. It gave freedom to the children of slave women born after promulgation. Their mothers' masters were responsible for raising the children until the age of 8, and after that they could have their services until the age of 21 or they could hand them over to the state for $600,000 réis. Abolition became official on May 13, 1888, when the royal princess, Isabel de Bragança, sanctioned Law no. 3.353, passed by the General Assembly of the Empire, declaring the end of slavery in Brazil. See www.senado.gov.br. "Legislação."
8. Antônio Frederico de Castro Alves (1847–1871) died at age 24, a victim of tuberculosis, leaving behind his unfinished work *The Slaves*, a series of poems on slavery, the most famous of which is titled "The Slave Ship" (1868). He is known as the poet of the slaves. See www.academia.org.br.
9. In slang, "dog" means "devil."
10. Music by the group Ilê Aiyê. Lyrics written by Paulinho Camafeu.
11. In 2013, Alberti presented a detailed lesson plan using oral and other sources on affirmative action as a final paper for a distance-learning course on the uses of archival documents in classrooms. See, Public Archive of São Paulo (Arquivo Público do Estado de São Paulo): http://www.arquivoestado.sp.gov.br/difusao/pdfs/ACOES_AFIRMATIVAS_Verena_Alberti.pdf.
12. The percentage has since been modified to 20 percent for black students, 20 percent for students coming from public schools, and 5 percent for disabled persons. These numbers refer solely to universities from the state of Rio de Janeiro. About the procedure of Law no. 3,708, ratified on November 9, 2001, see Michelle Peria. For federal universities, the Law no. 12.711/2012,

approved on August 2012, assigns 50 percent of the vacancies gradually (over four years) to students coming from public schools and low-income families, also taking ethnic identity into account.
13. For a more detailed discussion of these questions derived from The Holocaust Educational Foundation's DVD, "Recollections..." see Alberti 2011.
14. See http://slitoolkit.ohchr.org/data/downloads/fishbowl.pdf.
15. A detailed, step-by-step description of the activity in Portuguese may be found at: http://www.arquivoestado.sp.gov.br/difusao/pdfs/ACOES_AFIRMATIVAS_Verena_Alberti.pdf.

Works Cited

Alberti, Verena. "Histórias Dentro da História" [Stories within History]. *Fontes Históricas*. Ed. Carla Pinsky. São Paulo: Contexto, 2005. 155–202.

———. "Oral History Interviews as Historical Sources in the Classroom." *Words & Silences: The Journal of the International Oral History Association*, 6.1 (December 2011): 29–36. Web.

———. "Controversies around the Teaching of Brazilian 'Black History.'" *Challenging History in the Museum: International Perspectives*. Ed. Jenny Kidd, Sam Cairns, Alex Drago, Amy Ryall, and Miranda Stearn. Surrey, England: Ashgate, 2014.

Alberti, Verena and Amilcar Araujo Pereira. "A Defesa das Cotas como Estratégia Política do Movimento Negro Contemporâneo" [In Defense of Quotas as a Political Strategy of the Contemporary Black Movement]. *Estudos Históricos*, 37 (2006): 143–167. http://bibliotecadigital.fgv.br/ojs/index.php/reh/article/viewArticle/2249].

———. *Histórias do Movimento Negro no Brasil: Depoimentos ao CPDOC*. Rio de Janeiro: Pallas, 2007a.

———. "O Movimento Negro Contemporâneo." *Revolução e Democracia: 1964. As Esquerdas no Brasil*. Vol. 3. Ed. Jorge Ferreira and Daniel Aarão Reis. Rio de Janeiro: Civilização Brasileira, 2007b. 637–669.

Araújo, Maria Raimunda. Personal interview. Recorded in São Luís, Maranhão, September 10, 2004.

Bethencourt, Francisco. *Racisms: From the Crusades to the Twentieth Century*. Princeton, NJ: Princeton University Press, 2013.

Bhavnani, Reena, Heidi Safia Mirza, and Veena Meetoo. *Tackling the Roots of Racism*. Bristol: Policy Press, 2005.

Damasceno, Caetana. *Segredos da Boa Aparência: Da "Cor" à "Boa Aparência" no Mundo do Trabalho Carioca (1930–1950)*. Seropédica: UFRRJ, 2010.

Fernandes, Florestan. *A Integração do Negro à Sociedade de Classes*. São Paulo: Editora Nacional, 1965.

Hasenbalg, Carlos Alfredo. *Discriminação e Desigualdades Raciais no Brasil*. Rio de Janeiro: Graal, 1979.

The Holocaust Educational Trust and the Shoah Foundation Institute of the University of Southern California. "Recollections of Eyewitnesses Remember the Holocaust." 2007. Interactive DVD.

Maio, Marcos Chor. "The Unesco Project: Social Sciences and Race Studies in Brazil in the 1950s." *Portuguese Literary & Cultural Studies*, 4–5 (2000): 51–64.

———. "Unesco and the Study of Race Relations in Brazil: National or Regional Issue?" *Latin American Research Review*, 36.2 (2001): 118–136.

———. "Florestan Fernandes, Oracy Nogueira, and the Unesco Project on Race Relations in São Paulo." *Latin American Perspectives*, 38 (2011): 136–149.

Mattos, Hebe Maria. "O Ensino de História e a Luta Contra a Discriminação Racial no Brasil." *Ensino de História: Conceitos, Temáticas e Metodologia*. Ed. Martha Abreu and Rachel Soihet. Rio de Janeiro: Casa da Palavra, 2003. 127–138.

Medeiros, Carlos Alberto. Personal interview. Recorded in Rio de Janeiro, April 15, 2004.

Mendes Pereira, Amauri. Personal interview. Recorded in Rio de Janeiro, October 31, 2003.

Ministry of Education. "Diretrizes Curriculares Nacionais da Educação Básica." Brasilia: Secretaria da Educação Básica, 2013. 501. Web.

Nogueira, Oracy. *Tanto Preto, Quanto Branco: Estudos de Relações Raciais*. São Paulo: Queiroz, 1985.

Pereira, Amilcar A. "Circulação de Referenciais: Brasil, Estados Unidos e África." *O Mundo Negro: Relações Raciais e a Constituição do Movimento Negro Contemporâneo no Brasil*. Rio de Janeiro: Pallas/FAPERJ, 2013.

Peria, Michelle. *Ação Afirmativa: Um Estudo Sobre a Reserva de Vagas para Negros nas Universidades Públicas Brasileiras: O Caso do Estado do Rio de Janeiro*. Masters dissertation, Universidade Federal do Rio de Janeiro, 2004.

Reis, João J. and Flávio Gomes. *Liberdade por um Fio: Historias dos Quilombos no Brasil*. São Paulo: Companhia das Letras, 1996.

Santos, Joel Rufino dos. "O Movimento Negro e a Crise Brasileira." *Política e Administração*. Special edition, Vol. 2 (July–September 1985): 285–308.

Shopes, Linda. "Making Sense of Oral History." *History Matters: The U.S. Survey Course on the Web*, February 2002. http://historymatters.gmu.edu/mse/oral

Stuurman, Siep and Maria Grever, eds. "Introduction: Old Canons and New Histories." *Beyond the Canon: History for the 21st Century*. New York: Palgrave, 2007. 1–16.

CHAPTER 10

Images and Words: Photography and the 1968 Student Movement in Mexico

Alberto del Castillo Troncoso

In certain parts of Latin America, constructing a collective memory has acquired tremendous importance in recent years as an understandable consequence of the severe state oppression suffered by the civilian population. This memory-building process has gone through several stages and face-lifts, alternately advancing and retreating according to the different circumstances of time and place, from military dictatorships and authoritarian regimes to periods of political transition to democracy.[1]

History and memory are important factors in analyzing the revision of these types of processes. The two concepts are complementary, but they serve different purposes. As Necoechea (31) reminds us, history is first and foremost a discipline that aspires to be objective and attempts to interpret a given reality. Memory, on the other hand, attempts to legitimize the past, transcending the individual sphere to construct a collective frame of reference and weave stories about the identity of social groups.

The nonlinear path of memory, with all its gaps as well as continuities, has found one of its most important outlets for expression in photography. The 1960s witnessed student movements in various locations around the world. However, in Mexico those protests ended with a civilian massacre in the Plaza de Las Tres Culturas, on October 2, 1968, in the Tlatelolco district, when thousands of soldiers opened fire against snipers, later proved to have been sent by their own government (Hobsbawm 34–37).

The whole thing was documented by photographers, and their work helped create a collective imagery that would powerfully influence Latin American political thought in the decades that followed. Today, half a century later, it is paradoxical that we know so little about the worldview of those who shaped that imagery, which filled the front pages of newspapers around the world during the critical juncture of '68 (del Castillo 2012, 45–46).

This chapter essentially aims to analyze a combination of the photographers' oral testimonies, 40 years after the fact, and compare them with some of the images that they had produced (Thomson and Freund 17–21). It is important to note that the interpretation of oral and graphic testimonies is shaped, not only by the photographers' intentions but also by the editorial use made of their images by others. This contradiction is a basic premise for interpreting how oral stories and graphic sequences are read (Orme 15–17).

We should also remember that Tlatelolco is a place of paradigmatic significance in Latin American memory. This predominantly indigenous neighborhood in Mexico City marks the location of the last major battle of the Aztecs against the Spaniards in the sixteenth century. On that very spot, an archaeological site coexists with the Church of Santiago and a mid-twentieth-century apartment block. The entire site is a densely packed space, uniquely conducive to the exercise of remembrance, as Octavio Paz pointed out (35–37).

The civilian uprising of 1968 began in late July as a protest against the state's repressive military and law enforcement tactics, spearheaded by students from the country's two leading universities: the National Polytechnic Institute (IPN) and the National Autonomous University of Mexico (UNAM). Over the next two months, thousands of young people took to the streets, voicing the need for the rule of law, in a country governed by a state party regime without democratic checks and balances. It was a reactionary movement that introduced new forms of public protest, but it was brutally crushed by the government on the afternoon of October 2, 1968, just ten days before the Olympic Games were due to begin.

As mentioned earlier, an important group of photographers recorded the civil unrest that flooded the streets of Mexico City and were largely responsible for bringing it to the attention of international public opinion. In October 1968, Mexico's politicians unanimously applauded the massacre and repression of the student protests. The nation's congressional representatives and senators voiced their approval of the slaughter, and the directors of all national media, including the newspapers and periodicals, were openly supportive of President Gustavo Díaz Ordaz and his powerful secretary of the interior, Luis Echeverría Álvarez.

Nearly half a century later, the president of Mexico has hailed the events of '68 as a "key" episode for Mexican democracy, and the Mexican Congress has instructed that the student movement be written in "gold letters" alongside the names of the nation's greatest patriots, like Pancho Villa and Emiliano Zapata. Those once vilified as "terrorists" have become the heroes and martyred founders of the country's new political system. The coordinates of political correctness shifted drastically in a few short years, shaping the collective memory of all social actors. In this context, a museum has been built in that very square to commemorate those historic events. However, its contents are not limited to the events of October 2, and the institution aims to develop a bold audiovisual program and identify the links between Mexico '68 and other student movements across the globe.

This museum, the Tlatelolco University Cultural Center, is part of the UNAM and offers a permanent exhibition devoted to the 1968 student movement in Mexico and its context. What makes it unusual is the fact that it stands on the very spot of the October 2 massacre, and in that respect it is more like a memorial, complete with a display of assorted period artifacts. Consequently, the museum explores historical memory from a broad perspective that goes beyond the boundaries of conventional political vision and adopts a critical stance, distancing itself from any idealizing rhetoric. It explores the background and rationale for those events without recourse to communist conspiracy theories and international intrigue, instead, presenting the facts of the '68 movement as a process that can be understood and explained by a series of internal factors linked to the state's monopolistic control of its citizens. The museography is based on two central pillars: collecting new oral testimonies and presenting a photographic recapitulation of images published in the press at the time. This dialogue between images and words is usually corroborative, but in some cases the two contradict each other or approach an issue from different angles (Shudson 25–29).

A few years ago this venue had hosted an exhibition titled *Miradas en Torno al 68* [Visions of '68], which featured new oral and photographic testimonies and juxtaposed recent interviews of several photographers active at the time with some of their most significant photographs, most of which had never been published before. This chapter reflects on the use of these testimonies and images in the context of this museographic mise-en-scène. In this chapter I have revisited Elizabeth Jelin's concept of "vehicles for memory" (27–31), according to which certain objects not only represent but also incorporate the past, becoming privileged instruments in the construction of meaning and historical significance. It is highly significant that this type of knowledge and praxis is circulating and being re-signified in today's new museographic settings, designed nearly half a century after the events of '68.

In 2008, I conducted a series of interviews, in collaboration with Beatriz González, of some of the photographers of Mexico's '68: Enrique Metinides, Daniel Soto, Héctor García, Rodrigo Moya, Aarón Sánchez, María García, and Enrique Bordes Mangel. The goal of these interviews was to contextualize the photographers' participation in the coverage of those events (del Castillo 2012: 15–18). I compared and contrasted my analysis of the photographers' work with a critical examination of their oral testimonies. This exercise revealed clues that point to a narrative of the events that does not tally with the official or conventional versions, reviving the debate about different uses of the past and revealing other elements that can help us understand and interpret it (Traverso 47–51).

For this chapter, I chose to focus on three individuals whom I consider to be pivotal figures, even though one of them (Soto) is relatively unknown to the general public. The differences between the career paths and public profiles of these three photographers are considerable. For Daniel Soto and Rodrigo Moya, this was the first time they had given their account of the events, whereas Enrique Metinides had done so on several occasions over the last four decades. The narratives of the first two took exception to certain aspects of the official version, while the perspective of the latter served to corroborate a stereotypical image of the events. All three accounts are points of reference in the spotlight of public opinion, influenced by different political leanings. Their narratives express a microcosm that illustrates the different trends in journalistic coverage of the events, which generally portrayed the students as criminal agents of social unrest, but it also hints at a tendency toward social criticism that became more pronounced in the following decades, redefining the concepts of citizen participation and the limitation of power.

Criminalizing the Student Protest: Enrique Metinides

Like the famous Ukrainian-born New York crime photographer Weegee (Arthur H. Fellig), Metinides is considered one of Mexico's greatest police reporter-photographers of the twentieth century. North American and European museums have taken an interest in Metinides's work, making him one of the most renowned Mexican photographers in international circles. He spent practically his entire career at *La Prensa*, a sensationalist daily newspaper with a large circulation and significant influence among Mexico City's working-class population.[2]

La Prensa was among those that heralded the "conspiracy theory" trumped up by the authorities, who insisted that sinister communist forces were at work behind the scenes, manipulating the students in order to prevent the Olympics from being held. The paper's pro-government leanings were apparent in the political slant of its reporting, and in the editor's decisions regarding which photographs of different events were published. This editorial policy was part and parcel of Díaz Ordaz's governmental strategy. In fact, several editorials in the paper were pseudonymously penned by important members of Mexico's political class, such as Mario Moya Palencia and his boss, the powerful secretary of the interior, Luis Echeverría, who used a regular column called the "Political Granary" to lambaste the opponents of the government. This column vilified the students and set the tone for other social actors (Rodríguez 28–31).

In '68, Metinides covered several pivotal moments of the student uprising, including the October 2 massacre. His photographer's eye, specialized in capturing crime scenes, approached the student movement with a similar attitude, zooming in on the bloodiest, most shocking effects of the tragedy while omitting the underlying causes and reasons for the violence. This added a rationalizing component to his images, which conveyed the same anticommunist messages governing the paper's editorial policy. A seasoned career professional, over the years Metinides has constructed a conventional testimonial discourse regarding his participation in the events of '68, a narrative dominated by several salient facts. The first is the fact that he has adopted a heroizing rhetoric that portrays the reporter as a victim of adverse working conditions and a context of political repression:

> From the moment the troubles began, they didn't give us a single day of rest. We didn't have the right to get sick, eat, sleep, nothing. And we had to put up with being attacked. All that, and our photos didn't even end up getting published. (Metinides in del Castillo 2012: 46)

His narrative is also strongly influenced by his outlook as a reporter specialized in covering the police beat; he does not stop to reflect on the causes of the violence and instead emphasizes the shocking results of the tragedy, which peaked with the October 2 massacre. The photographer's testimony, given four decades later, allows us to take a closer look at these facts and underscore these considerations, which indicate that his position is aligned with the official discourse:

> I still see news reports on television, I've recorded some of them, and I've seen that there was going to be some kind of coup d'état against the Mexican government, and they began bringing people in earlier, because I remember that even before '68 there were attacks. I even got sent to a house in the Condesa district where there were 8 corpses that had been blown to smithereens while making bombs, and I still have a photo of a restaurant that was there on Avenida Reforma where they planted a bomb...I remember the Supreme Court where they also placed a bomb. In the Zócalo there were lots of anti-government attacks, so I'm convinced it was another attempt to overthrow the government, which wanted to put a stop to it somehow and that led to the October 2 massacre. (Metinides in del Castillo 2012: 37)

The way that the photographer associates the student movement with the government's idea of a communist conspiracy theory and the rise of powerful, mysterious dark forces working to topple the government is quite telling. In Metinides's oral testimony, the enormity of the state's crime dissipates in the dark labyrinth of the Cold War.

A series of photographs taken by Metinides was featured on the front page of *La Prensa* on September 25, 1968, the day after the military occupation of the Polytechnic Institute, which ultimately resulted in the deaths of several students. The sequence shows a medical team rescuing one of the soldiers attacked by the students. The event is narrated in four frames, and the emphasis is on the tragic outcome. However, on this occasion the subject is not a domestic dispute or crime of passion, the bread and butter of the sensationalist crime sections printed in Latin American papers at the time (known as *la nota roja* or "red news" because of the bloody images), but a very different kind of violence, which the photo caption attributes to the student rebellion (see figure 10.1). The succinct headline "Blood Was Spilled" underscores the absence of any other attempt to rationalize or explain this type of event.

The visual education imparted by the sensationalist press over several decades gave such messages the ring of truth and served to impress the

Figure 10.1 "Blood Was Spilled." *La Prensa*, September 25, 1968.
Source: Photo by Enrique Metinides. Public Domain. Courtesy of Alberto del Castillo.

official version of events on a wide audience. In this context, the editorial manipulation of the photographer's images provides interpretative clues that allow us to understand the stereotype created by Metinides himself, with a conservative moralizing message that criminalized the subjects of his photographs, particularly the women, and stigmatized their behavior.

Denouncing the State's Crime: Daniel Soto

In 1968 Soto was the chief photo editor for *El Universal*, one of the founders of Mexico's modern press and which, during the 1960s, was aligned with the government. Soto worked at the daily for more than 20 years, giving him ample opportunity to coordinate the photographic strategy that would guide his colleagues through the challenge of capturing one of the most important moments of the 1960s.

From his strategic position at the newspaper, he covered the first student protests in August, and later witnessed the official military operation that deployed 10,000 soldiers to occupy the Central University City Campus, as well as the efforts to control press coverage of this episode and ensure that it toed the party line. Most of the Mexico City press justified the campus occupation as a necessary measure, although it was criticized by the country's intelligentsia (Volpi 97–98). Soto's testimony in this chapter, given for the first time after four decades of silence, contradicts the government's official story regarding freedom of the press and media coverage of the events. He confirms that the press coverage of this episode was, in fact, a state-mandated operation designed by the office of the Secretary of the Interior, Luis Echeverría Álvarez, head of Mexican homeland security.

The photojournalists sent to cover the event came straight from the Secretary's headquarters. On arriving at the university campus, military officers organized a tour for the photographers. Among other things, they were shown classrooms scrawled with irreverent messages that supposedly proved that the students had ties to the Cuban Revolution and insultingly referred to President Díaz Ordaz as a "gorilla," a term frequently used to describe military dictators of that period.

El Universal's coverage parroted the official discourse and accused the students of planning an armed mutiny against the government. This coverage divided Mexican public opinion into two camps: those who backed the government (the majority), and those who defended the autonomy of the university community (an intellectual minority).[3] The front page of *El Universal* led with a single photograph by Soto, showing the armed forces positioned opposite the university president's office (see figure 10.2). In this professional shot, the photographer confines the frame to three military tanks and a few soldiers on the main esplanade; in other words, he merely shows the military elements present at the scene of the events, without negative connotations, as the photo does not illustrate any direct acts of repression against the students.

Figure 10.2 Military occupation of the Central University City Campus. Front page of the daily *El Universal*.
Source: Photo by Daniel Soto. Public Domain.

Soto's photograph merely depicts the context of the operation. However, his personal testimony half a century later adopts a rhetoric based on the photographer's participation as a subject. Unlike Metinides's victimized subject, in this case the narrator employs an ironic tone, portraying himself as a photographer who confronts the powers-that-be without any illusions of heroism and achieves his goal almost by accident in comical circumstances. Speaking in an informal, highly ambiguous tone that completely belies the seriousness of the episode, Soto describes his encounter with another photographer in the midst of the military takeover of the university grounds. The two colleagues spied each other across the human barrier that the soldiers had formed around the campus. Soto was behind the line and his colleague was outside, but this did not prevent them from holding a peculiar conversation, which ended when the photographer feigned a farewell handshake in order to slip his friend a precious roll of film:

> They wouldn't let us out. It was already half past midnight and the material needed to be delivered to the paper. So, the cordon of soldiers was there on Avenida Insurgentes, and I was trying to get out and talking to the soldiers,

but they wouldn't let me. "You can't pass here! We have orders to let no one leave," they told me. I told them I was a journalist and that the government itself had brought me to the university campus on a bus. "Well, we don't know anything about that. Nobody gets through here," they replied. And then I saw one of the boys who worked with me as a photographer for *El Universal*, who was called Javier Rivera, on the other side of the military line. I'd already removed the film from my camera and I had it hidden in my hand. I said to him, "Hi there, what brings you here?" "Oh, you know, I want to see if I can get into the campus," he replied. "Well, then, how's it going?" I said, stretching my arm between the heads of two soldiers to shake his hand. He immediately felt the roll in the palm of his hand and understood what I was trying to tell him. Then I said, "Go on, get going!" and he went and delivered all the material to the newspaper on time. (Soto in del Castillo 2012: 74)

One of Soto's photographs, which did not appear in the newspaper, focuses on the eyes of one of the students arrested during the occupation. Hands on his head, the student's facial expression and attitude are anything but an image of defeat; in fact, the message that comes across seems more like an advertisement for the concept of civil resistance. Such an image would not have sat well with the government authorities, which may explain why the paper decided not to publish it.

For the purposes of this argument, the contrast between the published and unpublished photos highlights the fact that the editor's opinion carried more weight than the photographer's intention, but it also suggests that the author of the images was playing a double game.

On the night of October 2, Daniel Soto received official orders to hand over all records of the massacre to government agents, presumably to be destroyed or be used by the state intelligence services. Instead of obeying, Soto and his colleagues rushed to conceal part of their graphic material, and thanks to their quick thinking some of this uncensored reportage survived and eventually came to light in later issues of the newspaper over the past 50 years.

The primary motivation behind this momentous decision was not the political convictions of the photographer and his colleagues—whose political activism was nonexistent as they were not affiliated with any party—but rather a sense of their professional duty to safeguard the images as documentary records of a historic event, which they knew from experience to be of paramount importance. Theirs was an act of civil disobedience in the broadest sense of the term, a personal rebellion against state authoritarianism in such an extreme situation as the October 2 massacre.

Criticizing and Presenting the Facts: Rodrigo Moya

Moya's unusual background made him an exception among the photojournalists of his day. He was a photographer with openly antigovernment leanings, who engaged in communist political activism and refused to take part in the traditional co-optation system that was the norm in those years, instead choosing to move in the most relevant artistic, theatrical, and literary circles of late 1950s Mexico (del Castillo 2011).[4]

> Every photographer is shaped by various influences: sometimes local, sometimes the guidance of a teacher, sometimes reading material. I was a photographer who read about photography. Photo books were not as common and abundant as they are now; every once in a great while a book would come out, and, well, you followed the great photographers. In my particular case, the teachings of Nacho López and Guillermo Angulo and the art critic Antonio Rodríguez. (Moya 45)

These influences are important signifiers that allow us to understand the photographer's point of view and the visual culture he brought to bear on presenting the facts. Moya forged his own genealogy and charted a personal and professional course that led him to several major landmarks in the history of photojournalism in Latin America—such as Nacho López, the most important Mexican photographer of the late twentieth century—and the world, zooming in on Walker Evans as the preeminent North American documentary photographer in the 1930s, and one of the most legendary figures in the history of international documentary photography (del Castillo 2006).

The sequence of photos depicting the march led by Javier Barros Sierra, president of the UNAM, on August 1, 1968, represents one of the most symbolic episodes in the entire student movement that year and has pride of place in Moya's archives. The president's decision to head a pacific protest against the brutality of the Mexican army and the repression of student demonstrations on previous days gave the student revolts at the Polytechnic Institute and the UNAM the stamp of legitimacy, elicited widespread popular sympathy and support for their cause, and consolidated the university's

Figure 10.3 Protest march of President Barros Sierra, August 1, 1968, annotated by Marcelo Brodsky.
Source: Photo by Rodrigo Moya. Courtesy of Rodrigo Moya Photo Archives.

political project over the following months. In a word, it lent rationality and weight to a protest movement which, prior to the president's involvement, had been fairly limited in its scope.[5]

The narrative appeals to the logic of the photographer's work, marked by a critical determination to create a documentary record and the use of sequences, an unconventional photojournalistic practice in those years. It is also an exercise in introspection and a reflection on the profession itself:

> Here I went to the top of a building and waited for them to come, knowing their route because I'd been with them one kilometer back. I ran ahead of them, always looking for a rooftop; I asked permission to enter an apartment building, I went up, got the high-angle shot; here I took a foreshortened shot, on a diagonal, where you see the posters. Here I went down again, rushing downstairs, and then I got them from a low angle, and I went walking with them in the rain that had begun to fall. So that was how I felt a demonstration should be shot, getting inside a demonstration

and really feeling it from the inside, from various angles. It's an act of love. I contain the demonstration, envelop it, but actually it's the demonstration that envelops the photographer. It was a personal record, and I had this passion for those movements, for an ideological attitude. So I took part and attended, but there was no intended recipient. Until now, those photos have been in limbo. I think it's the first time they've been photographed together like this. (Moya 27)

The account is a veritable mission statement, in which the photographer ponders his work and even likens his bond with the demonstration to an erotic relationship. Subjectivity and politics are intertwined in these musings, where words and images meld together and complement each other.

Another pivotal moment captured by Moya was the burning of the gorilla (a symbol of brutal repression in twentieth-century Latin America) representing Mexico City's chief of police, General Cueto, whose paws are crushing and trampling on the Mexican Constitution, the symbol of legality and the rule of law (see figure 10.4). This image glorifies the irreverent attitude of citizens toward the powers-that-be. The symbolism is obvious if we consider the fact that, in Mexico, the gorilla is an allegory of the president's absolute power. In one of the most important episodes of '68, the establishment was subjected to sacrilege and ridicule on the very doorstep of the National Palace. As Octavio Paz wrote:

> In certain fiestas the very notion of order disappears. Chaos comes back and license rules. Anything is permitted: the customary hierarchies vanish, along with all social, sex, caste, and trade distinctions. Men disguise themselves as women, gentlemen as slaves, the poor as the rich. The army, the clergy, and the law are ridiculed. Children and madmen rule. Obligatory sacrilege, ritual profanation is committed. Love becomes promiscuity. Sometimes the fiesta becomes a Black Mass. Regulations, habits, and customs are violated.... Therefore the fiesta is not only an excess... it is also a revolt. (57)

Steeped in symbolic significance, both of these episodes were acts of civil defiance against the state regime's authoritarian power. The first was represented by the leader of the nation's greatest university, who raised the flag of legality to decry the arbitrary military invasion of the hallowed halls of higher learning and the streets of Mexico City. The second illustrates the students' festive form of protest, which dramatized political events and highlighted the

Figure 10.4 Burning of the gorilla, August 13, 1968.
Source: Photo by Rodrigo Moya. Courtesy of Rodrigo Moya Photo Archives.

contrast between the irrational behavior of the authorities and the rational legality of the university.

It is no accident that Moya's lens retrieved and recreated these particular moments of '68; he had already leveled his irreverent gaze at the authorities in other major social movements that occurred throughout the 1960s in Mexico and Latin America. Through this new lens, '68 can be reinterpreted as a struggle for symbols among different sectors of the social and political spectrum and as a link that connects it to student movements in other countries. The photographer's oral narrative sheds light on his images, revealing new details and helping us decipher their symbolic meaning (del Castillo 2012).

In offering this double oral and visual testimony for the first time in four decades, Moya makes an original contribution to our understanding of the events of '68, constructing a more heterogeneous framework in which to review an occurrence etched in bold letters on the official timeline of recent history.

Half a Century of Hindsight: '68 from a Distance

This type of research is instrumental in the formation of exhibition halls, museums, and similar spaces, which act as triggers of collective memory (Fleury and Walter 31–33). In this context, the historical vision of '68 has changed radically in Mexican politics: the state-controlled press that stigmatized the students as rabble-rousers in the service of communism has been replaced by more politically independent media, and '68 is now recognized as a crucial moment that paved the way for a new democratic regime, though this does not make it immune to other types of political manipulations and uses.

The testimony of these photographers must be read in the light of such contradictions and paradoxes. Scenes captured then under dangerous circumstances and from a reactionary or pro-government stance are now perceived as part of a nation's documentary heritage and reminders of an exemplary episode of civil action. This brings me to one of the most relevant aspects of this project: an analysis of the testimony-image link in order to debunk some of the myths propagated by the official imagery of '68 and prompt the revelation of new information and perspectives on this episode.

The oral and graphic narratives of these professional photographers offer interesting highlights and shadows that provide insight into one of the most pivotal moments in contemporary Latin American history. Soto's and Moya's accounts qualify the official version of the facts, adding information in an ironic, critical tone, while Metinides's perspective reiterates a conventional version of the events.

In incorporating these plural voices and images, the museum of '68 has become an important point of reference for the people of Mexico City, as well as an oral and visual documentation center that appeals strongly to young audiences. Reflecting on this theme through the convergence of oral testimonies and photographs not only enriches the historiography of a vital subject in Mexico's recent past, but also serves to build bridges and connect with generations that did not live through the conflict.

Whether this venue becomes a space of regeneration or a forum for the perpetuation of myths will depend on its ability to expand the horizon of '68 to include an entire decade and its flexibility in comparing and contrasting local events with experiences in other parts of the world. This space strives to offer something more than a conventional review of history, bent on correcting the "errors" of human memory. Such proposals challenge the veracity of conventional history, subordinated to the power of the written document and little accustomed to debating with museographic spaces.

For all of these reasons, reflecting on the pertinence of the imagery of '68 with regard to the memory of later crimes committed by the state is an important and timely undertaking. The most recent of these atrocities was the massacre of 43 students from the Ayotzinapa Normal School on September 26, 2014, in southern Mexico, raising international concerns about the collusion of Mexican government authorities and municipal police officers with paramilitary groups linked to the drug cartels, in what amounted to a crime of the state.[6]

The photographer Marcelo Brodsky is responsible for one of the subtlest museographic references and readings of the events of '68 and their symbolic connection to this recent massacre, reworking one of Moya's best-known photographs of the student demonstration on August 1, 1968 (see figure 10.3), and relating it to the Ayotzinapa debacle in 2014 by identifying their common denominator: the participation of the state in crimes against humanity.[7] The renowned Argentinean photographer sees a clear link between the 1968 student revolt, which voiced the need for the rule of law, and the civilian protests over the 2014 Ayotzinapa crimes.

Brodsky's alteration of Moya's photograph was shown at *Paris Photo* in November 2014, confirming the importance of the imagery built up around '68 as a benchmark for situating these types of events, which stir up international public opinion regarding governmental involvement in crimes against civilians. The work's presence at this fair, one of the world's most prestigious photography showcases, brought the subject to the attention of a vast global audience. As Huyssen (2002) has pointed out, in the case of *Buena Memoria* [Good Memory], Brodsky's handwriting affects the interpretation of the image, lending its subjects a ghostly aura. The Ayotzinapa murders cast a shadow over the smiling faces of the students marching with their president, simultaneously reminding us that their celebration will end in tragedy on October 2.

In this chapter, I have attempted to rethink '68 through a series of oral and visual testimonies that capture the dynamics of the events which unfolded back then, and to show how this past extends into the present with rereadings and new interpretations that allow these images to take on new meaning and circulate in order to shape a collective memory.

This kind of endeavor represents a point of reference that has rarely been used in the history of Latin American photojournalism. I have aimed to highlight its usefulness for the practice of historiography and emphasize the political need to contextualize testimonies with other kinds of graphic documents, even though images and words share an ethical perspective rooted in research itself. In this respect, I agree with Ruben Chababo, director of the Museo de la Memoria [Museum of Memory] in Rosario, Argentina, when he says:

> heeding the unsettling rumors that belie the myth, far from being discredited and accused of threatening the memory of history's vanquished, should be seen as a hazardous yet equally glorious act of according human status—with all that this implies—to those whom history has humbled. (12)

Notes

1. In recent history, the memory-building process involves different ways of viewing and dealing with the past. Two extreme examples are Argentina, where judicial proceedings were initiated against a considerable number of soldiers who committed crimes against humanity during the dictatorship; and, in the case of authoritarian states, Mexico, where impunity seems to be the general rule in such matters. This underscores the importance of obtaining new testimonies that allow us to see facts and events in a different light (Franco and Levin 17–21).
2. As González (2012) notes, the newspaper *La Prensa*, with editor in chief Mario Santaella at the helm, exemplifies the collusion that characterized the relationship between the press and the Mexican government during the heyday of the Institutional Revolutionary Party (PRI) in the mid-twentieth century.
3. It is interesting to analyze the photojournalistic coverage of the military occupation in Mexico and compare it with other similar episodes registered in Latin America in the 1960s—in particular, the "Night of the Long Batons," when the military police took over the University of Buenos Aires on July 29, 1966—which loom large in the continent's public consciousness. These images suggest the possibility of creating a vast oral and photographic archive dedicated to this darker side of Latin American political history.
4. This career move introduced him to the world of theater, where he documented dozens of rehearsals and performances directed by Juan José Gurrola, Héctor Azar, and Juan Ibáñez with the assistance of other leading personalities like the sculptor Juan Soriano and the poet Octavio Paz, who helped transform the stages of Latin American dramaturgy by designing

bold visual proposals that met with great success on the European stage. A case in point is Ibáñez's production of the play *Divinas Palabras* by Ramón del Valle Inclán, which won the first prize at the World Theater Festival in Nancy, France, in 1964.
5. The president's leadership and backing of the student rebellion was the exception to the rule. This did not happen in any other student movement in '68, because university presidents were universally regarded as part of the establishment. Only in Mexico, where the university community had a history of being openly critical of the revolutionary government's authoritarian regime during the first half of the twentieth century, was it conceivable for a university president to throw his support behind the students and become the government's political intermediary (Ramírez 19–20).
6. The students were arrested by Mexican police who, acting on the orders of José Luis Abarca, mayor of the city of Iguala in the state of Guerrero, handed them over to a paramilitary group known as "Guerreros Unidos" or "United Warriors." In response, students all across Mexico organized walkouts and protests were held around the world. Today, these young people are officially listed as "missing."
7. At the top of the photo, Brodsky wrote in red chalk, "43. No to another Tlatelolco." And in the lower left-hand margin he added, "The boys were stopping in Iguala on their way to participate in the march in Mexico City marking the anniversary of the Tlatelolco massacre, held on October 2, 2014."

Works Cited

Brodsky, Marcelo. Personal interview by Alberto del Castillo. Buenos Aires, Argentina. December 2014.

Chababo, Rubén. *Apuntes Sobre el Heroísmo*. Santiago de Chile: Ediciones del Museo de la Memoria y los Derechos Humanos, 2014. Print.

del Castillo, Alberto. *Rodrigo Moya. Una Visión Crítica de la Modernidad*. Mexico City: Conaculta, 2006. Print.

———. *Ensayo sobre el Movimiento Estudiantil de 1968. La Fotografía y la Construcción de un Imaginario*. Mexico City: Instituto Mora/Instituto de Investigaciones sobre la Universidad, 2012. Print.

Fleury, Beatrice and Jacques Walter, eds. *Memorias de la Piedra. Ensayos en Torno a Lugares de Detención y Masacre*. Buenos Aires: Ejercitar la Memoria Editores, 2011. Print.

Franco, Marina and Florencia Levín, eds. *Historia Reciente. Perspectivas y Desafíos para un Campo de Construcción*. Buenos Aires: Paidós, 2007. Print.

González, Beatriz. *Imágenes y Representaciones del Movimiento Estudiantil de 1968 en el Periódico* La Prensa. Diss. Universidad Simón Bolívar, Caracas, Venezuela, 2010. Print.

Hobsbawm, Eric. *Historia del Siglo XX*. Barcelona: Crítica, 1994. Print.
Huyssen, Andreas. *En Busca del Futuro Perdido. Cultura y Memoria en Tiempos de Globalización*. Mexico City: Fondo de Cultura Económica, 2002. Print.
Jelin, Elizabeth. *Los Trabajos de la Memoria*. Madrid: Siglo XXI, 2002. Print.
Moya, Rodrigo. Personal interview by Alberto del Castillo, Cuernavaca, Mexico. August 10, 2008.
Necoechea, Gerardo. *Después de Vivir un Siglo*. Mexico City: Ensayos de Historia Oral, INAH, 2005. Print.
Orme, William A. *A Culture of Collusion: An Inside Look at the Mexican Press*. Miami: North-South Center Press, 1997. Print.
Paz, Octavio. *El Laberinto de la Soledad*. Mexico City: Fondo de Cultura Económica, 1999. Print.
Ramírez, Ramón. *El Movimiento Estudiantil de México. Julio-Diciembre de 1968*. Mexico City: Era, 1969. Print.
Rodríguez, Jacinto. *La Otra Guerra Sucia*. Mexico City: Random House, 2007. Print.
Schudson, Michael. "News, Public, Nation." *American Historical Review* 107.2 (April 2002): 25–47.
Thomson, Alistair and Alex Freund. *Oral History and Photography*. New York: Palgrave, 2011. Print.
Traverso, Enzo. *El Pasado: Instrucciones de Uso*. Buenos Aires: Prometeo, 2011. Print.
Volpi, Jorge. *La Imaginación y el Poder. Una Historia Intelectual de 1968*. Mexico City: Era, 1998. Print.

CHAPTER 11

"A Living Museum of Small, Forgotten and Unwanted Memories": Performing Oral Histories of the Portuguese Dictatorship and Revolution

Joana Craveiro

"A Living Museum of Small, Forgotten and Unwanted Memories" is a set of seven performance-lectures that challenge official, unofficial, and personal narratives of three key moments in Portugal's twentieth-century history: (1) the Portuguese New State Dictatorship that lasted for 41 years, from 1933 to 1974[1]; (2) the 25th of April Revolution, the coup that toppled this dictatorship in 1974[2]; and (3) the popular revolutionary process during 1974–1975, known as the Ongoing Revolutionary Process (or PREC).[3] My aim in creating this performance is to examine the relationship between past events and the way we remember them in the present, especially when looking at the recent commemorations in Portugal of the coup's fortieth anniversary. How these commemorations unfolded and the prolific production of representations and narratives that accompanied them provided important source materials for this project.

The performance of "A Living Museum..." has seven parts: (1) "Small Acts of Resistance;" (2) "Invisible Archives of the Portuguese Dictatorship" (3) "Broken Portuguese;" (4) "Fragments of a Revolutionary Process;" (5) "Taken by Surprise" (6) "When Did the Revolution End?" and (7) "Memory/ Postmemory." I have performed some of these parts at academic conferences in Portugal and abroad,[4] however, the full performance was first presented in Lisbon, in November 2014. Using mainly oral testimonies and private archival documents, I uncover and display subjective stances regarding the memories of people who experienced these events firsthand, as well as those who did not (what Marianne Hirsch names the "postmemory generations").[5] One of the strategies I use to achieve this is to hold an open forum debate after each performance, to promote audience dialogue about the conflicting understandings we still hold today through our memories of these events and the historical facts.

The process of turning oral history testimonies into performance and presenting them to an audience that also includes many of the interviewees themselves, creates what Della Pollock terms as "an especially charged, contingent, reflexive space of encountering the complex web of our respective histories" (1). Members of the audience come with their own particular perspectives on the events themselves, and the performance enables a coming together of these divergent views and memories. At the same time, this reflexive audience space speaks to the absence of public inscription of these memories and rescues them from oblivion. Modeled on the popular assemblies[6] that characterized the revolutionary period in Portugal between 1974 and 1975, the post-performance debates become a space to voice and discuss conflicting perspectives, frameworks, and prejudices, as well as official and unofficial narratives. The live confrontation of performer, audience members and interviewees in these debates creates a "transformational process" (Pollock 2) for all parties involved. This transformational process is what this chapter seeks to describe and analyze.

Introducing the Museum and the Archivist

Description of the set: Over a desk center stage, a small video camera is installed. Sitting at the desk, the Archivist of the museum (myself) conducts the audience through her notebooks, which are projected on a screen behind her, containing titles, images, and subtitles, forming a possible narrative of the events (see figure 11.1).

Figure 11.1 Part 1, "Small Acts of Resistance."
Note: Performed in Lisbon, November 2014.
Source: Courtesy of João Tuna.

In constructing "The Living Museum," I purposefully intend to challenge traditional ideas of history, organization, cataloguing, and displaying of past events. I seek to do this by looking at the nature of the artifacts themselves—private archives and personal testimonies—and displaying them live. The physical presence of the objects is extremely important. At the same time, this museum is paradoxical. According to the International Council of Museums (ICOM), a museum is a place, which traditionally "acquires, conserves, researches, communicates and exhibits the tangible and intangible heritage of humanity."[7] However, this museum is set upon conserving what seems, at first, to be unimportant and irrelevant. Here lies one of the crucial aspects of this project: to give voice to that which would not otherwise be visible or valued. And, moreover, to do it *live*.

The role of the character that I play—the Archivist—is key. In *Performing History*, Freddie Rokem defines the actors in historical performances as hyper-historians.[8] Along these lines, the Archivist—claiming she is not a historian—presents herself as a collector, an organizer of the archive, a documentarist. The Archivist starts with her own family history: forbidden books at her parents' home; a box full of pamphlets, stickers, books, and newspapers to be donated by her father to the 25th of April Documentation Center; a story about her grandfather listening to Radio Moscow, an underground resistance radio station during the dictatorship (1926–1974); the emblematic funeral of Ribeiro Santos, a student murdered by the Political Police (PIDE)[9] in October 1972, that the Archivist's father and mother attended.

There is something forensic about the Archivist. She links her desire to reconstruct a national past to understanding her own identity. She declares, "It all started when I asked myself how could a dictatorship last that long? It was like asking who am I, where do I come from—and what remains within me of those times?" [From performance-lecture #1 "Small Acts of Resistance"]. This reconstruction of identity bears similarities with Anna Deavere Smith's work on reconstructing an American identity through the collection of testimonies, conveying conflicting views on the same subject.[10]

The Structure of the Performance

The full performance of the seven pieces lasts four and a half hours, with a break for dinner halfway through. It follows a linear chronology from 1933 (the beginning of the New State Dictatorship) to 2014 (the commemoration of the fortieth anniversary of the revolution), and as performances continue in 2015 and 2016, I incorporate newer and more recent data. Each performance-lecture works independently. The sentence "This investigation continues in order to render the invisible visible," serves as the transition between each part. Together, the seven performance-lectures work as a mosaic of perspectives over 41 years of Portuguese history. The performance, presented by the Archivist (the alter ego of the performer), unfolds as follows:

> **#1 "Small Acts of Resistance"**: serves as an introduction to the ideological framework of the New State Dictatorship. It focuses specifically on the censorship of media and the arts. The dictatorship is generally referred to as a time of darkness, poverty, illiteracy and conservative values. I was interested in finding hidden acts of resistance within the regime, those

that "prudently avoided any irrevocable acts of public defiance" (Scott 17). I say "hidden acts" because the history of the "declared" political resistance to the regime has been investigated widely since 1974. The purchase and reading of forbidden books was one such hidden form of resistance. Amaro's *Massacres na Guerra Colonial (Massacres in the Colonial War)*, about the Portuguese wars in Africa[11] was one of these forbidden texts, containing official documents of operations in Mozambique. I interviewed José Ribeiro, who published this book in 1976. Despite being published in the post-dictatorial period, its release was nonetheless very fraught. José, who also owned a famous resistance bookshop in Lisbon, was sued by the Portuguese government for publishing the book. This led me to question the relationship of the Portuguese state to the memory of the Colonial War, and the silence that still surrounds this 13-year conflict that left profound scars on a whole generation of Portuguese men and their families and descendants.[12] I approach the subject of the Colonial War by enacting a testimony by a former commandant in the Guinea war, Carlos N., as a parenthesis during the performance of Part #1.

#2 "Invisible Archives of the Portuguese Dictatorship": This second performance-lecture focuses on state repression, namely, by the PIDE. It draws on written and published testimonies of former political prisoners about the torture they had suffered (figure 11.2). Fernando Rosas states that the regime was able to last as long as it did due to an efficacious combination of "preventive" and "repressive violence"(196–210). By using the title "Invisible Archives," I highlight the methods used to erase these acts of violence from public view, during and after the dictatorship. One example is the absence of any memorial inscription on the building that housed the headquarters of the PIDE in Lisbon, which today is a luxury condominium.[13] This process of "rendering invisible" is also apparent in the lack of transitional justice or reparations during the post-dictatorial period for former victims of state repression.

#3 "Broken Portuguese": is conducted as a radio program. This performance recounts some of the stories behind the 25th of April 1974 coup. The coup was carefully planned and led by captains of the Movimento das Forças Armadas (Armed Forces Movement)—most of them quite young. Radio transmissions played a crucial role in bringing about the coup. Officers learned about the progress of the operation through radio signals in the form of specific songs, which remain symbols of the revolutionary coup today, such as José Afonso's "Grândola Vila Morena."

Figure. 11.2 Part 2, "Invisible Archives of the Portuguese Dictatorship."
Note: Performed in Lisbon, November 2014.
Source: Courtesy of João Tuna.

#4 **"Fragments of a Revolutionary Process"**: The 25th of April, 1974 military coup gave rise to a popular movement normally referred to as the Ongoing Revolutionary Process (PREC), which surprised even the military.[14] It is commonly understood that this process came to an end with another coup on November 25, 1975. The history of this 19-month period has been subject to various ideological interpretations, and to an established, negative narrative of it as a time of excess, dangerous popular power, and naivety. In my research, however, I came across many testimonies that point in a different direction. Namely, that this was experienced as a time of real change in people's lives, through the direct and concrete actions of ordinary people who organized together despite formal political affiliations. A common thread of excitement, hope and utopia runs throughout these testimonies, and the revolutionary period is commonly described as a "celebration," a "party," that is, a joyful and happy time. Coming after the dinner break, this performance-lecture analyzes these memories, attempting to convey the excitement of the PREC. The audience is invited to participate in a popular assembly and vote, followed by the performance of select testimonies. Then, the performance is abruptly interrupted by the sentence: "In the middle of the celebration, *this* happened." *This* refers to the decolonization process and the return of thousands of Portuguese from the former colonies. This interruption transitions into the next performance-lecture.

#5 "Taken by Surprise—The Story of a Family": At this point, I narrow the focus of the performance to tell the story of Family A, who lived in Angola until 1975 and abruptly returned to Portugal on the eve of the revolutionary process. This focus on a single family story stands in deliberate contrast to the previous act, which included as many as six testimonies. In focusing on one family, I attempt to humanize the story of the so-called returnee (in Portuguese, *retornados*) from the former colonies. The returnees have often been treated as a homogenous group, as "reactionary," "conservative," "pro-regime," and "racist." Following an introduction to some of the problematic issues concerning colonialism and the decolonization process itself, this performance conveys the difficulties of Family A's return, as well as some of the hardships they experienced in Portugal. It also lays bare some of the contradictory and problematic aspects of their story and beliefs: anticommunism, racism, and willful ignorance of politics among some family members. The story of the Family A illustrates that decolonization is an extremely complex topic, subject to different positions within families themselves, and that returnees cannot be treated as a homogeneous group that shares identical values.

#6 "When Did the Revolution End?" This piece presents and questions several theories and beliefs regarding the end of the PREC. The radicalization of all parties, political forces and civil society during this period, gave rise to increasing instability that led to the second coup on November 25, 1975.[15] The conflicting narratives about this event prevent us, even today, from fully grasping what really happened. Nowadays, this second coup is commemorated by certain segments of Portuguese civil and military society as a landmark event in the move toward democracy. In the years that followed, up until today, there has been a progressive revision of the meaning of the events that took place during the revolutionary process, and of the 25th of April Revolution itself. The performance-lecture raises a question mark as to what really happened *back then*, leading into the next part, which deals directly with our relationship to these events *today* (see figure 11.3).

#7 **"Memory/Postmemory"**: Built as an epilogue, this performance questions how the revolution is commemorated today and what features are obliterated from that commemoration. The public space has been erased of certain memories, like the political murals that used to cover the walls of Lisbon. Following the recent official and unofficial commemorations of the fortieth anniversary of the 25th of April Revolution (in April 2014), this performance displays some of the contradictions that are still apparent in the Portuguese people's relationship to these events.

* * *

After this, a post-performance open discussion takes place. Although not formally a part of the performance itself, it works nonetheless as a conclusion to the full performance of "A Living Museum of Small, Forgotten and Unwanted Memories."

Two Sides

As a whole, my performance piece tries to move beyond the dichotomized history that still dominates many of the narratives of these periods, which places the left wing on the side of the victors and the right wing on that of the losers. In fact, this performance uncovered so many ideological nuances among the supposed winners that it challenged the very idea that the revolution was a victory for the entire Left from the beginning and throughout the revolutionary process. As the performer, I unveil, together with the audience, in a process of "shared authority" (Frisch), other dimensions of these historical periods and their official narratives, which still comprise several problematic and unresolved elements.

Challenging a two-sided historicity does not evade, however, the matter of my own partiality and personal investment, confirming Alessandro Portelli's assumption that "oral history can never be told without taking sides, since sides exist inside the 'telling'" ("What makes..." 41). In fact, an autobiographical, participant voice runs throughout the performance. As the performer, I state from the beginning where my political background lies, and I deconstruct and question my position throughout the performance in sentences like, "I remember my father calling my mother a Maoist. And he didn't mean it as a compliment" (#2 "Invisible Archives").

The Use of Testimonies

Testimonies are a key element of this performance. I use them to intertwine historical facts, photographs and other memorabilia. In a sense, they are a key part of what makes this a "living" museum. In the performance, I give the full context of how the testimonies were collected, underlining from the beginning that I will be displaying a mosaic of multiple voices. As Anna Deavere Smith states, "It takes ultimately many people to tell the story of a community or the story of a society."[16] These voices—pieces of what Christian Boltanski has termed "small memory" (107), may not be found in any official history textbook, but they are the core of "A Living Museum of Small, Forgotten and Unwanted Memories." In fact, I avoid telling the history of military or political protagonists, to focus instead on how ordinary unknown people lived the events before and after the 25th of April Revolution.

The testimonies used in "A Living Museum" were collected in Portugal, between 2012 and 2014. I interviewed people who had experiences of activism and political resistance during the New State Dictatorship, people who actively participated in the PREC, members of my family, and some foreigners who came to Portugal expressly to witness the revolution first hand. I also conducted extensive interviews with people who returned from the ex-colonies after 1974. In total, I conducted over 50 interviews. More important than the number of testimonies collected, however, was the richness of the experiences and the depth of the interviews. These were lengthy life stories, of up to three hours each. My focus was to understand the emergence of political awareness and political activism, to capture particular acts of resistance before the revolution, and people's participation in the revolutionary process. My final question always revolved around when people felt that the revolution had ended.[17]

Every interview was unique in length and content. Some were held in public places, one was a guided tour of special places in the narrator's memory, and one was a group interview with a family of five. Interested in more than just the content, I was looking at the "performance qualities" (Abrams 130), of each interview, which I tried to incorporate in my own performance, in a process similar to Deavere Smith's methodology, "to say exactly what they said, more than word for word, utterance for utterance."[18] One audience member commented: "We could sense those people were there, alive, on stage." At the same time, the live performance of the testimonies produced reactions in the audience—either of empathy or rejection—some of which I will analyze in the following section, using the example of four testimonies.

Performing the Testimonies—Four Examples

Carlos N.

I first met Carlos briefly in September 2014. He talked openly about his past as a soldier in the colonial war and shared some of his memories of state repression during the dictatorship. Later, we arranged an interview, which lasted three hours. He told me he was an actor in a Portuguese theater company and had used some of his memories of the war in one of the shows. During the interview, he became visibly moved when relating his encounter with a dead enemy soldier:

> After a battle, what do I see? A young man, his shoelaces impeccably tied, the marks of sweat under his arms; in one pocket, a letter and a picture of his girlfriend; in the other pocket, a toothbrush and toothpaste. This meant we had won something, like a trophy. Still, he was a young man, fighting for an ideal.

It was a powerful and moving memory, expressed beautifully, almost, as if it had been prewritten, previously performed. Perhaps I was influenced by his constant references to his previous performances, where he had related his accounts of the war. I transcribed the narrative exactly as he recounted it, and I attempt to perform it exactly as I heard it, trying to convey Carlos's own performance of this memory.

Just 90 minutes before the opening of the show, Carlos knocked on the door of the venue, with a large travel bag in hand. Inside, there were all sorts of objects, mementos, letters, and a G3 bullet from his commission in Guinea during the colonial war. Some two hours later, when performing Carlos's testimony, I would reproduce his description of some of the objects as well as the history he recounted of this bag, which had lain unopened in the basement of his house for so many years.

Later on that same night, during the closing debate, an audience member asked if the soldier I talked about was part of my family. She then recounted how her father's story was very similar to that man's. Carlos raised his hand to speak: "That soldier is me." The woman was startled and turned around to look at him, and so did the rest of the audience: Carlos was a real man, and he was there in the flesh.

Aurora Rodrigues

A left-wing activist imprisoned and tortured in 1972, Aurora's testimony was published in 2011 (Rodrigues). It is a verbatim transcript of a long testimony that Paula Godinho and António Monteiro Cardoso recorded, transcribed, and edited. I did not personally interview Aurora Rodrigues, but used her published testimony as an example of someone who had been the victim of brutal state repression during the dictatorship.

Aurora came to watch the performance of "A Living Museum" on November 15, 2014. In the debate, she immediately stood up and introduced herself: "I am Aurora Rodrigues." Again, there was a silence, and all heads turned to Aurora as she confirmed in person the testimony I had just performed on stage: "I was imprisoned and tortured by the PIDE [Political Police]." It was as if she was attesting to the truth of what had been told. Moreover, she felt the need to add an important aspect that was missing from my selection of materials. In May 1975, in the midst of the PREC, she and 400 other militants in the party she belonged to—the MRPP[19]—were arrested by the military and spent three months in the same jail she had been confined to before the revolution. This attests to the complexities of the revolutionary process and of the tense relationship between certain segments of the Left with the military. Her experience questions the assumption that the 25th of April coup was consensually supported by all elements of the Left throughout. Aurora's arrest in May 1975, together with fellow militants, is still nowhere to be found in history textbooks and remains largely unknown to the general public. One audience member, turned skeptically and almost angrily to Aurora: "Are you telling me you were arrested after the 25th of April by the military?" Aurora responded affirmatively, but the audience member laughed in disbelief. The next day, I decided to add this story to the performance. I could not forget how Aurora had introduced the subject: "There is something that you haven't mentioned; and according to *your* chronology this event took place during the PREC." Aurora's comment showed that the chronology of the events themselves is also a product of subjective and ideological interpretation. What I was performing was, indeed, my own understanding of the chronology of events (*my* chronology), a product of the collective memories, practices and narratives that surround me daily, despite the attempts of "A Living Museum" to display a wider mosaic of memories in order to defy some of these hegemonic and persisting narratives, erasures, and omissions.

Teresa R.

Teresa wrote her testimony before our meeting, "in order not to get lost in the memories." I started the performance of her testimony with those exact words. Like Teresa had done while talking to me, I also read from a notebook, seeking to convey her exact performance—the same tone, the same laughs, the same irony she had displayed when being interviewed. Teresa's experience of the PREC was mainly focused on a housing project called SAAL,[20] whose mission was to build houses for people most in need. She worked on a specific block in Lisbon that contained over 4,000 shanty houses, and took part in many occupations of empty buildings to provide housing for very poor people. At a certain point in her testimony, she recounted the occupation of a flat in downtown Lisbon. Usually, the occupations were of vacant buildings, according to a list provided by the Town Hall. But this house was not empty; rather, it was filled with beautiful furniture from the ex-colonies. Teresa recounted how she had called the landlord and asked him to come, for they had mistakenly occupied his house. I reproduced Teresa's lightness and laughter in the performance of her testimony. Something in the way she spoke conveyed the general idea of the PREC as a sort of a celebration, a party; something I found in many other accounts.

In two of the post-performance audience discussions, two incidents occurred. In one instance, a man who was uncomfortable with what he had witnessed questioned why, of all the good things that happened during the PREC, I would choose to convey such a negative event as the housing occupations, which were an assault on private property. On another occasion, a woman, also uncomfortable, asked why the episodes of the occupations were performed in such a humorous way, as if to caricature them. She believed the occupations had been a very important and significant part of the PREC process, and I was not conveying that. Although these comments expressed opposite views, both nonetheless implied that the performance did not offer a fair judgment or appreciation of what "really happened" during the PREC. Both audience members tried to "set the record straight."

These interventions took place on two different days. Teresa happened to be watching both performances. She responded directly to the woman worried about making light of the occupations, saying:

> As one of the protagonists of the episode of the occupations, I must say Joana depicted it with precision. It was like a party indeed, a celebration, no one can imagine how it was like for those people who had been living in a shanty house for over 50 years, most of them with no toilets even, to go out into the

streets and literally take over the public space—the town hall, for example. Those 4,000 families live on within me, still. And it happened exactly as she depicted it: we occupied, and sometimes the places were not vacant and we would move to another one, all of this laughing, as in a celebration.

Teresa went into an on-the-spot analysis: "I think we all have representations of what happened according to our social origins and backgrounds, and when we see this show, it resonates personally with each of us." She summed up the process, whereby the performance was like a mirror to the audience, who were confronted with deep-seated beliefs and personal experiences, prompting them to revise their own remembrances, sometimes rewriting them, sometimes resisting change.

Family A

For the staging of this performance I use a photo album, which I leaf through while presenting each member of the family and their respective memories, culminating in their turbulent flight from Angola, just after the country gained independence in November 1975. Besides the interviews with the family, I had access to a handwritten notebook by M (1911–1993), the grandfather of the family, as well as three audiotapes of him reading his notebook.

Having worked before with memories of the so-called returnees from the ex-colonies, I knew these were problematic memories. With the end of the 13-year colonial war, the decolonization process had been part of the Portuguese Armed Forces' agenda, and it had been one of the major motivations for the military's overturn of the dictatorial regime. Moreover, anticolonialism had always been part of the left-wing resistance. We were now living in a "revolutionary" country in which those who had lived, worked, or had been born in the former colonies were represented as "reactionaries," "colonizers," "exploiters of the black people." On top of that, it is generally understood that the ex-colonists benefited greatly from government assistance programs. They were provided with lodging, money, and clothing on their return, and many were given jobs in public administration. However, there were also those who lost everything and upon return had to endure long-lasting poverty, living in temporary shanty houses for almost 20 years. They endured the discrimination of being called a "returnee." Women were discriminated against and insulted on account of their more "open" and "free" ways. Many, in fact, had never been to Portugal until then, and still refer to Africa, today, as their homeland. But it is not exactly the Africa of today, either; it is the Africa they *remember*.

In the post-performance discussion on November 13, 2014, two journalists in the audience publicly confessed that in 1974–1975, the return of circa one million Portuguese from the ex-colonies, in fact, had not really interested them. One even recalled an episode in Angola, where he deliberately chose to cover a story of a general who was taking over a city, while disregarding millions of people who gathered at the Luanda airport, waiting for the flight—called "the air bridge." He said that it took him many years to acknowledge that he had made a mistake and should have covered both events. The other journalist stated that the return of these people was considered a "side effect" of a main story, the "mainstream event" (his words) they were all engaged in, namely, the revolution and revolutionary process in Portugal. They were, therefore, very impressed with this part of the performance because it captured something that they still regret today.

Two days later, a woman angrily protested about the second half of the show, because of the story of that "family of returnees." She questioned why I had chosen to devote so much time to an episode that, in her opinion, depicted people who merely "got rich on account of exploiting others and stealing what didn't belong to them, in a country that wasn't theirs." The rest of the audience reacted by saying that we should look into "everything that happened" and "not erase certain episodes." During that same debate, another woman publicly confessed going to Lisbon airport in 1975 to pick up some friends who were coming to watch the revolution live, and how she had passed by those thousands of people crammed into the airport, not giving them a second thought, and how that had haunted her ever since.

I found out later that in the audience there were some children of people who had returned from the former Portuguese colonies. They remained silent, however. How should this silence be understood? As an inability to articulate their opinions and experiences? As an impossibility of reconciliation?

Some Conclusions: On Erasures, Reconstructions, and the (Im)Possibility of Reconciliation

Through this mosaic of testimonies from different angles about different issues, "A Living Museum of Small, Forgotten and Unwanted Memories" displays live fragments of a complex history and episodes that are still unresolved today. Remembrances and memories are by definition subjective, and continuously in the making.[21] Memories do not pretend to inscribe what really happened and thus challenge the whole idea of the existence of a single authoritative version of events. The "Living Museum" performances, together with its audiences, attempt to build an alternative history to the main narratives in circulation today. As such, I believe this project is able to address five major issues.

First, it shows that over these 40 years of post-dictatorship, the memory of that dictatorship has gradually softened. This slow shift has been occasioned by the state, the media, and certain trends in historiography. The lack of inscription of the memory of state repression in the public space,[22] combined with the invisibility of that repression that still prevails, has led the Portuguese to believe that their dictatorship was "*not that bad*." Comparative perspectives with other more brutal regimes are usually used to sustain such visions. The discussion of whether the Portuguese regime could indeed be termed "Fascist" is part of this ongoing process of revision.[23] By describing and analyzing concrete memories and aspects of state repression, namely, through the testimony of Aurora Rodrigues and others, together with a detailed description of some of the methods of torture used during the interrogations, the performance works as a reminder of an ever-present past. Not only does this past still live on in those who were victims of torture and could never quite overcome it, but also in those who gave information under torture to the PIDE, and are still haunted by that specter today. Because there was no transitional justice process as in other post-dictatorial societies,[24] victims feel that there was no reparation, and the perpetrators are out there in society, mingling with the rest of us. Unlike the HIJOS in Argentina,[25] who drew an alternative map of Buenos Aires, for example, pointing out where some of the perpetrators of state violence in Argentina lived, the Portuguese would not know how to do that—the perpetrators could be anywhere. In fact, in 1992 two former PIDE inspectors were commended by the first minister, Aníbal Cavaco Silva (now serving as the president of the Republic) for "exceptional and relevant services rendered to the nation."[26] One of these inspectors was one of Aurora Rodrigues's torturers, and this was one of the reasons that prompted her to publish her testimony.

The second major issue that the performance challenges is the idea that history is written by the victors. The performances suggest that there were different victors at different historical stages: the dictatorship, the revolutionary coup, and the revolutionary process, or PREC. For example: the military won on the 25th of April—but did they really win? The people, who were told to stay at home, invaded the streets. And then, for the next

19 months, the far-left seemed to win—but did they really win? And what about the former supporters of the regime—did they really lose? Were they brought to justice and convicted for their former actions? Many fled the country; others endured six-month or similarly short sentences; and still others are said to have easily escaped state prison.[27] Then, at the end of the revolutionary process—the November 25, 1975 coup—the moderates won and the radicals were beaten. But were they really beaten? Testimonies show accounts of engaged activism up to the beginning of the 1980s, as Teresa R. stated in one of the debates: "Why do you say 'the end of the Revolution'? I think the question should not be when did the Revolution end, but if indeed it ended at all. I would say it did not."

This idea of supposed winners and losers ties in with yet another idea, that of a two-sided history of these events. The performance is able, at points, to successfully break through that binary[28] and establish a field of multiple possibilities, expressed in the following exchange between audience members in one of the debates: "Did you ever think about conveying the history of the 'other side'?" asks one audience member. "What do you mean by 'other side'?!" reacts another, emphatically, "She [referring to me] has just shown that there are more than just two sides!"

Third, the performance also depicts and confronts the present relationship that people have with these events. These memories are not just about what happened then, but also and mainly about how we perceive *now* what happened *then*, for "the meanings attached to the past change over time and are part of larger, complex social and political scenarios" (Jelin *xv*). When the two journalists recounted their feelings about the returned colonists, they were conveying their present feelings, while reflecting on what they had felt *then*. Another woman I interviewed, M., put it plainly: "You are talking to someone who isn't the same anymore. Throughout the years, I have come to question it all [her political beliefs at the time of the 25th of April coup]."

Fourth, the performance addresses issues of reconciliation, a subject not easily discussed in Portuguese society. Reconciliation can also be applied to two other major events that form part of the performance: the Portuguese Colonial War and the decolonization process. Carlos N.'s testimony of the war clearly states that most men who fought it did not support it, and that they had a great respect for their enemies. As for the decolonization process, the deep-seated resentment and mistrust that this process generated is still apparent today, evidenced through a new wave of autobiographical novels, a recent radio program featuring testimonies,[29] and a soap opera.[30]

By performing the story of the Family A and discussing it afterward, I was able to confront audience members with their own fears, prejudices, and regrets, and perhaps to offer a glimmer of a suggestion that public reconciliation of all parties involved might be possible.

Finally, the performance uncovers and displays the deliberate attempts to erase and hide information about these periods. It reveals some of the revisions that have been in operation since the 25th of April 1974, while leaving blank spots so that audience members can fill them in with their own experiences. The performance offers an invitation at the end, to continue the "Museum." The Archivist states: "I have an appointment with my generation and others, so that we can continue this reconstruction" (#7 "Memory/Postmemory").

The proposal for continuation offered at the end of the performance, is conveyed through the sentence handwritten by the Archivist and projected on the screen: "This Living Museum continues." This proposition renders the performance a work in progress, handed to the audience as a possibility for some kind of action and continuous collaboration—between the performer and the audiences, including those interviewed and those whose testimony has yet to be collected. A woman asked if I was not afraid that this project could become a "never-ending black hole." I responded that I do not fear this because I believe that the possibility of progress and continuous addition to this puzzle (which I call a reconstruction) is in fact the one sure thing that can be offered to the people, what Portelli calls the "restitution" (2013: 69) of the researcher to the communities whose testimony he or she collected. This restitution entails the possibility of "amplification" of those voices, "breaking through the feeling of isolation and impotence and taking their discourses to other people and communities" (71). It is a way of challenging a state of latency and stagnation that some of those who fought hard for their utopias and ideals feel they have fallen into today. The performance conveys to them and to other generations a general sense of hope that their struggles have not been in vain. Portelli concludes his thoughts on reparation by claiming oral history to be "an art not only of what happened, but also of what didn't happen and what could have happened or should have happened. We stand in the terrain of memory as alternative" (74).

Here we are, once again, heatedly debating ideological points and stances concerning the revolution; here we are, together, trying to make sense of a common past—shattered by the fragmented versions and narratives, yes, but nonetheless common.

Figure 11.3 Part 6, "When Did the Revolution End?"
Note: Performed in Lisbon, November 2014.
Source: Courtesy of João Tuna.

An audience member commented on a social network: "I went home and I couldn't sleep afterwards, I was so excited!" During those long nights of the PREC, the activists didn't sleep either—there was no time. There was so much to transform.

Notes

1. The New State Dictatorship (1933–1974) was established in 1933, following on a previous military dictatorship in 1926 (National Dictatorship, 1926–1933). With the approval of the Corporative Constitution in 1933 and the rise to power of Oliveira Salazar, who had been the former minister of finance, this new regime would last until 1974. Marcello Caetano

succeeds Oliveira Salazar after his death in 1974, maintaining the same politics of Salazar's regime. See Raby for a thorough description of the regime (*Fascism and Resistance in Portugal*), and also Rosas (*Salazar—A Arte de Saber Durar*) and Torgal (*Estados Novos, Estado Novo*).
2. The revolutionary coup was staged by a segment of the Portuguese Armed Forces, known as the Movimento das Forças Armadas, in the early hours of April 25, 1974, which overturned the dictatorial regime. Also known as the "Carnation Revolution." For a full account and analysis see Rezola, *25 de Abril: Mitos de uma Revolução*.
3. This refers to the period following the 25th of April coup that lasted until November 1975, where the people took the streets, the fields, their working places and questioned it all through popular assemblies, demonstrations, strikes, neighborhood commissions, land and building occupations amongst other actions of direct democracy. I find D. L. Raby's description of this period particularly incisive (2006).
4. Fragments of "A Living Museum of Small, Forgotten and Unwanted Memories," in Portuguese can be seen at https://vimeo.com/103911152. It was presented at the Citemor Festival, Montemor-o-Velho, August 2014, in progress. A working version of the "Invisible Archives of the Portuguese Dictatorship" was presented in English at the Radical Archives Conference, at the Asian/Pacific/American Studies Institute, New York University, April 2014. It can be viewed at https://pad.ma/DYR/player/00:02:00. This version was later considerably changed in the process of creating "The Living Museum." Additional performances were presented at conferences in London, Skopje, Barcelona, Montréal and Bristol.
5. A term coined by Marianne Hirsch to describe a second and third generation connection toward an event (5).
6. Popular assemblies were a form of political organization and debate during the revolutionary process (PREC), whereby issues of general interest to specific groups were discussed and voted. These were used in several frontlines, such as workers commissions, neighborhood commissions and occupied estates. See John Hammond for a comprehensive study of these forms of popular power—*Building Popular Power, Workers' and Neighborhood Movements in the Portuguese Revolution*—and also Charles Downs, *Revolution at the Grassroots. Community Organizations in the Portuguese Revolution*.
7. http://icom.museum/the-vision/museum-definition/.
8. Rokem writes "The actors serve as a connecting link between the historical past and the "fictional" performed here and now of the theatrical event; they become a kind of historian, what I call a 'hyper-historian'" (13).
9. International Police of State Defense: the Political Police created by the regime. PIDE is the Portuguese acronym by which this police is mainly known.
10. See Anna Deavere Smith performances "Fires in the Mirror" (2011) and "Twilight LA" (n.d.). Smith invokes her grandfather's statement—"if you say a word often enough it becomes you."—as a starting point for her

methodology and research; and she adds: "Having grown up in a segregated city—Baltimore, Maryland—I sort of use that idea to go around America with a tape recorder, to interview people, thinking that if I walk in their words...I could sort of absorb America" (2005).

11. The Portuguese Colonial War, also known as *Overseas War*. Refers in general terms to the wars fought since February 1961 by the Portuguese military against the liberation movements in some of its colonial territories—namely, Angola, Mozambique, and Portuguese Guinea. For a full account on the origins of the conflict see Dalila Mateus and Álvaro Mateus, *Angola 1961—Guerra Colonial, Causas e Consequências*.

12. For a groundbreaking work on oral history of ex-combatants in the Colonial War see Ângela Campos, "Shifting Silence, Enduring Shame, Ambivalent Memories: an Oral History of the Portuguese Colonial War (1961–1974)." PhD thesis. University of Sussex, 2014. Print.

13. A small plaque states that on the 25th of April 1974, four people were killed by the Political Police in front of the building. However, no reference is made to the fact that the building itself had been the headquarters of the PIDE. This plaque was the initiative of a group of citizens and memory activists in 1980.

14. John Hammond writes, "In Portugal in 1974 and 1975, ordinary people challenged the social order forcefully, turning a military coup into an attempted revolution" (3).

15. A coup staged by moderate officers of the armed forces, together with right-wing parties, and the Socialist party, to put a stop to a supposed far left-wing coup led by the Communist Party to establish a communist regime in Portugal. Many conflicting versions of this event still prevail today. To this day, the Communist Party denies the preparation of any coup to seize power.

16. From https://m.youtube.com/watch?v=NkjADgWRq3Y.

17. The interviews conducted of the returnees from the former Portuguese colonies had a different script, focusing on their going to Africa—or being born there—and how they returned to Portugal and why, as well as their views on the 25th of April 1974 coup.

18. Anna Deavere Smith states: "I take something that they [the interviewed] said, and then I attempt to say exactly what they said, more than word for word, utterance for utterance, because I have come to see that it is in the way that utterances themselves are manipulated that identity comes forward" (2012).

19. MRPP (Movimento Reorganizativo do Partido do Proletariado. Lit. Reorganizing Movement of the Party of the Proletariat): Originally created in September 1970, a party of Maoist inspiration, set against the ideological line pursued by Portuguese Communist Party, which the MRPP believed was a revisionist party that needed "reorganizing."

20. SAAL (Serviço Ambulatório de Apoio Local [Local Ambulatory Support Service], 1974–1976): a project implemented in the first government after the 25th of April coup which aim was to find a solution to the dire housing

problem that existed in Portugal, where thousands of people lived in shanty houses.
21. Enzo Traverso writes: "Due to its subjective character, memory is never crystallized; it is close to an open shipyard, in continuous operation" (23).
22. As I was finishing this chapter, the Museum of Aljube (Freedom and Resistance) opened in Lisbon, on April 25, 2015. The Aljube was a former prison, which held many political prisoners during the dictatorship until it closed in 1965. As the first of its kind in Portugal, this museum may symbolize a new direction in the politics of memory in the country. The museum is an initiative of the City Hall.
23. For an in-depth discussion of this and the representations of the dictatorship see Torgal, *Estados Novos, Estado Novo*. Enzo Traverso also discusses the revision of the term "Fascism" in relation to Italy and Germany (129–147). And D. L. Raby writes: "The Portuguese régime... undoubtedly exhibited several fundamental characteristics of fascism; to describe it simply as 'authoritarian' or 'Iberian-corporatist' is to evade the question" (1988: 5).
24. Irene Pimentel (2013) has questioned if indeed there had been a lack of transitional justice concerning former agents of the PIDE. She concluded that there was an active impulse for justice just after the revolution and gives examples of several trials, that according to her were "forgotten." She suggests that, although limited, some "retributive justice" was performed, followed by some acts of "reparative justice" toward former anti-Fascist militants (111–133). My claim, nonetheless, is that those acts were rare and have not healed the memories of those who suffered under state repression during the dictatorship.
25. An organization created in 1995 in Argentina—Hijos por la Identidad y la Justicia contra el Olvido y el Silencio—aggregating children of the "disappeared" during the Argentinean military dictatorship and subsequent Dirty War of 1976–1983. See Diana Taylor for a description of the traditional "Escraches" as well as the alternative re-mapping of the city identifying the homes of the perpetrators as well as the public spaces of state repression (161–189).
26. Decree A-22/92-XII of 27–03–1992.
27. On June 29, 1975, 89 former agents of the PIDE successfully escaped from the high security prison of Alcoentre, in Portugal. It is still unclear today how they managed to escape.
28. Elizabeth Jelin writes: "Moments of political opening involve a complex political scenario. They do not necessarily or primarily entail a binary opposition between an official history or a dominant memory articulated by the state on one hand, and a counternarrative expressed by society on the other. Quite to the contrary, multiple social and political actors come to the scene, and they craft narratives of the past that confront each other, and in doing so, they also convey their projects and political expectations for the future" (29–30).

29. "Começar de Novo", Antena 1 Radio, 2013, dir. Iolanda Ferreira, http://www.rtp.pt/play/p1019/comecar-de-novo.
30. "Depois do Adeus", RTP1, 2013, dir. Sérgio Graciano and Patrícia Sequeira http://www.rtp.pt/programa/tv/p28774/e26.

Works Cited

Abrams, Lynn. *Oral History Theory*. New York: Routledge, 2010. Print.
Amaro, José, ed. *Massacres na Guerra Colonial—Tete, um Exemplo*. Lisboa: Ulmeiro, 1976. Print.
Boltanski, Christian. *Advent and Other Times*. N.p.: Centro Galego de Arte Contemporánea, 1996. Print.
Campos, Ângela. "Shifting Silence, Enduring Shame, Ambivalent Memories: An Oral History of the Portuguese Colonial War (1961–1974)." Diss. University of Sussex, Brighton, 2014. Print.
Carlos, N. Personal interview. Recorded in Lisbon, October 31 and November 13, 2014.
Downs, Charles. *Revolution at the Grassroots: Community Organizations in the Portuguese Revolution*. Albany: SUNY Press, 1989. Print.
Family A: Personal interviews with L., L., R., and S. Recorded in Viseu, January 19 and October 9, 2014.
Ferreira, Iolanda. "Começar de Novo." Antena 1 Radio. 2013. Web.
Frisch, Michael. *A Shared Authority: Essays in the Craft and Meaning of Oral and Public History*. Albany: SUNY Press, 1990. Print.
Graciano, Sérgio and Patrícia Sequeira. "Depois do Adeus." RTP1. 2013. Web.
Hammond, John. *Building Popular Power: Workers' and Neighborhood Movements in the Portuguese Revolution*. New York: New York University Press, 1988. Print.
Hirsch, Marianne. *The Generation of Postmemory: Writing and Visual Culture after the Holocaust*. New York: Columbia University Press, 2012. Print.
International Council of Museums (ICOM). "Museum Definition." 2007. http://icom.museum/the-vision/museum-definition/.
Jelin, Elizabeth. *State Repression and the Struggles for Memory*. London: Latin America Bureau, 2003. Print.
Mateus, Dalila Cabrita and Álvaro Mateus. *Angola: 1961—Guerra Colonial, Causas e Consequências*. Lisbon: Texto Editora, 2011. Print.
Pimentel, Irene Flunser. "A Extinção da Polícia Política do Regime Ditatorial Português." *Democracia, Ditadura—Memória e Justiça Política*. Ed. Irene Flunser Pimentel and Maria Inácia Rezola. Lisboa: Tinta-da-China, 2013. Print.
Pollock, Della, ed. *Remembering: Performance Oral History*. New York: Palgrave, 2005. Print.
Portelli, Alessandro. "What Makes Oral History Different." *The Oral History Reader*. 2nd ed. Ed. Robert Perks and Alistair Thomson. New York: Routledge, 2006. 32–42. Print.

———. *A Morte de Luigi Trastulli e Outros Ensaios*. Lisbon: Unipop, 2013. Print.
Raby, D. L. *Fascism and Resistance in Portugal*. Manchester: Manchester University, 1988. Print.
———. *Democracy and Revolution: Latin America and Socialism Today*. London: Pluto Press, 2006. Print.
Rezola, Maria Inácia. *25 de Abril: Mitos de uma Revolução*. Lisbon: A Esfera dos Livros, 2007. Print.
Rokem, Freddie. *Performing History, Theatrical Representations of the Past in Contemporary Theatre*. Iowa City: University of Iowa Press, 2000. Print.
Rodrigues, Aurora. *Gente Comum—Uma História na PIDE*. Castro Verde: 100Luz, 2011. Print.
Rosas, Fernando. *Salazar. A Arte de Saber Durar*. Lisbon: Tinta da China, 2013. Print.
Scott, James C. *Domination and the Arts of Resistance: Hidden Transcripts*. New Haven, CT: Yale University Press, 1990. Print.
Smith, Anna Deavere. "Four American Characters." Ted Talks. Feb 2005. Web.
———. *Fires in the Mirror*. Part 1. Youtube. January 17, 2011. Web.
———. "How Do You Get into Character?" Big Think. Youtube. April 23, 2012. Web.
———. Twilight: Los Angeles. Vimeo. N.d. Web. https://vimeo.com/17891143.
Taylor, Diana. *The Archive and the Repertoire*. New York: Duke University Press, 2003. Print.
Teresa, R. Personal interview. Recorded in Lisbon, April 23 and 26, 2014.
Torgal, Luís Reis. *Estados Novos, Estado Novo*. Coimbra: Universidade de Coimbra, 2009. Print.
Traverso, Enzo. *O Passado, Modos de Usar*. Lisbon: Unipop, 2012. Print.

Contributors

Estefanía Acién González is a doctoral candidate, writing an ethnography of Nigerian sex workers in Almería (Spain). She is a researcher at the Laboratory of Social and Cultural Anthropology (LASC) at the University of Almería, and also at the university's Center for the Study of Migration and Intercultural Relations, the Human Rights Association of Andalusia (APDHA), and the NGO Acción en Red. She conducts research and social intervention in the public and private sectors, and has taught employment workshops in intercultural mediation. She also teaches anthropology and migration at the university. She has coauthored two books on sex work research, and articles on ethnicity and identity, life histories, migration and residential issues, ethnic economy, gender, sexuality, economic strategies of migrant women in the sex industry, prostitution, and human trafficking.

Verena Alberti has worked since 1985 as a researcher at the Center for Research and Documentation of Brazilian Contemporary History (CPDOC) of the Getulio Vargas Foundation, Rio de Janeiro. She also teaches methods and techniques of teaching history at the School of Education at the State University of Rio de Janeiro (Universidade do Estado do Rio de Janeiro, UERJ), and teaches history at the German School of Rio de Janeiro. She has a doctorate in literary theory from Siegen University in Germany, and a postdoctoral degree in history education from the Institute of Education at the University of London. Her publications include books and articles on oral history, history of teaching, history of race relations, and history of the ideas about laughter.

Ángeles Arjona Garrido is professor of social anthropology at the University of Almería (Spain). She has a PhD in anthropology from the same university. She is the author of *Los Colores del Escaparate* (2006), and *Jóvenes Inmigrados y Educación en España* (2008). Her main lines of research are labor markets, ethnic economy, models of immigrant integration, gender, and second generation immigrants. She has authored and coauthored more than 40 articles in national and international journals including *Sociologia, Revista*

Española de Investigaciones Sociológicas, Sociología del Trabajo, Migraciones Internacionales, Papeles de Población, Polish Sociological Review, and *Revista Croata de Sociología*, among others.

Rina Benmayor is professor emerita at California State University Monterey Bay. She has taught courses in oral history, literature and Latina/o studies. She served as president of the International Oral History Association (2004–2006), and the Oral History Association (2010–2011). She has a doctorate in Romance Languages and Literatures from UC Berkeley and is the author of *Romances Judeo-Españoles de Oriente* (1979). She has coauthored and coedited *Latino Cultural Citizenship* (1997), *Migration and Identity* (1995; 2005), *Telling to Live: Latina Feminist Testimonios* (2001), and has published numerous oral history articles on women in the Puerto Rican migration, local community history, oral history pedagogy, and digital storytelling. She is currently producing a virtual oral history walking tour and is writing a family memoir.

Ângela Campos is research fellow in the Science Policy Research Unit (SPRU) at the University of Sussex (UK). She works on oral history in the SPRU History Project and is associated with the university's Centre for Life History and Life Writing Research. She serves on the executive council of the International Oral History Association and is a member of the Oral History Society. Her 2014 doctoral dissertation is titled "Shifting Silence, Enduring Shame, Ambivalent Memories: An Oral History of Ex-Combatants of the Portuguese Colonial War (1961–1974)." She has published in *Historia, Antropología y Fuentes Orales* (2006), *Lusotopie, Recherches Politiques Internationales sur les Espaces Issus de l'Histoire et de la Colonisation Portugaises* (2008), and *Estudos Históricos* (2009).

María Eugenia Cardenal de la Nuez is assistant professor at the University of Las Palmas de Gran Canaria. She teaches inequality and social exclusion and qualitative research methods at the Faculty of Social Work. Her PhD in sociology is from the University of La Laguna, Tenerife, Canary Islands. She researches life transitions as a structural, structured, and biographically experienced process and has published on youth transitions and migrant trajectories in the labor market. Methodologically, she follows the Biographic Narrative Interpretive Method, an interpretive analysis to biography in sociology. Her publications include *El Paso a la Vida Adulta: Dilemas y Estrategias ante el Empleo Flexible* (2006), and with Adriana Santos Diniz, "Los Sujetos, la Educación Superior y los Procesos de Transición: Aportaciones del Enfoque Biográfico," *Revista Lusófona de Educação* (2012).

Juan Carlos Checa Olmos is professor of sociology at the University of Almería (Spain). He received his PhD in sociology from the same university. He is the author of *Viviendo Juntos Aparte* (2007) and *Sin Trabajo y sin Esparto* (2007). He coedited *Convivencias entre Culturas* (2001), *La Integración Social de los Inmigrados: Modelos y Experiencias* (2003), and *Inmigración y Derechos Humanos* (2004). He has published in *Sociologia, Anthropologica, Revue Européenne Migrations Internationales, Papers, Ciudad y Territorio, Revista de Estudios Geográficos, Kinesiology, Antropological Notebook, Scripta Nova,* and *Revista Española de Investigaciones Sociológicas*. His main areas of research are spatial segregation, labor markets, models of immigrant integration, second generation immigrants, and return migration.

Joana Craveiro is a performer, writer, and artistic director of Teatro do Vestido, founded in Portugal in 2001. She is a PhD candidate at Roehampton University (London), with the support of a scholarship from the Portuguese Foundation of Science and Technology. Her research focuses on performance and transmission of political memory in dictatorial and post-dictatorial Portugal. She holds an MA in directing from the Royal Scottish Academy of Music and Drama; a BA in Drama, Escola Superior de Teatro e Cinema; and a BA (Hons) in anthropology, Universidade Nova de Lisboa. She is assistant lecturer in the Drama and Theatre Department of Escola das Artes e do Design, Caldas da Rainha (ESAD.CR), Portugal, since 2007.

Alberto del Castillo Troncoso is professor and researcher at the Instituto Mora and the National School of Anthropology and History in Mexico City. He has been visiting professor at the New School for Social Research, the University of Buenos Aires, and at universities in Pernambuco and Toulouse. His research is on the social history of photography in twentieth-century Mexico and Latin America. Recent books include *Conceptos, Imágenes y Representaciones de la Niñez en la Ciudad de México, 1880–1920* (2006; Azuela Prize); *Rodrigo Moya: Una Mirada Documental* (2011; García Cubas Prize); *Ensayo sobre el Movimiento Estudiantil de 1968: La Fotografía y la Construcción de un Imaginario* (2012; Honorable Mention LASA, RELAHO y Clavijero); and *Las mujeres de X'oyep: La Historia detrás de la Fotografía, CONACULTA* (2012; National Prize for essays in photography).

Pilar Domínguez Prats is assistant professor of history of social movements at the University of Las Palmas de Gran Canaria. She has a PhD in history from the Complutense University of Madrid. She was president of the International Oral History Association (2008–2010), and on the executive council (2004–2012). Her publications include *Voces del Exilio: Mujeres*

Españolas en México. 1939–1950 (1994) and *De Ciudadanas a Exiliadas: Un Estudio sobre las Republicanas Españolas en México* (2009). She coedited the *VI Jornadas Historia y Fuentes Orales* on social movements during the transition to democracy, and has essays in *El Mundo del Trabajo en Renfe: Historia Oral de la Infraestructura; Entreverse. Las Fuentes Orales: Fundamentos Teóricos y Metodología Práctica*; and *Memory and Cultural History of the Spanish Civil War*.

Vitor Sérgio Ferreira is postdoctoral research fellow at the Institute of Social Sciences, University of Lisbon (ICS-ULisboa), Portugal, with a grant from the Portuguese Foundation for Science and Technology. He has a PhD in sociology from the Lisbon University Institute—ISCTE (2006), specializing in sociology of communication, culture, and education. He is part of the Coordinating Board of the Permanent Youth Observatory, and teaches qualitative methods at the postgraduate level. His books include *Young People and Routes* (2011), *Life Course: Times and Transitions: Portugal at the Mirror of Europe* (2010), and *Marks That Demarcate: Tattoo, Body Piercing and Youth Cultures* (2008). He has published in international journals like *Youth & Society, Youth: The Nordic Journal of Youth Research*, and the *Journal of Youth Studies*, among others.

Miren Llona is professor of contemporary history at the University of The Basque Country UPV/EHU. She served on the executive council of the International Oral History Association IOHA (2008–2012). Her research focuses on the construction of identities from national, class, and gender perspectives. Her publications include *Entre Señorita y Garçonne: Historia Oral de las Mujeres Bilbainas de Clase Media, 1919–1939* (2002), "Los Otros Cuerpos Disciplinados: Relaciones de Género y Estrategias de Autocontrol del Cuerpo Femenino" (2007), "Patriotic Mothers of Basque Nationalism: Women's Action during the Spanish Second Republic in the Basque Country," (*Feminist Challenges in the Social Sciences*), and "From Militia Woman to Emakume: Myths Regarding Femininity during The Civil War in the Basque Country" (*Memory and Cultural History of the Spanish Civil War*).

Francisco Majuelos Martínez has degrees in anthropology and migration studies from the University of Almería. His 2014 doctoral dissertation is titled "Prostitución y Sociabilidad: El cliente en perspectiva emic." He is a researcher at the University of Almería's Laboratory of Social and Cultural Anthropology and collaborating researcher at the Center for the Study of Migration and Intercultural Relations. His research interests include migration, prostitution, and sociability. He has long experience working in social action programs, including with sex workers. He is the coauthor of the 2003 report "De la Exclusión al Estigma," edited by the Asociación Pro Derechos Humanos de Andalucía. His articles include "Trabajo Sexual y Economía inmigrante," (2012) in *Revista Internacional de Estudios Migratorios* and "Trabajadoras Sexuales Africanas: Entre el Estigma y la Crisis" (2014) in *Gazeta de Antropología*.

Joana Maria Pedro is full professor of history at the Federal University of Santa Catarina (UFSC), Brazil. She currently serves as dean of graduate studies at UFSC. She has a PhD in social history from the University of Sao Paulo and held a postdoctoral fellowship at the University of Avignon (France). Supported by the National Research Center (CNPq) in Brazil, her research focuses on gender relations and feminism. She is a researcher at the Institute for Gender Studies at UFSC and advises Master's and PhD students. Her most recent books, coauthored with Cristina Scheibe Wolff, include *Gênero, Feminismos e Ditaduras no Cone Sul* (2010), *Resistências, Gênero e Feminismos contra as Ditaduras no Cone Sul* (2011), and *Nova História das Mulheres no Brasil* (2012), coauthored with Carla Bassanezi Pinsky.

Amilcar Araujo Pereira is associate professor in the School of Education at the Universidade Federal do Rio de Janeiro, and has a PhD in history from the Universidade Federal Fluminense (UFF). In 2008, he completed a joint doctorate at Johns Hopkins University. He is the author of the book *"O Mundo Negro": Relações Raciais e a Constituição do Movimento Negro no Brasil* (2013). In 2015, he held a Fulbright-Capes fellowship to develop postdoctoral research in history education at Columbia University.

Janine Gomes da Silva is associate professor of history at the Federal University of Santa Catarina (UFSC), Brazil. She holds a doctorate in history from the same university. She is a researcher at the Institute for Gender Studies at UFSC and advises Master's and PhD students. Her most recent books include *Prostituição em Áreas Urbanas: Histórias do Tempo Presente* (2010) and *Gênero e Violência: Diferentes Narrativas sobre Mulheres em Situação de Violência em Joinville/SC* (2014), coauthored with Joana Maria Pedro and Marlene de Fáveri.

Magdalena Villarreal is senior researcher and professor at the Mexican Center for Advanced Research and Postgraduate Studies in Social Anthropology (CIESAS Occidente). She is a member of the National Research System and the National Academy of Science. She graduated from Wageningen University in the Netherlands, and has been visiting professor there, at the Centre for Development Research in Copenhagen and the University of California Santa Barbara. Her projects focus on development, poverty, gender, migration, finance, and money in California, Western and Southeastern Mexico, and Honduras. Her recent publications include *Antropología de la Deuda/The Anthropology of Debt* (2004); "Erratic Hopes and Inconsistent Expectations: A Critique of Economic Thinking on Alternatives to Poverty" (2009); and *Mujeres, Finanzas Sociales y Violencia Económica en Zonas Marginadas de Guadalajara* (2009).

Cristina Scheibe Wolff is associate professor of history at the Federal University of Santa Catarina, Brazil. She directs the graduate studies program in history and is a researcher at the Institute for Gender Studies. She has a doctorate in social history from the University of Sao Paulo and has held postdoctoral fellowships at the University of Rennes (France) and the University of Maryland. She is an editor of *Revista Estudos Feministas* and has received research grants from the National Research Center (CNPq) for work on gender relations in the resistance movements in the Southern Cone. Her most recent books, coauthored with Joana de Pedro, include *Gênero, Feminismos e Ditaduras no Cone Sul* (2010) and *Resistências, Genero e Feminismos contra as Ditaduras no Cone Sul* (2011).

Index

25th of April 1974 Revolution, 11, 207, 225n2
  and end of colonial wars, 20
  Left support for, 217
  Living Museum and, 211
  memory/postmemory of, 214
  Ongoing Revolutionary Process (PREC) and, 212–13, 226n14

Abarca, José Luis, 204n6
Abolition of Slavery Act (Brazil), 170
Aceves, Jorge, 114
Acién González, Estefanía, 8, 129–46
activism/resistance stories of Spanish trade unionism, 40–8
  collective memory and, 52
  and fight against injustice, 42–6, 51
  rank and file influence, 51–2
  rebel identity and, 41–2, 44, 46, 51
Acuerdo Básico Interconfederal (Basic Inter-Confederal Agreement), 51, 53n12
addiction, tattooing and, 153–4
affirmative action
  in Brazil, 168, 178–82
  curriculum materials on, 178, 184n11
Afonso, José, 211
Afro-Brazilian history, mandated teaching of, 168
Afro-Brazilian maroon *quilombola* movement, 168
Ahmed, Sara, 82, 87, 90n12
Alberti, Verena, 10, 12, 167–86
Almería, Spain, 8
  stigma of sex workers study in, 131, 144n11

Amaro, José, 211
American Dream. *See also* María's story
  debt and, 123–4
  framing and reframing, 124–5
  getting ahead and, 117–18
  Lupe and, 118
  undocumented farm workers and, 8, 111–27 (*see also* undocumented immigrants in California agriculture)
Andalusia
  economic conditions during Franco regime, 40
  labor leaders from, 44
  Pro Human Rights Association of (APDHA), 130
  protest culture in, 42–3
  and shift in UGT strategies, 51
Anderson, Kathryn, 94
Angola, Portuguese colonial war in, 19–20, 34n2
Angulo, Guillermo, 197
APDHA (Pro Human Rights Association), 130
Arana, Sabino, 79, 89n9, 89n10
Araújo, Maria Raimunda, 175–6, 182–3
Araujo Pereira, Amilcar, 167–86
Archivist
  introducing, 208–10
  role of, 210
  voice of, 214
Ardaya, Gloria, 65
Argentina
  Auger's narrative and, 67–8
  Boria's narrative and, 66
  and election of woman president, 64
  Oberti's narrative and, 68

238 / Index

Argentina—*Continued*
   trials of Dirty War participants in, 70
   women's narratives from, 60–2
Arjona Garrido, Ángeles, 8, 12, 129–46
Armed Forces Movement (Movimento das Forças Armadas), 211
armed struggles, women in, 5–6.
   See also women's narratives from Southern Cone
Asenjo, Father Pepe, 43
Association of Nationalist Women (Emakume Abertzale Batza), 84
attributed identity, defined, 95
Auger, Nélida (Pola), 67–8
authority, shared, 214
autobiographical narratives
   BNIM approach to, 94–5
   patterns in, 94–5
auto-bio-graphy, 10, 152, 159
Ayotzinapa Normal School, student massacre and, 202, 204n6
Azar, Héctor, 203n4
Azinheira, Joaquim, 19–20

Barba, Peces, 45
Barros Sierra, Javier, 197–8, 198f, 204n5
Basic Inter-Confederal Agreement (Acuerdo Básico Interconfederal), 51, 53n12
Basque culture
   stigma attached to, 79, 82–3
   subordination of, 80
Basque identity, *versus* other identities, 86, 90n15
Basque nationalism
   approaches to, 7
   Arana's concept of, 79, 89n10
   origins of, 79
Basque Nationalist Party (Partido Nacionalista Vasco), 79, 87, 89n6
Basque people, history of, 88n6
Becker, Harold, 106–7
Benmayor, Rina, 1–17
Bertaux, Daniel, 3, 94, 144n9

Bertaux-Wiame, Isabelle, 3
Bethencourt, Francisco, 177
Bilbao
   development in, 78, 89n7
   dichotomy of lifestyles in, 79–80
biographical approaches to sociology, 93–110, 149–66
biographical method of research, 143n7
Biographical Narrative Interpretive Method (BNIM), 7–8
   expression of Voice in, 107
   (*see also* Voice(s))
   lived life in, 97–8
   methodology of, 94–7
   SQUIN in, 96–7
Bizkaitarra, founding of, 89n9
Black Brazilian Front (Frente Negra Brasileira), 170
black movement in Brazil, 167–86
   affirmative action and, 178–82
   documentation of, 167
   educational materials about, 171
   historical underpinnings, 169–71
   and histories of race/racism, 171–8
   scope of research, 168
Black Rio movement, 175
black women's movement, in Brazil, 168
blackness, ugliness and, 176–7
Blessing (Nigeria), 132–3, 135, 139
Boas, Franz, 184n4
body. *See also* tattooed skin
   and adornments as social status, symbols, 85, 90n12
   emotions and, 78, 87, 88n3
   ideological messages inscribed on, 88
   memory's relationship with, 12
   nondualistic concept of, 88n3
   racialized, 12
body image, hedonistic economies and, 150
Bolivia
   Ardaya's narrative and, 65
   Escobar's narrative and, 63
   Suarez's narrative and, 60–1

Boltanski, Christian, 215
Bordes Mangel, Enrique, 190
Boria, Adriana, 66
Bornat, Joanna, 3
Brazil
    black movement in (*see* black movement in Brazil)
    and election of woman president, 64
    and feminization of universities, 63
    National Truth Commission report and, 70
    quotas in, 178–9, 184n12
    racism in, 10
    slavery in, 170
    teaching of Afro-Brazilian history/culture in, 168
    whitening project in, 169
bridging divides, disciplinary, linguistic, geographical, 1–2
Brodsky, Marcelo, 202, 204n7
Budgeon, Shelley, 94
Butler, Judith, 6, 68, 86

Caetano, Marcello, 224n1
California, prime agricultural development in, 111, 125n1
Camafeu, Paulinho, 184n10
Campos, Ângela, 4–5, 19–35
Canadian Oral History Association, 2
Canary Islands. *See also* Fernández Rodríguez, Justo; Travieso, Anastasio
    economic conditions during Franco regime, 40
    labor leaders from, 44
    and shift in UGT strategies, 51
Cardenal de la Nuez, María Eugenia, 1–17, 77, 93–109
Carlos N, Living Museum testimony of, 216, 222
Carnation Revolution, 20, 225n2
Carper, James, 106–7
Carrillo, Santiago, 49
Carvalho, José, 31

Castellanos, Pablo, 45
Castillo Troncoso, Alberto del.
    See del Castillo Troncoso, Alberto
Castro Alves, Antônio Frederico de, 172, 184n8
Catholic Action Workers' Brotherhood (HOAC), 42
Cavaco Silva, Aníbal, 221
Cenarro, Ángela, 40
Center for Research and Documentation of Contemporary Brazilian History (CPDOC), 167, 168, 183n1
Centro de Estudios Sociais (Center for Social Studies), 14n4
Chababo, Rubén, 203
Chamberlayne, Prue, 7, 94, 108n5
character identity, 107–8
Checa Olmos, Juan Carlos, 8, 129–46
Chile
    Díaz's narrative and, 65–7
    and election of woman president, 64
    Iglesias Saldaña's narrative and, 61
Christian socialism, Spanish protests and, 42, 53n8
CIESAS (Mexican Center for Advanced Research and Postgraduate Studies in Social Anthropology), 3, 14n4, 112
Ciriza, Alejandra, 68
Citemor Festival, 225n4
citizenship
    cultural, 113
    Mexican undocumented workers and, 121–2
    performing, 113
civil rights, Franco regime and, 37
civilian massacre in Tlatelolco district.
    See student massacre in Tlatelolco district
CLADEM (Latin American and Caribbean Committee for the Defense of Women's Rights), 67

Cold War, and US support of dictatorships in Southern Cone, 58–9
collective amnesia, Portuguese war and, 20
Collective Bargaining Act (1958), 37–8
collective identity
 in context of dictatorship, 3
 of socialist trade unionists, 39
collective memory
 constructing, 187, 189
 context and, 39
 identities and, 1, 4–6, 48
 student protest of 1968 and, 187, 189, 202
Colling, Ana Maria, 67
colonial wars in Africa. *See also* Portuguese colonial war
 ex-combatants' memories of, 4
combatants. *See also* ex-combatants of Portuguese colonial wars; Portuguese ex-combatant interviews
 in Portuguese colonial wars, 20–2
Comisiones Obreras, 38, 47
commemoration, 3
Communist Party, Workers' Commissions and, 47
Confederación Nacional de Sindicatos (CNS), 37
context, in creation of collective memory, 39
Convention on the Protection and Promotion of the Diversity of Cultural Expressions (UNESCO), 171
Cosenza, Gilse, 65–6
CPDOC (Center for Research and Documentation of Contemporary Brazilian History), 167, 168, 183n1
Craveiro, Joana, 11–13, 207–29
Cuesta, Josefina, 12
cultural citizenship, 113

culture of remembrance, 39, 53n6
Cunha, Daniel, 20, 26
curriculum materials on race/racism, 182–3
 affirmative action and, 178, 184n11
 benefits, 171–8, 173f, 174f
 "fishbowl" conversations and, 181–2, 181f
 interviews in, 172–7, 173f

da Silva, Janine. *See* Silva, Janine Gomes da
Davis, Angela, 177–8
decolonization, of Portuguese colonies, 212, 219, 222
del Castillo Troncoso, Alberto, 10, 187–206
democracy
 racial, 184n4
 Spain's transition to (*see* Spain's transition to democracy)
 and studies of collective memory/identities, 4
democratization, and social perception of past, 4–5
dialogic relationship between researcher and narrator, 13
Diana, Marta, 67, 68
Díaz, Gladys, 65–7
Díaz Ordaz, Gustavo, 189, 191, 194
dictatorship. *See also* Portuguese New State Dictatorship
 memories and, 5
dictatorships in Southern Cone
 regional plan of, 58–9
 US support for, 57
discourses, healing effect of, 77–92. *See also* gender subjectivity in Basque nationalism
discrimination, women's memories of, 61–4
Divinas Palabras (del Valle Inclán), 204n4
Domínguez Prats, Pilar, 4–5, 37–55

Downs, Charles, 225n6
Dubar, Claude, 93

Echeverría Álvarez, Luis, 189, 191, 194
economic migration, women's, 8–9
Ehrenberg, Alain, 162
El fil (the field), 119
El Universal, 194–5, 203n3
Elias, Norbert, 88n5
Emakume Abertzale Batza (Association of Nationalist Women), 84
emotion studies
  Basque nationalism and, 7
  embodied emotional dimensions of memory and, 12
emotions
  in construction of gender nationalist subjectivity, 77, 78, 87
  impact on body, 87
  written on body, 78, 88n3
enclaves of memory, 77
Entreverse (Llona), 14n5
ERP (People's Revolutionary Army), 61
Escobar, Silvia, 63
Estado Novo (New State), 20, 34n3. *See also* Portuguese New State Dictatorship
Eufemia (Brazil), 139
European Social Science History Conference, 3, 14n4
European Sociological Association, Research Network on Biographical Perspectives on European Societies, 14n3
Euskara language, 80
  protection and promotion of, 88n6
Evans, Walker, 197
ex-combatants of Portuguese colonial war, 4–5, 20–32. *See also* Portuguese ex-combatant interviews
  attitudes toward wars, 28–32
  and families of remembrance, 26–7
  historical neglect of, 23–4
  meanings of war experience, 23
  public's attitudes toward, 21
  struggles for public recognition, 21–2, 34n6
  traumatic memories of, 27–8
  veterans' groups and, 26, 34n8

Family A, Living Museum testimony of, 219–20, 223
Federal University of Santa Catarina (Brazil), 57
Fellig, Arthur H. (Weegee), 191
female body, memories of, 6, 64–6
feminist activism/movements
  during dictatorships of Southern Cone, 57–8
  influence of, 63, 69
feminist theory, embodied emotional dimensions of memory and, 12
Fernandes, Florestan, 170
Fernández Cruz, Emilio, 39
  election to Congress, 49–50
  resistance story of, 40–1, 46–7
Fernández Rodríguez, Justo, 39
  1977 elections and, 49
  resistance story of, 44–6
Ferreira, Vitor Sérgio, 9–10, 149–65
Ferrer, Lolita, 85
Figueiredo, Manuel, 24, 26
  interview of, 24
"fishbowl" conversations, 181–2, 181f
Fitas, Francisco, 25, 27
Flores, William V., 113
Forças Armadas Portuguesas (Portuguese Armed Forces), 19–20, 34n2
frameworks for American Dream, 124
  calculation toward, 125–6
  defining and negotiating, 114
  reworking meanings and interpretations, 114
Franco, Francisco, death of, 48
Franco regime
  protests and, 37–8, 42–4
  socialist trade unionism during, 40
  state of emergency and, 42, 53n7

Frente de Juventudes, 43–4, 53n9
Frente Negra Brasileira (Black Brazilian Front), 170
Freund, Alexander, 9, 14n2
Freyre, Gilberto, 184n4

Gaete Altamirano, Tomás, 107–8
Gamio, Manuel, 184n4
García, Héctor, 190
García, María, 190
"Gender, Feminisms and Dictatorships in the Southern Cone," 57
gender, in resistance movements, 57–8
gender identity, in Spanish trade unionism, 39
gender subjectivity, 6
gender subjectivity in Basque nationalism, 77–92
   historical context of, 78–80
   Trabudúa's story and, 80–7
gendered memories, 59–61, 69–70.
   See women's narratives from Southern Cone
"gendering" of history, 6
General Union of Workers (UGT), 38, 43, 53n1
   Fernández Cruz and, 47–8
   Fernández Rodríguez and, 45–6
   after Franco's death, 48
   Guillén and, 47
   labor militants in, 5
   shift in strategy, 50–1
   strategies of, *versus* Workers' Commissions strategies, 51
   ties to Socialist Party, 49
   Travieso and, 46
geographical boundaries, bridging, 2
getting ahead, meanings of, 117–21, 124–5. *See also* American Dream; undocumented immigrants in California agriculture
Giddens, Anthony, 154, 162
Gift (Nigeria), 135
Goffman, Erving, 143n4, 150

González, Beatriz, 190
González, Felipe, 49
gorilla symbol, burning of, 199, 200f
Gouveia, Avelino, 31
Gouveia, José, 31
"Grândola Vila Morena" (Afonso), 211
Guerra, Alfonso, 49
Guerreros Unidos (United Warriors), 204n6
Guerrilla Warfare (Guevara), 63
Guevara, Che, 63, 68, 69
Guillén, Miguel, 39
   resistance story of, 41–2, 47–8
   on shift in labor strategy, 50
Guinea, Portuguese colonial war in, 19–20, 34n2
Gurrola, Juan José, 203n4

Halbwachs, Maurice, 12, 39, 58
Hamilton, Paula, 12
Hammond, John, 225n6
Hernández, Moriana, 67
Hijos por la Identidad y la Justicia contra el Olvido y el Silencio, 221, 227n25
Hirsch, Marianne, 12, 208
Historia, Antropología y Fuentes Orales, 2
História Oral (Journal of the Brazilian Oral History Association), 2
Historia Oral: Ensayos y Aportes de Investigación (Aceves), 2, 114
Historical Memory Act, 38, 53n5
History and Gender Studies Laboratory (LEGH), 57, 71n2
HOAC (Catholic Action Workers Brotherhood), 43
Holocaust testimonies, pedagogical strategies for use of, 180
Huyssen, Andreas, 202

Ibáñez, Juan, 203n4
identity(ies). *See also* gender identity
   character of, 107–8
   collective memory and, 4–6

predicative *versus* attributed, 95
racial, oral narratives and, 175–6, 182–3
reconstructing through testimonies, 210, 225n10
stigmatized, 132–5
tattooed skin and, 151, 156–8, 162
identity construction, 1, 3
oral history and, 87–8
subjectivity and, 6–9
Iglesias Saldaña, Margarita, 61
Ilê Aiyê, 178, 184n10
image. *See also* photographers of '68 student massacre
power of, 10–11
relationship with narrative, 9
Imam (Morocco), 134
immigrants
prostitution and, 129–30
undocumented (*see* undocumented immigrants in California agriculture)
immigration, in Spain, 142n1
indigenous history, in Brazil's national curriculum, 168
Inma (Brazil), 135
Instituto de Ciências Sociais da Universidade de Lisboa (Institute of Social Sciences of the University of Lisbon), 3, 14n4
Instituto Mora, 3, 14n4
Instituto Nacional de Antropología e Historia (INAH) (National Institute of Anthropology and History), 3, 14n3
interdisciplinary collaborations, institutions supporting, 3
International Council of Museums (ICOM), museum defined by, 209
International Oral History Association (IOHA), 2
International Sociological Association, Research Committee on Biography and Society of, 14n3
Internet, videotaped oral narratives on, 10

interviews. *See also* oral history; testimony(ies)
challenges in pedagogical uses, 183
improvised, 94
for Living Museum, 215, 226n17
open-ended, 7–8
pedagogical strategies for, 180
of photographers of '68 massacre, 190
in study of race/racism in Brazil, 172–7, 173f
Isabel de Bragança, 184n7

Jack, Dana, 94
Jelin, Elizabeth, 4, 190, 227n28
João, 149, 157
Joffily, Olívia, 65
Jornal do Brasil, race/racism in, 176–7
Juliano, Dolores, 136, 138
Juventudes Católicas, 43

Kate (Nigeria), 133
Kaufmann, Jean-Claude, 163n1
knowledge, "new," 174, 183

La Prensa
Metinides photos and, 192–3, 193f
student protests of 1968 and, 191, 203n2
labor management juries, 46, 53n10
labor militants, in UGT, 5
labor movement, Workers' Commissions and, 47
labor protests, against Franco regime, 37–8
Latin America-Iberian Peninsula collaborations, 2
Latin American and Caribbean Committee for the Defense of Women's Rights (CLADEM), 67
Laverdi, Robson, 14n2
Law of the Free Womb, 172, 184n7
LEGH (History and Gender Studies Laboratory), 57, 71n2
lieu de mémoire, 9, 11, 12

linguistic divides, 2
"Living Museum of Small, Forgotten, and Unwanted Memories, A," 207–29
  25th of April 1974 coup and, 211
  dialogue with audience, 208
  dichotomized history and, 214
  implications for history, 221–2
  introducing, 208–10
  memory erasures and, 223
  performance components, 208
  performance structure, 210–14
  performances of, 208, 225n4
  PIDE and, 211
  PREC and, 212, 226n14
  and present relationship with past, 222
  reconciliation and, 222–3
  small acts of resistance and, 210–11
  "small memory" and, 215
  and softening of memory, 221, 226n20
  and use of testimonies, 215
"Living Museum of Small, Forgotten, and Unwanted Memories, A" (testimonies)
  Aurora Rodrigues, 217
  Carlos N, 216
  Family A, 219–20
  Teresa R, 218–19, 226n20
Llona, Miren, 7, 12, 14n5, 77–92
Lobo, Júlio, 31
Local Ambulatory Support Service (Serviço Ambulatório de Apoio Local), 218, 226n20
Lola's story, 93–109
  interviewer's encounter in, 95–7
  lived life and, 97–8
  narrative in, 98–106
  self-presentation in, 98–102
  "Voices" in, 102–6
López, Nacho, 197
López Gómez, Alejandra, 62
Loureiro, Manuel, 21
Lugo, Fernando, 71n5

Luis, reflections on tattooed skin, 149, 155, 160
Lupe, 118

Majuelos Martínez, Francisco, 8, 129–46
María (Dominican Republic), 133
Maria (Portugal), 150
Mariam (Nigeria), 133
María's story, 114–25
  American Dream and, 123–5
  background in Mexico, 115–16
  el fil and, 119–21
  framing of US life, 116–17
  getting ahead and, 117–21
  lack of citizenship rights and benefits, 121–2
  self-image of, 117, 121–2
Mariátegui, José Carlos, 184n4
Marques, José, 27–8
Martins, 57
masculinization, of activist women in Southern Cone, 66–8
Massacres in the Colonial War (Massacres na Guerra Colonial) (Amaro), 211
Mateus, Álvaro, 225n11
Mateus, Dalila, 225n11
mayordoma (forewoman), 111
McDonald, Kevin, 156
Medeiros, Carlos Alberto, 179
media, race/racism in Brazil and, 176–7
memory(ies), 1. *See also* collective memory
  competing, 4
  contested, 11
  in context of dictatorship, 3
  emotional charge and, 77
  enclaves of, 77
  erasures of, 223
  of female body, 6
  gendered (*see* gendered memories; women's narratives from Southern Cone)
  versus history, 187

individual, context of, 39
nonlinear path of, 188
of PREC, 213, 215, 217–19, 221
public, 4
public representations and, 3, 9–11
recovering, criticisms of, 39
reinterpretations of, 5
relationship with body, 12
relationship with past events, 207
small, 215
softening of, 221
subjectivity of, 22–3, 227n21
tattooed skin and, 158–61
traumatic, of ex-combatants of Portuguese colonial wars, 27–8
of war, genocide, dictatorship, 5
Mendes Pereira, Amauri, 172–3
mestizaje
 Brazilian pride in, 169
 Latin American proponents of, 184n4
Metinides, Enrique, 190, 195
 student protest photos and later testimony, 191–3, 193f, 201
Mexican Center for Advanced Research and Postgraduate Studies in Social Anthropology (CIESAS), 3, 14n4, 112
Mexican migrant farmworkers, American dream and, 8.
 See also American Dream
Mexico. *See also* student protests of 1968 in Mexico
 1968 Student Movement in, 10–11
 agricultural work in, 119
migration
 American Dream and, 112, 124
 economic, 3, 8
 and performance of citizenship, 113, 121
 sex workers and, 140, 144n8, 144n13
 studies of, in Spain, 143n6

Miguel, reflections on tattooed skin, 154, 156–8, 160–1
militancy, construction as male space, 64
military occupations in Latin America, media coverage of, 203n3
MIR (Revolutionary Left Movement), 61, 65
Miradas en Torno al 68 (Visions of '68), 190
Miriam (Brazil), 136
miscegenation, Brazilian pride in, 169
Montenegro, Antonio, 14n6
Moraga, Cherríe, 87
Morales, Evo, 71n5
Movimento das Forças Armadas (Portuguese Armed Forces), 211, 225n2
Movimento Reorganizativo do Partido do Proletariado (MRPP), 217, 226n19
Moya, Rodrigo, 190, 203n4
 student protest photos and later testimony, 197–201, 198f, 200f, 201
Moya Palencia, Mario, 191
Mozambique, Portuguese colonial war in, 19–20, 34n2, 211
MRPP (Movimento Reorganizativo do Partido do Proletariado), 217, 226n19
Mujica, José, 71
museum(s). *See also* "Living Museum of Small, Forgotten, and Unwanted Memories, A"; Tlatelolco University Cultural Center
 Metinides' work in, 191
 and student massacre of 1968, 201
 tattooed bodies as, 9
Museum of Aljube, 227n22

Nadia (Romania), 136, 137, 140–1
narrative
 gendering of, 6
 relationship with image, 9

nation, as emotional community, 79
National Autonomous University
  of Mexico (UNAM), Student
  Movement of 1968 and, 188
national identities, construction of,
  78–80
National Labor Union.
  See Confederación Nacional
  de Sindicatos (CNS)
National Polytechnic Institute (IPN),
  Student Movement of 1968 and,
  188
National Truth Commission report, in
  Brazil, 70
nationalism, Basque. *See* Basque
  nationalism
nationalist discourses
  connection with emotion and
    collective memory, 84
  and restoration of dignity, 83–4
nationalist identity, middle class
  identity and, 84–8
nationalist subjectivity, 77–9
Necoechea, Gerardo, 14n2, 14n6
negritude, ugliness and, 176–7
Newsletter/Boletín (of International
  Oral History Association), 2
"Night of the Long Batons,"
  203n3
Nogueira, Oracy, 169–70
Nora, Pierre, 11–12

Oberti, Alejandra, 60, 68
Olga (Ecuador), 134, 137
Ongoing Revolutionary Process
  (PREC), 207, 212
  analyzing memories of, 213
  Aurora Rodriguez and, 217, 221
  controversy over, 222–3
  end of, 213, 226n15
  interviewees' memories of, 215
  popular assemblies and, 225n6
  Teresa R and, 218–19, 226n20
open-ended interview, 7–8

oral history. *See also* interviews;
    testimony(ies)
  BNIM approach to, 94–5
  contributions of, 32–4
  curricular uses of, 168 (*see also*
    curriculum materials on
    race/racism)
  development of, 4
  historical research and, 33
  identity construction and, 87
  interdisciplinary approaches to, 2–3
  lived life/narrative (told story) in,
    94–5
  major themes in, 1 (*see also*
    memory(ies); representation;
    subjectivity)
  performing, 207
  sides in, 214
  on stage, 11
  visual turn in, 9
Oral History and Public Memories, 12
Oral History Forum d'histoire orale, 2,
  14n2
"Oral History of Socialist Trade
  Unionism, The," 38
oral history scholarship, lack of access
  to, 1–2
oral narratives, educational benefits of,
  171–2. *See also* curriculum
  materials on race/racism
Ortiz, Fernando, 184n4

Palerm, Juan Vicente, 112
Palma, Victor, 31
Paraguay, Kanonnikoff Flores' narrative
  and, 62
participant observation technique,
  130–1
Partido Nacionalista Vasco (Basque
  Nationalist Party), ideology of, 79
Passerini, Luisa, 41, 70
Patience (Nigeria), 134
pau de arará, 71n6
Paz, Octavio, 188, 199, 203n4

Pedro, Joana Maria, 4–6, 57–73
"Pedro Mari," 86, 90n14
People's Revolutionary Army (ERP), 61
Pereira, Amilcar, 10, 12
performance. *See also* "Living Museum of Small, Forgotten, and Unwanted Memories, A"
  memory and, 59
  public, 3, 9–11
performance studies, 3
Performing History (Rokem), 210, 225n8
Perrot, Michelle, 59
persona, reframing of, 8
photographers of '68 student massacre. *See also* Metinides, Enrique; Moya, Rodrigo; Soto, Daniel
  photographs *versus* oral testimonies of, 190
photography
  1968 student movement in Mexico and (*see also* student protests of 1968 in Mexico)
  editorial use of, 188
PIDE. *See* Political Police (PIDE)
Pimentel, Irene, 227n24
Pinto, José, 31
Piteira, Joaquim, 24–5
  interview of, 24–5
Plaza de Las Tres Culturas, civilian student massacre in, 188
political ideology, emotional power of, 7
Political Police (PIDE), 211, 217, 225n9
  justice for agents of, 227n24
  murder of Ribeiro Santos, 210
  prison escape by agents of, 222, 227n27
  repression by, 211, 226n13
  Rodrigues' testimony and, 217
  torture of prisoners, 221
Polixene Trabudúa's story, 80–7
  background, 81–2
  enclaves of memory in, 80–1
  shame, emotion, and transformation in, 81–4
  Spanish cultural hegemony in, 82
Pollock, Della, 208
popular assemblies, Portuguese, 208, 225n6
Portelli, Alessandro, 3, 7, 22, 102, 107, 214, 223
Portugal
  1974 revolution in, 11 (*see also* 25th of April 1974 Revolution)
  end of dictatorships in, 4
  housing crisis in, 218–19, 226n20
  oral history in, 2
  Political Police (PIDE) in (*see* Political Police (PIDE))
  popular assemblies in, 208, 225n6
Portuguese Armed Forces (Movimento das Forças Armadas), 225n2
Portuguese colonial war, 226n11
  areas of, 19–20, 34n2
  attitudes toward returnees following, 219–20
  ex-combatants of (*see* ex-combatants of Portuguese colonial war)
  memorial legacy of, 19–22
  political polarizations over, 20–1
  Portuguese population affected by, 20, 34n4
  public memory of, 20
  reconciliation after, 220, 222–3
  shame over, 20, 34n5
  state's relationship with, 211
Portuguese colonies, decolonization of, 212, 219, 222
Portuguese dictatorship/revolution, performing oral histories of, 207–29. *See also* "Living Museum of Small, Forgotten, and Unwanted Memories, A"
Portuguese ex-combatant interviews
  approach to, 22–4
  Artur Santos, 28, 30
  Avelino Gouveia, 31

Portuguese ex-combatant
  interviews—*Continued*
 common themes of, 24–32
 contributions of, 32–4
 Daniel Cunha, 26
 Francisco Fitas, 25, 27
 Joaquim Piteira, 24–5
 José Carvalho, 31
 José Marques, 27–8
 José Pinto, 31
 Júlio Lobo, 31
 Manuel Figueiredo, 24, 26
 participant valuing of, 29–30
 plural forms of speech in, 30
 Victor Palma, 31
Portuguese New State Dictatorship,
  207, 224n1. *See also* Estado Novo
  (New State)
 fascism and, 221, 227n23
 lack of inscription in public space,
  221, 227n22
 Living Museum intro to, 210–11
Portuguese Red Ibero-Americana
  Resistencia y Memoria
  (RIARM), 2
Portuguese revolution of 1974.
  See 25th of April 1974 revolution
postmemory, 12
 of 25th of April coup, 214
postmemory generations, Hirsch's
  concept of, 208
powerlessness, Portuguese
  ex-combatants and, 24–5
Pozzi, Pablo, 14n2
PREC. *See* Ongoing Revolutionary
  Process (PREC)
predicative identity, defined, 95
Pro Human Rights Association of
  Andalusia, 130
professional identity
 and bad working conditions, 93
 building, 93–109 (*see also* Lola's
  story)
 factors in development of, 93–4
 for graduates with precarious jobs,
  93, 102, 107
 key elements in development, 106–7
 prostitution. *See also* sex workers;
  stigma of sex workers
 immigrants in Spain and, 129–30
public education, videotaped oral
  narratives in, 10
public memory, influence of, 4, 13
public representation
 memory and, 3, 9–11
 tattooed skin as, 9–10

qualitative research methods, 143n6
 in study of sex workers, 130–2
quotas
 Brazilian law and, 179, 184n12
 Brazilian universities and, 178

Raby, D. L., 225n3
race/racism, capitalism and, 170
race/racism in Brazil, 10
 avoidance of, 170
 CPDOC oral history project and,
  167
 educational materials about, 171
 histories of race and, 171–8
race relations, academic analysis of,
  169–70
racial democracy, 184n4
racial identity, oral narratives and,
  175–6, 182–3
racial prejudice, Nogueira's classification
  of, 169–70
Radical Archives Conference, 225n4
Ramos, Arthur, 169
reconciliation, after Portuguese colonial
  war, 220, 222–3
Red Latinoamericana de Historia Oral
  (RELAHO), 2
reframing
 of cultural models of reference, 125
 of past self, 7
 of persona, 8

remembrances
  collective, 30
  complexities of, 30, 32
  families of, 26
  Portuguese colonial war and, 11, 20, 24, 29, 33–4
rememoration, 4, 59
representation, 1
  creative spaces of, 9
  and performance, 207–30
  public, 3, 9, 29
  social, 157
  of tattooed body, 157, 163
  visual, 9, 149–66, 158, 187–206
  of women as mother, 68
representational strategies, 9
research
  biographical/oral history method, 143n7, 144n9
  ethnographic fieldwork, 112–14, 141, 144n7, 163n1
  informal conversation, 131, 144n10
  mixed methods, 131, 143n6, 143n7
  qualitative methods, 130, 143n6
researchers, dialogic relationships with subjects and, 13
resistance, small acts of, in Living Museum performance, 210–11
resistance discourses, gender/masculinity, femininity in, 60
resistance movements in Southern Cone
  gender configurations in, 58
  gender issues in, 57–8
  women in, 4, 57–73 (*see also* women's narratives from Southern Cone)
Revolutionary Left Movement (MIR), 61
Rezola, Maria Inácia, 225n2
Ribeiro, José, 211
Ricoeur, Paul, 4, 12, 157
Rivera, Javier, 196
Rodrigues, Aurora, Living Museum testimony of, 217, 221
Rodríguez, Antonio, 197
Rokem, Freddie, 210, 225n8

Roman Catholics, socialism of, 42
Rosas, Fernando, 211, 225n1
Roseneil, Sasha, 94
Rosenwein, Barbara, 79
Ruiz, Solís, 44–5

SAAL (Serviço Ambulatório de Apoio Local), 218, 226n20
Salazar, Oliveira, 224n1
Salazar dictatorship, end of, 20
Salvador y Sebastián, 43
Sánchez, Aarón, 190
Santos, Artur, 28, 30
Santos, Ribeiro, 210
Sapriza, Graciela, 66
school curricula. *See also* curriculum materials on race/racism
  oral history in, 10
Scott, Joan, 6, 70
Second Spanish Republic (1931–1939), 78, 84. *See also* Spain
self, reframing/reinvention of, 6–7
selfhood, tattooed body and, 10, 152, 157–9, 162
self-presentation, in Lola's story, 98–102
Serviço Ambulatório de Apoio Local (SAAL) (Local Ambulatory Support Service), 218, 226n20
sex workers
  legal status in Spain, 130, 143n2
  media portrayals of, 134, 144n13
  self-legitimation and, 135–6
  stigma and (*see* stigma of sex workers)
sexual violence, in women's narratives from Southern Cone, 65–6
shame/guilt
  Elias' definition of, 88n5
  over Portuguese colonial wars, 20, 34n5
  of Portuguese ex-combatants, 23, 29–31, 33
  sex workers and, 129, 133–6, 141–2

shame/guilt—*Continued*
  subordinated communities and, 78, 81–2, 87
  transformation of, nationalist discourse and, 81–4, 87
shared authority, 214
Shilling, Chris, 154
Shopes, Linda, 12, 180
shuttlework, Portelli's concept of, 102
Silva, Janine Gomes da, 4–6, 57–73
slavery, in Brazil, 170
Slaves, The (Castro Alves), 184n8
Smith, Anna Deavere, 210, 215, 226n18
Smith, Anthony, 84
social inequality, in Brazil, 167.
  See also race/racism in Brazil
social relief schools, Spanish, 40–1
socialism, Christian, Spanish protests and, 42, 53n8
Socialist Workers' Party (Spain), 1977 elections and, 49
Sofia (Nigeria), 134, 137, 138
Sofía (Venezuela), 139
Sonia (Nigeria), 138
Soriano, Juan, 203n4
Soto, Daniel, 190
  student protest photos and later testimony, 194–7, 195f, 201
Soto Roy, Alvaro, 107–8
Southern Cone. *See also* women's narratives from Southern Cone
  authoritarian regimes in, 57
  and election former resistance members, 71n5
  and election of women presidents, 64
Spain
  adverse economic conditions, 93–7
  civil war, 87
  elections of June 15, 1977, 40
  employment insecurity, 93
  end of dictatorships in, 4
  first democratic national elections in, 49
  growth in immigration, 142n1
  legal status of sex workers in, 130, 143n2
  Second Spanish Republic, 78, 84
  trade union leaders in, 4
Spain's transition to democracy, 38, 53n2
  socialist trade unionism and, 40
  vision of, 48–51
Spanish socialist trade unionism, 37–55
  activism/resistance stories, 40–8
  (*see also* activism/resistance stories of Spanish trade unionism)
  after Franco's death, 48
  historical archives of, 38, 53n4
  leaders in Spanish Parliament, 49, 53n11
  oral history of, 38–9
Spanish Syndical Organization, 46–7
Spanish transition to democracy, socialist political culture and, 50–1
speech, patterns of, 95
SQUIN (Single Question aimed at Inducing Narrative), 96–7
stereotyping
  and middle class aspirations of Basque women, 85, 90n13
  photojournalism and, 190, 193
  of Portuguese ex-combatants, 33
  racial, 134
  of socialist trade unionists, 51
  tattooed bodies and, 151–2
stigma
  Basque rural origins and, 79, 82–3
  manifestation of, 132–5
  participation in Portuguese colonial wars and, 28
  tattooed skin and, 150–1
  types of, 143n4
stigma of sex workers, 8–9, 129–46
  Blessing (Nigeria), 132–3, 135, 139
  and challenges of studying stigmatized populations, 130–2
  Eufemia (Brazil), 139
  Gift (Nigeria), 135
  hierarchy of values and, 137–8

identity and, 132–5
Imam (Morocco), 134
Inma (Brazil), 135
Kate (Nigeria), 133
María (Dominican Republic), 133
Mariam (Nigeria), 133
Miriam (Brazil), 136
Nadia (Romania), 133, 136, 137, 140–1
Olga (Ecuador), 134, 137
Patience (Nigeria), 134
research methodology, 130–2
Sofia (Nigeria), 134, 138
Sofía (Venezuela), 139
strategies for combating, 135–40
success story, 140–1
Tessy (Nigeria), 138
storytelling, tattooed skin and, 158–61
struggle for subjectivity, 156
student massacre in Tlatelolco district, 10–11, 188
contemporary *versus* later official responses to, 189
Metinides's photographs and testimony, 191–4
Moya's photographs and testimony, 197–201
photographers documenting, 190
photographic images of, 188–90
Soto's photographs and testimony, 195–7
student protests of 1968 in Mexico, 10–11, 187–205
Ayotzinapa massacre and, 202
and constructing collective memory, 187
criminalizing, 191–3
El Universal's coverage of, 194, 203n3
in hindsight, 201–3
impetus for, 188
La Prensa's coverage of, 192–3, 193f
Suárez, Adolfo, 49
Suárez, Miriam, 60–1
subjectivity, 1
BNIM and, 94

emotions in construction of, 77–8
existential phenomenology and, 88n1, 88n2
gender, 6 (*see* gender subjectivity in Basque nationalism)
identity construction and, 6–9
interviewee, 94–5
of memory, 22–3, 227n21
nationalist, 77–9
of oral history narratives, 87
struggle for, 156
tattooed skin and, 156–7, 160, 162–3
Susana, reflections on tattooed skin, 150, 153, 154

tattooed skin, 12, 149–65
as construction of identity, 156–8
increased incidence of, 149
meanings, 151
narratives of, 9–10
as reflexive project, 153–6
research methodologies, 151–3, 163n1
stigma of, 150–1
transformed social significance of, 150
as visual auto-bio-graphic narrative, 158–61
Tavares, Flavio, 64
Taylor, Diana, 227n25
Teresa R, Living Museum testimony of, 218–19, 222, 226n20
Tessy (Nigeria), 138
testimony(ies). *See also* interviews; "Living Museum of Small, Forgotten, and Unwanted Memories, A"; oral history; photographers of '68 civilian student massacre; Portuguese ex-combatant interviews; *specific interviewees under* undocumented immigrants in California agriculture; *specific women under* stigma of sex workers
of Emilio Fernández Cruz, 39–41, 46–7, 49–50

252 / Index

testimony(ies)—*Continued*
  Holocaust, 180
  of Juan Ramón Troncoso, 39, 42–4, 50–1
  of "Living Museum," 11
  of Maria, 114–25
  of Miguel Guillén, 39, 41–2, 47–8, 50
  of Polixene Trabudúa, 80–7
  of silenced social actors, 4
  of socialist trade unionists, 44, 51
  of women resistance members of Southern Cone, 60, 65–6
Third World Conference against Racism, Racial Discrimination, Xenophobia and Related Intolerance, 178–9
Thomson, Alistair, 2–3, 9, 22–3
Tiago, reflections on tattooed skin, 156–7, 159
Tlatelolco district
  civilian massacre in (*see* student massacre in Tlatelolco district)
  historical significance of, 188
Tlatelolco University Cultural Center, exhibition of, 189
Tomás, 123
Torgal, Luís Reis, 225n1, 227n23
torture
  by PIDE, 211, 221
  in women's narratives from Southern Cone, 65–6
Trabudúa, Polixene, 7, 89n7
  background of, 78
  story of (*see* Polixene Trabudúa's story)
trade unionists, in UGT, 5
transition to democracy. *See* Spain's transition to democracy
translations, lack of, 1–2
traumatic memories, of ex-combatants of Portuguese colonial wars, 27–8
Traverso, Enzo, 12, 227n21, 227n23
Travieso, Anastasio, 39
  resistance story of, 46
  Vertical Union and, 48

Troncoso, Juan Ramón, 10, 39, 51
  resistance story of, 42–4
  on shift in labor strategy, 50–1

UGT. *See* General Union of Workers (UGT)
UNAM (Universidad Autónoma de México), 188–9
undocumented immigrants in California agriculture, 111, 125n2. *See also* María's story
  American Dream and, 111–27
  and child's presentation to society, 117, 126n9
  citizenship responsibilities and, 113–14
  farm labor conditions and, 118–19
  frameworks created by, 114
  Lupe, 118
  mortgage payments, 115, 125n6
  payment of taxes, 121, 126n20
  research method, 112–13
  rights and obligations of, 113
  Tomás, 123
  treatment of women, 118, 124–5
UNESCO. *See* United Nations Educational, Scientific and Cultural Organization (UNESCO)
Unión Sindical Obrera (Workers' Trade Union), 42, 53n8
United Nations Educational, Scientific and Cultural Organization (UNESCO)
  antiracist studies of, 169–70
  Convention on the Protection and Promotion of the Diversity of Cultural Expressions, 171
United States, and support for dictatorships in Southern Cone, 57–9
United Warriors (Guerreros Unidos), 204n6
University of Buenos Aires, military occupation of, 203n3

University of California, Santa Barbara, 112
Uruguay
  and feminization of universities, 63
  Hernández's narrative and, 67
  López Gómez's narrative and, 62

del Valle Inclán, Ramón, 204n4
Vallejo, Rafael, 47
Vasconcelos, José, 184n4
Vertical Union. *See also* Confederación Nacional de Sindicatos (CNS)
  demolition from within, 48
  after Franco's death, 48
  power of, 43, 44
  UGT growth and, 46
Viglietti, Daniel, 68
Villa, Pancho, 189
Villarreal, Magdalena, 8, 111–27
Visions of '68 *(Miradas en Torno al 68)*, 190
voice(s)
  of sex workers, 141
  undervaluing of, 29
  unheard, 34
Voice(s)
  in Lola's narrative, 102–6
  restrained *versus* passionate, 103, 104, 106
  significance of capitalization, 95, 102

war veterans. *See also* ex-combatants of Portuguese colonial war
  diverse recollections of, 4–5

Weegee (Arthur H. Fellig), 191
Wengraf, Tom, 7, 94, 108n5
Williams, Rhonda, 95, 102, 107
Wolff, Cristina Scheibe, 4–6, 12, 57–73
women
  in armed resistance movements, 4
  and identity construction, 3
women presidents, democratically elected, 6, 64
women's economic migration, 8–9. *See also* stigma of sex workers; undocumented immigrants in California agriculture
women's narratives from Southern Cone, 57–73
  common themes of, 58–9
  gendered memories and, 59–61
  interview methodology, 58
  losses in, 68
  and male *versus* female roles, 63–4
  masculinization of, 66–8
  and memories of discrimination, 61–4
  and memories of female body, 64–6
  similarities/dissimilarities, 69
Words and Silences, 2
Workers' Commissions
  role of, 47
  strategies of, *versus* UGT strategies, 51
Workers' Trade Union (Unión Sindical Obrera), 42, 53n8
Worker's Vanguard, 43

Zapata, Emiliano, 189

The manufacturer's authorised representative in the EU is Springer Nature Customer Service Centre GmbH, Europaplatz 3, 69115 Heidelberg, Germany. If you have any concerns regarding our products, please contact ProductSafety@springernature.com

Printed and bound by CPI Group (UK) Ltd, Croydon, CR0 4YY
23/03/2026
02076673-0020